Here's just some of what y

pages of this breakthroug

- ➢ Dealing with parents that are unhappy with playing time or positions.

- ➢ How to handle and approach youth umpires to get them on your side.

- ➢ Crazy little strategy tips that make a huge difference in travelball tournaments.

- ➢ Why you should consistently treat each player different.

- ➢ Creative offensive and defensive plays.

- ➢ Recruiting new players from rec ball leagues and other travelball teams.

- ➢ Tournament and game strategies adapted for travelball rules and formats.

- ➢ Why doing things by "The Book" doesn't always work in the youth game.

- ➢ Keeping other coaches from recruiting your players.

- ➢ Managing playing time in tournaments to keep everyone happy while winning.

- ➢ How to make travelball coexist with rec ball, school ball and other sports.

- ➢ Baseball specific strength, speed & conditioning exercises tailored for youth players.

- ➢ Why home runs are evil in the youth game.

- ➢ Curveballs and kids.

- ➢ Why Bill Walsh-style practices are best for young players.

- How to keep your team together over several seasons.

- Teaching plate discipline and the mental approach at the plate.

- Ethics of sign-stealing.

- Why you should remove the word "umpire" from your team vocabulary.

- Dealing with difficult parents of outstanding players.

- Matching positions with the right physical tools.

- Ground rules and policies all new players and parents should know.

- Importance of intelligent, aggressive base running.

- Why coaching parents is as important as coaching kids.

- Pitching staff strategies that are best in tournaments.

- Why it is critical for you to keep team stats.

- Teaching "relaxed focus" to players and coaches.

- Why every young player should play multiple positions.

- Constructing the most productive batting order.

- Why your best assistant coach is sometimes made out of metal.

- Avoiding "package deals", "daddyball" and "sugar daddies."

- Hosting a travelball tournament as a fundraiser.

- A close encounter with a dad named Cal Ripken, Jr.

- AND MUCH, MUCH MORE!

TRAVELBALL

How to Start and Manage a Successful Travel Baseball Team

Ron Filipkowski

Harmonic Research Associates

Sarasota, Florida USA

Travelball: How to Start and Manage a Successful Travel Baseball Team

Submit all requests for reprinting to:

Harmonic Research Associates
Post Office Box 1657
Sarasota, Florida 34230-1657 USA

Published in the United States of America by Harmonic Research Associates.

http://www.HarmonicResearchAssociates.com

ISBN-10: 1-933198-29-X

ISBN-13: 978-1-933198-29-3

EAN: 9781933198293

ACKNOWLEDGEMENTS

This book is for all "my boys" on the Meteors who made this possible. You are all great baseball players today and even finer young men. I will never forget the time we spent together at the tournaments and in practices. We learned a lot from each other!

I also dedicate it to all the Meteors parents. You stuck by me and were loyal to the program and each other. Although we did not always agree on everything, we stuck with each other because we loved being a part of something so special that we created together. Thank you for your time and dedication to do whatever it took to put your sons on a path to greatness.

Finally, but most importantly, this book is dedicated to my wonderful wife Jackie. You were a "baseball widow" for 9 years, but you never complained and always supported my crazy obsession with travel baseball and the Meteors. You are the most important person in my life and I love you more every day. Now I'm out to the golf course with the girls!

–Ron Filipkowski

TABLE OF CONTENTS

FOREWORD

I must confess, when I first decided to start a travel baseball team, I thought it would be a piece of cake. My son was turning thirteen and he wanted to play at the highest level possible. I quickly found a nice field down the street, had tryouts and we were off and running. We were named the Georgia Roadrunners.

It took me about one month into the season before I realized that Travelball was a different game than anything I had ever played and as the head coach I was absolutely CLUELESS!

I think my reasons for being so overconfident in the first place stemmed from having a fairly impressive baseball resume. After all, I had played for the USA Team, won a National Championship at LSU, played in the big leagues for 14 years, won over 100 games, pitched for four different teams in the playoffs and made the '99 All-Star Team. Baseball was such a huge part of my life. And not just playing the game, but also watching games, practicing long hours, doing specialized drills, studying hitters on video tape, evaluating different pitching deliveries, eating right, training right, talking to umpires, talking to fans and talking baseball with countless teammates.

As far as coaching goes, I had learned from some of the greatest college coaches around. And while playing professional baseball, I had the privilege to play for some dynamic leaders, names like Bobby Cox, Mike Scioscia, Terry Francona and Charlie Manuel.

But what I didn't know was the simple fact that baseball instruction was just a small part of what was truly required out of a Travelball head coach.

To my surprise, I had stepped into a full time CEO job that was more like running a small business. There were uniforms to be ordered, sponsors, hotels to be booked, fundraisers, deposits for tournaments, a web-site to be made, different rules at each of the tournaments, different interpretations of those rules, disgruntled parents calling about their sons' playing time, a disgruntled player practicing with a different team, middle school baseball, time limits to games, complaints about alcohol, complaints about no alcohol, coaches from different teams trying to steal players, umpires that were absolutely horrible, coaches that abused arms, coaches that flew in ringer players from Iowa, nice parents that lost their minds when the game started, teenage hormones, fights in the stands, police, players that pouted and threw temper tantrums, players that stopped trying in school, players that were consistently late, players that got hurt playing whiffle ball, players that had swim tournaments and family reunions and sunburns and on and on...

I don't mean to paint a dreadful picture here, because when the smoke cleared and the season was over I had an absolute BLAST! I am just saying that there were a lot of problems that I had no idea how to handle or fix regardless of my extensive baseball knowledge and past.

And there was no book at the local bookstore that had the answers to any of this stuff, which at times left me feeling helpless. What I needed was someone who had trudged up the hill before me and had come away with experience to give me some answers and much-needed help.

In TRAVELBALL Ron Filipkowski is that help and he is that experience. Ron no doubt speaks from the heart, having burst onto the scene ten years ago when this kind of baseball was just beginning to evolve.

He answers those same questions I had, the ones that pop up year after year, which will make you a more organized and better leader. I have learned so much from Ron throughout this book and will be applying many of his principles to my team again this year.

If you are a travel baseball coach at any level you don't just want this book, you desperately NEED it!

It is that good!

—Paul Byrd

INTRODUCTION

What is travelball? It is a question I have been asked a thousand times by relatives, acquaintances, friends, and co-workers. The first few times I gave long answers that explained what it was to me. However, once I was involved in it for a few years, my answer changed to a very short one: Travelball is whatever you decide to make it. Travelball teams are like fingerprints – I have never seen two exactly alike, not even my own teams!

The emphasis of this book is clearly on travel baseball. However, the concepts I write about – handling parents, players and officials, recruiting players, fundraising, creating a website, hosting tournaments are equally applicable to travel teams in every sport. Elite-level travel teams have become the rage in almost all youth sports. I wrote this book hoping that it could help youth travel coaches in all boys and girls sports.

When my first son became old enough to start playing organized sports, I had no predisposition to have him play a particular sport, or to spend most of his time playing one sport. Like most people of my generation, I grew up playing just about every sport imaginable, including hockey on frozen-over cranberry bogs. We did not realize we were the last generation to play most of our games unorganized – in the streets, on the playgrounds. Now, almost all sports are organized into leagues and most top athletes specialize in one sport. I do not necessarily believe this is a good thing, but it is reality.

I signed my son up for everything starting at four years old. By the time he was eight years old he had played football, baseball, soccer, swimming, tennis, golf and basketball. I sat back as a dad on the sidelines and watched. If you had told me then I would end up leading an elite travel baseball program for over ten years I would have thought you were crazy. However, two things happened that set me on that path, and subsequently led me to write this book.

First, it was obvious to me that my son was gifted in baseball. It seemed to come naturally and easy to him and he excelled right away. He is a good athlete, so he was competent in every sport he played, but baseball was clearly his best sport. Too many parents steer their children into sports that interest them, even though that is not the best fit for their child and is not necessarily what that child is interested in. I did not want to be one of those parents. Even though he continued to play other sports through high school, I let him gravitate towards an emphasis on baseball because that was what he wanted and that is where his natural abilities took him.

The second thing happened when he was eight years old. The little league we signed up for needed one more volunteer to be a head coach for 7-8 year olds. The league director asked me if I would do it. I had never coached youth sports before and was very reluctant. I only agreed because he told me that he was going to give me three dads that really knew the game and were willing to be assistant coaches. He was true to his word, and I had a blast that season.

I was hooked!

I played and knew baseball, but never at the college or professional level. I bought a few books, watched a couple of videos, went to a day-long coaches' clinic, and then did the best that I could that first season. I thought that I did an acceptable job, but I did not realize how little I knew or how many mistakes I made until much later. When my son was chosen for the 7-8 year old All-Star Team, I was able to watch the top coaches in the league in action during those practices. I realized right away that the practices I had run all year were totally inadequate.

The next year I eagerly signed up to be a head coach. This time I was determined to throw myself into the job 100%, and I went to the bookstore and online about bought everything I could get my hands on to make me a better coach. My coaching improved as did my teams, which dominated the 9-10 year old league at our local park. However, I still had no idea what I was doing and was in reality not a very good coach. I just didn't realize that yet.

I began to notice that many of the older 11-12 year old players at our park wore different helmets than those issued by the league. Some helmets were blue, some red, some grey, and these players stood out for more than just their helmets – they were obviously the best players in the league. When I asked why they wore different helmets, I was told these were "AAU" or "travelball" players – kids who played on elite travel teams on the weekends.

Naturally I wanted to get my son onto one of these travelball teams, but there were none at our park for his age group (at that time, age nine). I looked in the newspaper and saw that a team from the next town over – the Braden River Hurricanes, was looking for a new player. I took my son up to try out and he was chosen for the team.

I quickly realized that the world I had just entered was completely different from rec-ball or little league. The kids played year round, played against top competition, had private hitting/pitching coaches, and were all good. I knew right away that this was what I wanted to do with my son, and he loved it too.

That year I sat in the stands, watched and learned. I saw some things I liked, many I did not like, and began to think how I could start a team at my park and improve on what the Hurricanes were doing. Towards the end of that year I had made up my mind, I was going to start a travelball team at Twin Lakes Park in Sarasota and I was going to try and recruit the best ten year olds I could find at the park.

It was clear to me that none of the many books I had read about coaching baseball, including those about youth baseball, were much help when it came to forming and managing a travel baseball team. I could not find a single book that addressed the hundreds of issues that a travel baseball manager had to deal with. Making a schedule, recruiting players, dealing with parents and umpires, fundraising, playing time, tournament strategy, creating a team website, and dozens of other serious problems went unaddressed in even the best books written by college and professional coaches who did not have to worry about such things.

In fact, serious travel baseball is a relatively new phenomenon that had no mass appeal until only the last ten years or so. I suppose that accounts for the lack of instruction materials specifically designed for travel baseball coaches.

So, I jumped into it and learned from trial and error. My oldest son's team I now refer to as my "guinea pigs." Unfortunately for them, they had a coach who was very dedicated but also very misguided in many areas. I did the best I could with them, and I am very proud of the way they turned out. They are all enjoying great success in high school.

By the time I was finished with them and they were off to high school at fifteen, I felt I finally had a full understanding of what it took to do this the right way. When I started my second "Meteors" team for my third son when he was eleven, things went a lot smoother and I was a lot more confident that I knew the best approach to achieve success.

I got the idea to write this book while coaching this second Meteors team. As Chairman of the Florida AAU Baseball Coaches' Committee, I fielded hundreds of questions every season from coaches all around the state. I realized that many were motivated, well-intentioned and just as lost as I had been.

I decided that I wanted to write a book to answer their questions and help them avoid the mistakes I made. I wanted to write the kind of book that would have changed my entire approach to coaching if I had read it when I first started.

Certainly I do not have all the answers. But I have coached over 800 travel baseball games in more than ten years at the very highest level of travelball and I have learned a lot in that time period.

I hope you enjoy this book and that it helps put you on a path to a successful and enjoyable time as a travel baseball coach. If you do it right, there will be few things in life you will love more.

—Ron Filipkowski

Sarasota, Florida

November 2010

CHAPTER 1:
<u>WHO DO YOU WANT TO BE?</u>

I stared in shock and disbelief as Alan Davis' grand-slam home-run cleared the centerfield fence. The parents in the stands of the Sarasota (North) 9-10 Little League All-Star were going crazy! The most unlikely kid had just eliminated our heavily-favored Sarasota (West) team from All-Star district play.

Alan Davis was the smallest kid on the field for either team. He had never hit a home run before. He would play baseball for several more years, but he would never hit a second one. The home run he hit as a ten year old changed my entire approach to coaching travel baseball.

After the ball cleared the fences I looked at my assistant coaches and said, "Well, we lost. But you know what, that kid is never going to forget this moment for the rest of his life. He is going to tell his grandkids about it fifty years from now."

They looked at me like I was a moron. I was in as much pain as they were, undoubtedly more, but ultimately this is about kids and if I was going to be have my season end in defeat, I was at least glad it ended in a way that gave a lifetime memory to a young man.

The drive home was an epiphany. We had put together the "Manasota Meteors" travel baseball team one year before. Like everybody else, we had watched the "Little League World Series" on TV and were bitten by the "All-Star" bug.

I have yet to meet a little league coach who doesn't dream of being on ESPN coaching his team. Unfortunately, this event on national television has corrupted Little Leagues across the country. Little league is supposed to be baseball for everyone – whether you can throw, catch or have ever played, you should still be able to sign up for little league and have an enjoyable experience and get better. However, too many little leagues are all about one thing – All-Stars and getting on TV in August. Players who are not "all-star material" get ignored. I confess that I was once one of those coaches who focused too much on All-Stars my first couple of years.

Like thousands of other coaches all over the country, I started my travelball team to improve the rec-ball All-Star team of our park and give us a better chance to go deep into All-Star competition. Who knows, I thought, maybe we could even make it to Williamsport when we were twelve? I realized after Alan Davis' ball left the park that this was a very misguided approach.

My assistant coaches and I had just spent the past year drilling and practicing, year-round, our future 9/10 All-Star team. You cannot do that under Little League rules, and so the way around the rules is to start a travelball team. Thousands of coaches have exploited this loophole, and virtually every one of the so-called All-Star teams you see on TV are travelball teams that play together year-round. A little league team who tries to make it to Williamsport without a roster dominated by travelball players has virtually no chance today. That is just reality.

We had nearly 100 practices that year. We ventured about and played the best teams from the big cities in our State – the top programs from Tampa, Orlando, Jacksonville, Lakeland, Miami, Ft. Myers and

Ocala. We felt after twelve months of that, there was no way a team full of little leaguers like the Sarasota (North) All-Star team could beat us.

But, baseball is funny game. Like hockey with a hot goalie – one great pitcher can beat a great team. One bad break, error, or call by the umpire can change a game. The worst team in major league baseball, year in and year out, wins over a third of the games they play. In Major League Baseball, even the best team loses sixty games a year. That's what makes the outcome of an individual baseball game so unpredictable.

Then you factor in that you are dealing with kids, not men. You may not realize when you came to the ballpark that your starting pitcher was up until three a.m. last night playing X-box. Or that your leading hitter twisted his knee on a skateboard that morning. That your catcher can't play because he got a "D" in Spanish. And your shortstop is going to have to sit out because he cussed at his mom on the way to the game. Suddenly you ask yourself, do I want to build my entire program – thousands of hours, dollars, and gallons of sweat – around winning a single tournament when any one of these things can end it all after a single loss?

I suddenly felt liberated. No longer would I care about the Williamsport lottery crap-shoot.

So, if that was not the goal, what was it going to be? Why would we continue on with our program? To win travelball tournament trophies? That would be even more unfulfilling and misguided.

The more I thought about it, the more I realized that the purest and best purpose of a travelball team is to prepare kids to be great high school baseball players. For less talented players, it could give them a chance to make their high school team. After that, how far they could go in the game would depend on their talent and work-ethic.

I decided the purpose of my program would be to prepare my players to have great high school careers. With that long-term goal in mind, I changed everything I was doing with the Meteors. After I changed my objectives, I had to recalibrate what I was doing to

33

accomplish the new goal of producing great high school freshman ballplayers.

As I said in the introduction, travelball is whatever you make it. More specifically, teams embark on the path dictated by the head coach or manager. The first decision you have to make, before you decide on a team name, assistant coaches, or recruit a single player – is what kind of team do you want to be?

What objectives are you trying to accomplish? Once you make that decision, then you can put in place policies and a program to accomplish your goals. I will now summarize the different kinds of programs and approaches I have seen so that you can decide which category best suits you.

Elite National Program

These are teams that are comprised of players from a broad region or large metropolitan area. Sometimes these programs even play tournaments with players who come from multiple states. These programs may be "nationally ranked" by websites such as www.travelballselect.com. These ranking websites try to identify and recognize the top programs and players in the country at each age group. These are teams that have 7-8 truly outstanding players, 3-4 pitchers that would be aces on most other travelball teams, and no weaknesses in their lineup or defense. Less than one percent of travelball teams fit into this category.

Competition at this level of travel baseball can be rewarding, exciting, infuriating and frustrating all at the same time. It is very rewarding because your players face the very best of the best when they play tournament games against these teams. When they are a part of an elite national program they are also playing *with* great players – something that tends to raise their individual skill level. The expectations are also higher, and children tend to live up to the expectations we have for them so long as they are realistic.

This level of travelball is also very exciting. The events you play are the highest caliber and most hyped. The tournament formats are brutal and require you to run a gauntlet of 6-7 great teams to win it all. You may face everybody's best pitcher in every game. People often gather around these "big games" from the lower divisions and other age brackets to watch. They are also increasingly being televised, webcast, and covered by websites who report on travelball.

Playing at this level can also be very infuriating and frustrating. This is what I call the "Wild West" of travelball – teams that often have revolving-door rosters, pick up players for one weekend or even one game, and fly in players from other states. You may draw a team in a major national event that you had played a couple of months before and feel confident that your team will do well against them. However, that team now has seven new players and a new "ringer" pitcher that was flown in from another state.

Unfortunately, it is very common for these programs to pay the travel expenses of parents and players of great players as young as ten years old. There are entire programs made up of these "mercenary" players funded by deep-pocketed sponsors or a wealthy head coach who will pay whatever he needs to in order to win that weekend. It may be shocking to find out that this is true, but it is very common at every age group at this level of baseball.

My Meteors teams have been an elite national program for the past several years. I am proud to say that we never paid the travel expenses of "pick up" players and never flew in players from other States. Having a team play at this level was certainly not what I set out to do initially, but that is where I decided to take the program and I have never regretted it for a second.

To compete at this level, you can start with a nucleus of players from a single area, and make that area your home base for practices. However, you must reach out to the surrounding towns and cities in your region to find a few great players to fill out your roster.

This is especially true if you are from a small town or mid-size city and you are trying to compete with teams from Miami, Atlanta, Dallas, Los Angeles, Cincinnati, etc. Ideally, you want to draw players from no larger than a ninety-minute radius from your practice facility. I have found that is about as far as a supremely dedicated parent is willing to drive for a baseball practice.

If you decide to try and compete at this level, do the best you can with the players you have. Don't ever pay the travel expenses for "mercenary" players or fly in players from other states. This is insane, and is the dark side of travelball.

Don't be a contributor to the proliferation of this brand of youth sports madness. Be loyal to your players and they will be loyal to you. Treat this as a marathon, not a sprint, and your team will stay together until high school.

Strong Regional Team

These are programs that draw players from multiple towns or cities in close proximity. They play in the upper or "majors" divisions in tournaments and expect to compete and do well in big weekend events in their home state. They are usually not deep enough in pitching or their lineup to win a major national event. They are capable of beating an elite national team when they have their ace on the mound, but generally cannot compete against them if they have to start one of their other pitchers. Roughly twenty percent of the travelball teams in the United States fall into this category.

The advantages of taking players from outside your town and stepping up to this level is that your players play tougher competition and generally get to play more games when they go to a tournament because the more you win the more you play. This will allow your son and the players from your hometown to face a higher caliber of competition than they would otherwise be able to if you limited your roster to local players. Additionally, these teams will face a lot more "ace" pitchers from opposing teams than teams that are primarily community-based, and the best way to become a good hitter is to consistently face quality pitchers.

The disadvantages of regional programs are that you may lose some of the camaraderie that accompanies a team of kids who go to the same school and live in the same town. The players on strong regional teams will also be attending different high schools, so they will not play together after age fourteen and tend to lose contact with each other. Nevertheless, if you have the commitment and drive to do it, the positives associated with this type of program far outweigh the negatives.

Community-Based Team

The overwhelming majority of travelball teams are community-based. They may draw players from multiple leagues or parks, but generally all of their players come from the same town or city. These teams commonly play in a separate division from the elite national or strong regional teams. Although they are capable of beating these teams from time to time, most of the time they are unable to compete against elite programs that draw players from a broad region or large city.

I have observed four kinds of approaches within this grouping of teams.

The first kind of community-based team is the most common. It is formed to make a particular rec-ball All-Star team better by practicing and playing more together.

The second approach is to put kids who will be going to the same high school together at a young age. These teams are influenced by and sometimes even coached by their future high school coach.

The third are newer teams who aspire to become elite national or strong regional teams.

The last group is teams who are basically made up of players whose parents view them as travel baseball players even though no objective coach on any other team agrees with their assessment!

None of these approaches, except possibly the latter, is wrong or misguided. Each has its own purpose and most of the people who participate in travel baseball belong to a community-based team. These teams can share a common bond and sense of togetherness that other kinds of programs never develop. Lifetime friendships are often formed as these kids spend as much time together away from the field as they do on it. They can also play with and against each other in high school. These kinds of teams can be very rewarding if you don't lose your sense of perspective and do not set unrealistic expectations.

Communication

Communication with the parents on your team is absolutely critical. If your team is going to stay together and succeed over the long term you must constantly communicate with parents. You must do it sometimes at practices, before and after games, send out emails between events, and in postings on your team website. All the parents may not agree with you 100% of the time, but at least they will understand your perspective and good intentions.

Once you decide what kind of team you strive to be, you must communicate that clearly, honestly and directly to the parents of the players you recruit. Parents will listen closely to every single word you say or write in an email. I have had my own words read or quoted back to me many times by parents. They have sent me emails I sent out years before to show that I was doing something different than I said long ago.

If you tell the parents you are going to be a community-based team, they are going to agree to come onto the team under those parameters. If you then start to bring in players from outside your city after the first season, they are going to be unhappy right away because you have broken your promise to them. Conversely, if you recruit elite players from outside your town with the promise that you are going to have an elite national team, you better have success or they will be gone.

The bottom line is not to make promises you can't keep. If you want to start out as a community-based team but you hope to someday become a strong regional team, then you either tell the parents that up front or do not make any promises regarding what kind of team you are going to be long term. It is certainly better not to say anything at all than to mislead them. Ideally, you want to decide what kind of team you want to be before you even get started, communicate that to the parents, and stick to the plan over the long term.

CHAPTER 2:
<u>CHOOSING A HOME FIELD</u>

Choosing a field to practice and play on may seem obvious and simple, but this can be a very difficult and delicate decision that is critically important and should be thought through. I had to learn the hard way that making an unwise decision in this area can really come back to haunt you.

Ideally, you want to have your team practice and play at an independently-owned or municipal complex where you are not tied, wedded or anchored to any other baseball league or organization.

If there is only one principle you follow out of the hundreds in this book it is to be *independent* in all respects whenever possible. You must view your program as a *private baseball club* where you as the head coach have complete control over its direction and fate. You must never allow an outside entity have control over any aspect of your team unless you have no other choice. Whenever you compromise on this point, you will live to regret it.

Most travel baseball teams practice and play their games at facilities controlled by travelball "organizations" or by rec-ball leagues like Little League, Pony, Cal Ripken or Dizzy Dean. They make a variety of agreements in order to use the fields.

Rarely is it just money. Usually these organizations or leagues will want something else. A travelball organization may want you to adopt their name, colors, participate in their fundraisers and tournaments, etc. That may sound like something you can live with, but you are giving up your independence – even in a small way – and soon the strings that are attached to this arrangement may become more difficult to live with.

Rec-ball leagues typically want something more onerous – your players. They will want a certain percentage or all of your players to agree to play in their league, on their all-star team, etc.. This is the arrangement I agreed to when I first started the Meteors.

I can tell you from my own experience and that of hundreds of other coaches that this is more often more trouble than it is worth. Now your pitchers are going to be used by a little league dad who may decide to teach him a slider and have him throw it forty times a game. They might give him some new batting "tips" that are anything but helpful. I pulled my hair out my first three years of travelball because I agreed to this arrangement. The things that happened with my players drove me crazy – and that was only from the things I knew about!

My affiliation with Little League finally ended when we were twelve years old. My players had played All-Stars for the league at 9, 10 and 11 years old and were the best players in the league at twelve. We planned to play at the AAU National Championship in Minnesota in late July of that year.

The problem was that if our Little League All-Star team advanced past Districts and Sectionals the players would then have to choose whether to leave the All-Star team or abandon Minnesota. Since a trip to Minnesota requires the parents to commit vacation time and money far in advance, they elected not to play All-Stars and to give the other kids in the league a chance to play.

Needless to say, I became the most hated person at this park and the parents on my team were made to feel very uncomfortable. I received a lengthy email from one parent who told me that I had ruined his son's lifetime "dream" of going to Williamsport! I wanted to tell him that his son would not have even been chosen to play All-Stars if my players were on the team, but I left it alone. I decided right then that I would never associate my team with a rec-ball league or any other organization again.

The ideal way to operate is to contact the municipal Parks and Recreation Department in the area where you live and find out if you can pay for or reserve a practice field directly through their office. Most have fields available somewhere and can make something available to you.

They may not be the nicest fields in town, but I know many travelball teams who have moved into a run-down county ballpark and put a lot of sweat equity into it themselves and improved it greatly. If you plan on having a strong regional or elite national team, try to find a practice field centrally located for your players and one that is relatively close to an interstate or highway. Don't just pick the field closest to your own house if there is a better option to shorten the drive for the majority of your parents.

If you are able to obtain a field independent of any league or organization, you will have a much better experience and eliminate a lot of headaches that other teams experience right from the start.

CHAPTER 3:
RECRUITING THE RIGHT PLAYERS AND PARENTS

When I first started coaching, I was arrogant enough to believe that I could make *any* youngster a great ballplayer. I was certain that if he just came to practice, worked hard, and listened to what I said, he would become a great player.

I had that much faith in my ability as a coach and the approach our program was going to take.

I could not have been more wrong.

Of course the thing I overlooked was the component of natural God-given talent. It does not matter how good your coaching staff is, how hard the player works and how much you practice – some kids are just not born with what it takes to be an outstanding baseball player.

This was the most difficult thing for me to accept, but once I did that my life as a coach became a lot easier because I stopped trying to fit square pegs into round holes.

No "Package Deals"

This is an area where you can learn from my mistakes and nearly every other experienced coach. At some point in time you will be pitched a "package deal" for a player.

This happens when there is a really good player you want to recruit onto your team. However, he will not come onto the team unless you also agree to take his "best friend" who is not a very good player and will not help your team.

Sometimes the two sets of parents are best friends and help each other with rides and hotels and insist that if you want one you have to take the other. You should avoid making these "package deals." These arrangements have never worked out for me and I have not seen it work too well for others over the long term.

Travelball is competitive baseball. A lot of time and money is invested in forming a team where the players benefit by playing at a very high level. If the priority for a player or his parents is playing with their friends, then a rec-ball league is the best fit for them.

Don't worry too much about losing the player you really want if you say, "No." My experience is that when push comes to shove he will ultimately separate his baseball from his friend if your team is truly where he wants to be.

Notice also that the title of this chapter includes "recruiting parents." The parents on your team have as much of an impact on your success or failure as the players and coaches. Great parents can be your biggest allies and support system. Difficult parents can tear your team apart. I have passed on several great players because I did not want their parents disrupting our team.

I once had a guy who called me several times about his son coming onto our team. His son was an outstanding player who would help us a great deal, but his father was crazy and would disrupt a unified group of parents.

When he persisted, I finally said to him, "Mike, if you get killed in a car accident, I'll take your son."

He never called again.

Athletes First, Ballplayers Second

I adopted, "Athletes First, Ballplayers Second" as the Meteors team motto during the second year of our program. The phrase reflects my philosophy on the kinds of kids you want to recruit as well as our training program.

Whenever you evaluate a potential player to recruit onto your team, always try to look at him not for the kind of player he is now, but the kind he has the potential to be. You want to build your program around players with "high ceilings."

These are players who, because of their raw athletic ability, have the potential to become great players even though they are not that skilled yet. There is athletic ability and there is skill. Skill can be taught through proper fundamentals and repetition. Athletic ability is innate. As the old saying goes, "You can't teach speed."

If given the choice between a good ballplayer who is a mediocre athlete, or a great athlete who is a mediocre ballplayer, I'll take the great athlete every time. There are a lot of kids 9, 10, 11 years old who are excellent baseball players because they have been drilled by their dads or had private instruction since they were four years old. However, these kids may also be small, slow, overweight or have weak arms. Then there are other kids who are big, strong and fast but are not good players simply because they are just taking up the game or their parents have never worked with them.

If you put together of team of lesser athletes who have been extensively drilled, you will do better in the short term. However, I recommend you sacrifice the short term and take the excellent athletes who just need good coaching. If you build your team around a nucleus of outstanding athletes, and you have a good practice program, you will quickly surpass the teams ahead of you.

There are also a lot of biases and prejudices out there which are not necessarily true of every player. Not all kids who are small at nine years old will be small at fourteen. Some kids are late bloomers. Not all kids who are overweight at a young age will be overweight in their teenage years. Some kids who are slow get faster when they get older. Evaluating athletes is not an exact science.

Look how much time, money and expertise professional teams put into evaluating players before their drafts – yet they still guess wrong on a high percentage of players. You are going to be wrong from time to time and kids are going to surprise you over time. However, if you start your team with a majority of big kids with strong arms who run fast, more likely than not you are going to be in good shape over the long term.

That is not to say that all small or slow players cannot be productive players. The beauty of baseball is that it is possible to play it at a very high level even though you are not big, strong and fast. That is why I believe baseball is a better sport for a young man to play than football or basketball. But the likelihood of success if you are small or slow or have an average arm is diminished. Yes, there are a handful of Dustin Pedroias and David Ecksteins in professional baseball. But they are a distinct minority in a league filled with players over six feet tall who are strong and fast.

I have spoken with a number of coaches over the years who tell me they always take a good look at the child's parents to try and forecast his future size or strength. In other words, if the parents are short or overweight they will assume the child will be the same in the future even though he is not now.

I have found that this is a somewhat unreliable method. I have seen a lot of kids grow a good deal bigger and stronger that both of their parents. Also, many kids may have an adopted parent that neither you nor even he are aware of. I would advise you not to spend too much time looking at the height or weight of a child's parents when you are deciding whether to take a player.

Some coaches will take a couple of overweight, slow kids under the presumption that they can make them a catcher or corner infielder – positions where speed is not necessarily at a premium. I do not agree with that approach. I want my players to be interchangeable parts on the diamond – capable of playing multiple positions and all able to play the outfield. You just don't want to take players who are only able to play one position. There are a number of reasons for this, but I'll give you just one example from my own experience why I advise against taking these players.

Let's say you take a slow, heavy player to play first base for you. It is clear to you that this is the only position where he can be a productive player. The next year you have an opportunity to pick up a great left-handed pitcher. However, the dad of the lefty wants him to play first base when he is not pitching.

What do you do? If you take him onto the team, what are you going to do with your current first baseman? If he was more athletic, you could move him around to third base or right field and allow him to play a variety of positions. Everybody would be happy and your team would be better off. However, if he can only play first base, he effectively blocks anybody else from playing that position as long as he is in the game. You will have a lot easier time keeping everybody happy with their playing time and positions if you have versatile athletes who can play multiple positions.

There is an even bigger premium on good athletic ability during the thirteen and fourteen year old years when you move off the smaller fields and play on regulation-size dimensions. I have seen slow players get thrown out at first base from centerfield because it took them so long to get down the line after a hit.

Remember, at these age groups the outfielders will be playing a lot more shallow than in high school or the major leagues because most kids can't drive the ball over 300' at that age. These outfielders playing close to the infield will be able to force out players on the bases who lack speed.

Nothing is more frustrating for players, parents and coaches than when a kid hits a rope into the outfield for an apparent hit but then gets thrown out at first by an outfielder. It becomes very difficult for slow players to get base hits at this age level because essentially every player on the defense is an infielder when a batter lacks decent speed.

Assembling a "Cast of Characters"

Athletic ability is not the only thing you should consider when evaluating a player. Team chemistry and attitude is very important to a successful program.

In my experience, most teams adopt the personality of their head coach. If the head coach is fiery and intense, players on that team tend to act that way over time. If he is laid back and cerebral, they will tend to be less rowdy than other teams. This is not true of all the players on a team, but many players and parents tend to follow the behavioral example of the head coach.

Although the head coach sets the tone, each player has his own unique personality and it is critical to have an element of leadership come from the players.

Some will be very quiet and shy. Others will be loud and outgoing. Some will be fiery leaders who will exhort their teammates to do better while others will keep to themselves and focus on their own individual games. There is no "right" or "best" personality to have in a ballplayer. There are players in the Hall of Fame who fall into each of the categories I listed above. What I think is most important to great team chemistry is diversity – a few players of each type of personality who get along with each other.

I think it is important to have some quieter players. You can't have a whole team of loud, assertive kids or they will drive each other and you crazy. However, if you have an entire team of quiet, laid-back kids you also have a recipe for disaster because sometimes teams need to be fired up at certain points during a game, tournament or season. Sometimes the coaches can try and do this, but most times the best people to motivate a team are the players themselves.

I would much rather have a fired up kid pumping up his teammates than an assistant coach or parent trying to do it. This is especially true with each year the kids get older. A 13-year-old may tune out an adult, but he will rarely ignore his team captain.

The one type of personality you definitely do not want on your team is the prima donna. These are the kids who think they are the greatest players to ever walk the face of the earth – and they have no problem letting everybody know it. Many of these players are in fact very good, and can help your team a great deal from a talent standpoint, but they are cancerous to a travelball team.

First of all, they typically will not listen to instruction or constructive criticism because they think they already have all the answers. They also will be detested by their teammates because they will often point out all the areas of the game in which they are superior to them. They will refuse or resist doing the little things to help win ball games such as a sacrifice bunt or taking a pitch to allow a player to steal a base. They also will never accept spending time on the bench to allow other players a chance to play.

These players' personalities are easy to identify and most coaches do not take a prima donna player onto their team because they were fooled. They take these players because of their talent and natural ability, despite their obnoxious attitudes. This is one case where you should overlook talent, because even one of these players can disrupt your entire team.

I think it is important to have the majority of your kids be fun-loving and smile a lot. After all, this is a game and it is supposed to be fun. I also believe baseball is a game that is best played in a loose, relaxed, but focused fashion. If you have a team of players always uptight or worried you are not going to be successful. Having a happy, relaxed, fun dugout can be a blessing.

Parents and coaches put enough pressure on kids playing on elite teams to succeed. If the players have the personality to weather that kind of pressure and keep a smile on their face they will become productive players. Once again, the head coach largely sets the tone in this regard. If you want your players to be serious and intense at all times then they will be or will try to be. What I am saying is that this approach is fine for football, but usually is not a trademark of a successful travel baseball team.

Commitment and Work Ethic

Baseball, like golf and tennis, is a game of skill that requires hours and hours of practice and repetition. Therefore, all successful players must be committed to work hard on improving their game even on their own when you are not practicing. The workout habits of great professional players like Albert Pujols and Evan Longoria are legendary – arriving four to five hours before games to practice and lifting weights after games. Youth players are certainly not going to go to that extreme, but you at least want players who will show up to practice on time and work hard from the first minute of practice until the end.

It is difficult to identify which players will have a good work ethic and full commitment when you are recruiting them. This is particularly true when you are relying on a day or weekend tryout to select players. That is why I don't like "tryouts" and have never used them to select players.

I like to watch players over a period of time when they play on other travelball teams or rec-ball teams. I watch little things like whether they run on and off the field, is their shirt tucked in, do they run out every hit, etc.? At a tryout, players will always hustle and give 100%, so they can fool you. As the old saying goes, "character is how you behave when you think nobody is watching."

Scouting the Parents

I evaluate a child's parents at the same time I am watching him perform on the field. When I am interested in a player, I will spend a good deal of time quietly sitting or standing near his parents so that I can watch and listen to them without being noticed. I am trying to find out if they are criticizing the coach when he does not deserve it.

Are they harassing or yelling at the umpire? Are they critical of the other players on the team when they make a mistake? Are they constantly shouting instructions or berating their son? Are they yelling at the opposing coaches or parents? These are the kinds of parents you need to identify *before* you take a player onto your team.

I believe in "coaching the parents" at the same time I instruct players. Many parents simply do not know how to act in a competitive situation towards coaches, players, opposing players or umpires. It is possible to change parents' behavior by talking to them one on one and by explaining the things you will not tolerate. Many do not even realize they are doing these things, and will stop if your make them aware of it. Some do not even know that these kinds of things are counterproductive.

Of course some may just be so bad that you know it will be pointless to even try to change their behavior. Again, the temptation is to want to take the talented player, but if the parent is a lunatic the negatives will far outweigh the positives.

The most common problem I see in all youth sports is a parent "in the ear" of a child while he is playing. Every pitch of an at-bat the parent shouts instructions or "tips" to his son – often things that are different from what the coach is telling him.

I have seen this countless times. When I have talked to dads who have done that on my teams, some of them are not even aware they are doing it. Others insist that their constant advice shouted out to their son is actually beneficial, and that their son *actually wants* them to do it!

Of course, every time you pull the child aside and ask him about it, he will sheepishly tell you that his parent is driving him crazy. Suggest to these parents that their advice may be very valuable, but they should wait until *after* the game to give their son instruction. How many major league hitting coaches do you see yelling out to the hitters from the dugout adjustments between pitches?

In my experience, every time one of these parents misses a game, their son performs better. I do not think that is a coincidence.

No Sugar Daddies!

One of the worst things you could possibly do is take a player onto the team you really don't want simply because his parent offers to pay some or all of the expenses of your team. There are plenty of these guys around. Sometimes they will be very up front and tell you that they will pay for certain things or "sponsor" the team, but their son must play a certain position and/or has to be starter.

More likely though, they will try to hide their true intentions. They will assure you that they just want their son to "be on a good team" and that there are "no strings attached."

However, there is no such thing as something for nothing and these parents *always* expect something in return. If their son is not a starter or they perceive a slight in any way, you will begin to hear about all the money they are paying. If you put your program in a position where you have come to rely on their money, you are in trouble. Once you start to favor a player because his parent is paying the bills, it will cause dissention and you will lose your whole team.

Beware the "Hostile Takeover"

There are also dads in travelball who try to go onto teams intending to someday take that team over from you or lure your best players to leave the team after the season. I have experienced this and almost all other travelball coaches have as well.

These are usually guys who were head coaches of other travelball teams or of rec-ball teams but for a variety of reasons they have lost their head coaching position on that team. Like an investor on Wall Street, they will look for prosperous teams with talent to "buy into" by moving their son, who may be a talented player, onto that team. Then they spend the entire season quietly undermining you or trying to lure your players to come onto the "new" team they are going to form after the season.

Whenever you take a former head coaches' son onto your team, make very sure that his intentions are pure and he is coming onto your team solely because it is the best thing for his son.

Commitment and Dedication

Parents of travelball players are asked to make a huge commitment of time and money to ensure that their child gets the most out his ability. Be honest with them about that, and be sensitive to the fact that each parent's personal situation is different. You will have some parents who are "baseball nuts" and live and breathe everything you want to do. You may have others who are indifferent or even dislike baseball but they are following their child's desires.

It is important to have your finger on the pulse of your parents to make certain that you are not "burning them out" with your game and practice schedule. Find a reliable parent who is a non-coach to report to you what the parents think and feel. If you are oblivious to that, you will find yourself unexpectedly losing good players when it can be avoided with better communication.

Many parents of talented players decide not to participate in travelball for financial reasons or because of busy work schedules. Participation on a travelball team is expensive when you add up driving to practices and games, hotels, equipment, food, etc.. Many parents feel they just can't afford it, and they may be right.

I have never wanted to lose a talented player because of money, but I also think it is bad for team morale to pay the travel expenses of certain players (sometimes called "putting them on scholarship" by travelball coaches). Try to find a way to make it work financially by having parents share rides and hotel rooms. I have "team bats" that everybody can use so parents don't have to shell out $400.00 every season for a new bat. I also do a lot of fundraisers so that we have no team dues and parents do not have to pay for uniforms or tournament entry fees.

The people you bring onto your team, both players and parents, will become part of your "baseball family." You may find that you end up spending as much time with them as you do with your "real" family. Choose wisely and be as cautious who you bring into your baseball family as you would be about who you bring into your home. These are the most important decisions you will make as a travelball coach and will affect everybody associated with your team. If you make good choices on personnel, you are well on your way to success.

How Many Players?

The ideal number of players depends on what kind of program you intend to have. Generally, if you expect to play a lot of games each weekend, you need a larger roster. If you want to compete at the elite national level, you will need at least 13-15 players. This may seem like a lot, but you will need depth when playing in big national events, particularly at pitcher and catcher. These teams expect to play 5-7 games at a weekend event, and are playing the highest level of competition.

A strong regional team will ideally have 12-13 players. These teams may play some Sunday doubleheaders and usually a couple of tournaments a month. They expect to play at least 4-5 games when they enter tournaments so they need depth, but not quite as much as elite national programs.

Community-based teams generally play weekend doubleheaders and only a few tournaments per season. If you take too many players on these teams, there are just not enough innings to go around to keep everybody happy. These teams usually work best with 10-12 players, but ten can be dangerous because if a couple of guys get hurt or sick you can't put a team on the field. I would suggest 11-12 players so that you can keep everybody happy with playing time and still have enough to give you a small bench in case of illness or injury.

CHAPTER 4:
<u>CHOOSING ASSISTANT</u>
<u>COACHES</u>

You should choose your assistant coaches from the dads of the players you select for the team. If you do the reverse, it can get you in trouble. I have seen a lot of head coaches take a lesser player because that child's father is a good baseball guy and will be helpful as a coach. I have also seen managers want to coach with a good friend, but that friend's son is not a very good player.

Again, if your priority is to coach with your friends, then your local rec-ball league is the place to go. If you take your friend's son onto the team so you can coach together, every inning he is on the field and a better player is on the bench is an inning where you have a disgruntled parent in the stands.

The most important rule my assistant coaches must agree to abide by is this: *NO DADS ON THE FIELD*. What this means is that once they agree to become a coach, they must not act like a dad during the practices or games. On most teams, you can instantly tell when a coaches' son comes to bat. The coach/dad will immediately become more animated and vocal, shouting instructions and tips to his son. I have seen coaches say virtually *nothing* during games to any player on the team other than their own son.

You just cannot have this from your coaches. I want them to treat every player exactly the same so that a neutral observer could not tell which player is their son. I have often had coaches I played against many times ask me which player my son was, or mistakenly think one of my players is my son when he is not. Every time this happens it makes me smile because it reassures me that I am not being a "dad on the field."

If possible, you want to find the best "baseball guys" with good demeanors as your assistant coaches. In travelball, there is no set number of coaches you must have or are allowed to have. I have seen teams with two coaches and I have seen teams with six or seven dads lined up in front of the dugout on coaching buckets.

I believe the ideal number of assistant coaches is three, each with specific, defined areas of responsibility. I use every dad willing to help during practices – the more help you have the better then – but during games the most you need is four coaches.

I think it is good to have coaches with different personalities and, if possible, areas of baseball expertise. I like to have one coach as a fiery motivator. Another who is calm and reassuring to the players. You also need a coach who is a meticulous about details and is an observant scout of your opponents. It is also important to have assistants that compliment your personality and get along with you. Conflict between coaches on the same team during a game or practice can be a nightmare for a team.

Once you decide on who your coaches are going to be, it is very important to give them clearly defined areas of responsibility. Delegation of authority and accountability are important in any successful organization. You should let your coaches know right up front what their role is on the team. Talk to each of them first and find out what they are interested in doing. Ask them what position they played in high school, college or pro ball.

If you have a former college or professional pitcher on your coaching staff, this is a huge plus because a pitching coach is your most important assistant. If you don't have this, take the coach most interested in pitching and give him only that role to play. Encourage him to read books and videos on mechanics, handling pitchers, and calling pitches. Tell him to seek advice and learn from professional pitching coaches in your area. A good pitching coach is critical to a successful travelball team.

On my teams, one coach is considered the "offensive coordinator." This coach is responsible for producing runs. If the team is not scoring runs over the course of the season, he is accountable. I keep track of the average runs scored and the average runs allowed during the season and let my coaches know when I am not happy with one or both of these numbers.

The "offensive coordinator" coaches third base, because this is the coach that gives offensive signs, controls base-runners and should be the only coach allowed to talk to a hitter during an at-bat. This coach does not have to be the "hitting coach" during practices, but he must oversee the hitting coach and ensure that the players are getting the proper amount of swings in practices. On both of my teams, I was the "offensive coordinator."

As I stated previously, another coach should be designated as the "pitching coach" and he should not have any other responsibility during games other than handling the pitchers. No other person should be permitted to talk to a pitcher during a game – except to offer words of encouragement. Do not let a pitcher's parent or another coach yell out "tips" or advice on mechanics or anything else while he is on the mound during a game. Good pitching coaches are generally calm and patient because that is what pitchers need. It is the most stressful position on the field for a player, and when he comes off the field he needs to hear a calm, reassuring voice. You do not want your "fiery motivator" as your pitching coach!

The third coach should be your bench coach/scorekeeper. Many teams have a parent sitting in the stands keeping score. I have learned that is not ideal. You want the scorekeeper readily accessible to the other coaches, and sitting close to the pitching coach at all times. The head coach or third base coach may need information from the scorekeeper for a variety of reasons. When you have to run and look for your scorekeeper in the stands, it is often too late by the time you finally get the answer you are looking for.

This coach should also be your bench coach – he is responsible for everything that goes on in the dugout. He should pull players aside and talk to them after they have screwed up or made an error and are sulking. He also has to make sure the dugout is orderly and the equipment is not scattered.

I also never want a parent or sibling wandering into a dugout during a game and the bench coach is responsible for that. On my teams the bench coach is also accountable for how the players on the bench are behaving. I expect players who are not in the game to be following the game and not being either disruptive or pouting. The bench coach is a very important role on a team and is not to be overlooked when choosing coaches.

Finally, the fourth coach should be your "defensive coordinator." He is responsible for positioning the infielders and outfielders when each opposing hitter comes to the plate. He should also be the person primarily responsible for instructing the players on defensive fundamentals and team plays such as bunt defenses and outfield relays during practices. He should be the person who, in consultation with the pitching coach, calls out defensive plays and coverages such as first-and-third plays. This coach or your bench coach is ideally positioned to serve as your "fiery motivator" when that is needed during a game or tournament.

The assistant coaches are the right arm of the manager. It is impossible to run all the aspects of a travelball team yourself. You must have loyal, hardworking, dedicated assistants who believe in you and your program.

CHAPTER 5:
TEAM ORGANIZATION AND ADMINISTRATION

The following are what I refer to as the "necessary evils" of travelball.

These are the things that I personally find the least enjoyable about travel baseball.

The good news is that there may be people associated with your team who truly enjoy doing these things or who want to contribute to the team in some way but are not qualified or chosen to be coaches.

You should delegate as many of these things as possible to a "Team Mom" or other non-coach who wants to help out.

What's In a Name?

Naming your team is certainly something you can do on your own. I have also seen coaches allow the players to choose the team name.

Usually when the players do it, you ask all of them to come up with a name, you pick the best (and appropriate) three "finalists," then have the players vote on those three to decide the name of the team.

It is common to see travelball teams named after major league teams– they will have the name of their town or city followed by "Yankees," "Red Sox," "Cardinals," "Reds," etc.. However, I always thought the best names for travelball teams were ones that were unique or humorous.

If you start out with a cool name that the kids like, it will already make them feel like they are part of something special. I liked the "Meteors" name because there was no other baseball team in the country that used that name. Our logo is a large "M" with a white baseball flying through it, with flames trailing off the baseball through the "M." It was designed by a Meteors' mom and is truly one of a kind!

I have seen a lot of really cool and unique names that kids and coaches have come up with. The two suggestions I would make when choosing a name are:

1. Be original.

2. Pick a name your players like.

Our two biggest rivals in Florida for my first Meteors team were the "Apopka Black Sox" and the "Dirtbags." Joe Renda, the Black Sox coach, liked the Oakland Raider-like, renegade theme of "Black Sox" and I thought it was a great name.

My friend, Coach Pete Saez, came up with "Dirtbags" at one of his first practices when he looked at his players gathered around and saw shirts untucked, long, straggly hair, earrings, bellies hanging out, mismatched socks, and said, "You guys look like a bunch of dirtbags!"

The players all laughed and they loved it! They started calling themselves "Dirtbags," and when it came time to buy uniforms, that's what ended up on the jerseys.

Appointing a Treasurer

I strongly advise that you not be the person primarily responsible for handling team funds. A lot of money flies into and out of travelball team bank accounts. Many parents know exactly how much money has come in through dues and fundraisers, but they don't fully realize how expensive things are and how much money goes out on a weekly basis.

When you get to the end of the season and there is no money left, some parents will accuse coaches of stealing money or taking it for their own purposes, even though that is not the case. Avoid putting yourself in that position by appointing a non-coach as Team Treasurer.

Unfortunately, some head coaches who control all the money *do* improperly take money from the team. They will justify it in their own minds because of how much work they are doing for the parents and kids, etc.

I have always viewed this as stealing from kids, and that is about as low as you can get. Obviously, when these guys get caught, that is the end of the program.

You should involve as many different parents as you can in the operation of your team. It gives them a "stake" in the team and makes them feel more a part of what you are doing instead of just an observer.

Choose a parent that is honest and has no personal financial difficulties to be your treasurer. Ask them to manage the team bank account and handle all the money collected from parents, sponsors and fundraisers.

Each month they should give a full accounting of all the money taken in and paid out via email to all the parents so everybody can see exactly what is raised and what is being spent. If you handle it this way, you will never have any disputes over money.

Forming a 501I(3) Non-Profit

When you and your treasurer go to open your team bank account, the bank will want to have your "Tax ID" number and your "Articles of Incorporation." You can get your Federal Tax ID number by visiting this website and following the simple instructions:

http://www.irs.gov/businesses/small/article/0,,id=98350,00.html

I also suggest you make your team a "not-for-profit" organization so that it becomes tax-exempt under section 501I(3) of the federal tax code. You can find instructions on how to form a tax-exempt, non-profit organization here:

http://www.irs.gov/charities/article/0,,id=96109,00.html

Some organizations like the Amateur Athletic Union (AAU) may provide information on how you can make your team a non-profit under their umbrella for less money and time filling out forms. You may want to explore this option with the different sanctioning organizations for travel baseball in your area.

Your "Articles of Incorporation" can be very simple. There is not much formality required, just a few basic requirements that are all fairly straightforward, and your local librarian can help you get any information that you may require.

Once you have a team name, prepared your "Articles of Incorporation" and have your "Tax ID" number, you can now go to a bank and open up your team account.

When you are setting up your team bank account, I suggest you also request a debit card for yourself so that you can pay for tournaments, equipment and other things online.

You do not have to form a 501I(3) to open up your bank account, and many teams do not do this because they consider it a hassle. However, once you become "tax exempt" you can buy all your uniforms and equipment sales tax-free. Your parents can make purchases through the team and save on taxes. You can also make your hotel reservations using this and save a ton of money on tourism and sales taxes.

Dues, Fundraisers, and Sponsors

Travel baseball teams are private clubs and have to pay their own way. That is the price to pay for independence from rec-ball leagues.

You will need money for team registration fees, tournament entry fees, baseballs, umpires, uniforms, equipment, insurance, the list goes on and on. When I started out as a community-based program, we kept our expenses low and our team budget was about $3,000.00 per season. Once we became an elite national program and began to play a heavy tournament schedule, the budget climbed to about $13,000.00 a season. These amounts did not include the travel expenses of the individual parents – only the expenses of the team.

There are primarily three ways to finance a travelball team if you do not wish to pay for everything yourself or take a "sugar daddy" approach that I have previously advised against. You can collect dues from the parents, have team fundraisers, or you can have individuals or businesses sponsor your team. I have used all three separately and in combination at different times.

Collecting dues from the parents is my least favorite approach. Travelball is already an expensive proposition for the parents just in travel expenses. If you are forced to add team dues on top of it you may lose some good players over money.

If you elect to finance the team with dues from parents, my suggestion is to collect monthly or quarterly dues rather than one lump sum. It is a lot easier for parents with limited income to pay $25.00 a month for a year rather than $300.00 at one time.

Sponsors are fantastic if you can get them. Generally, these are businesses or individuals who will gift you money with no expectation of anything in return. Businesses owned by parents or their employers are always good prospects, as well as sporting goods or uniform stores. I have received as little as $50 and as much as $2,500.00 from businesses to sponsor my team.

You can recognize your sponsors by including them on your team website, putting them on team T-Shirts or listing them on a banner that you hang on the outside of your dugout. Be certain to give a plaque to your larger sponsors or a card to the smaller ones at the end of the season.

I have found that the sponsors like to know how the team did that season and what you spent their money on. Designating an individual sponsor's money for a particular purpose – "You paid for our entry fee in the 'September Slugfest' and we came in second place!" makes them feel special and lets them know their contribution had a tangible impact.

Here is a sample fundraising letter I sent to one of our sponsors:

Manasota Meteors

240 N. Washington Blvd.
Sarasota, FL 34236
(941) 366-5848

August 16, 2005

Sarasota Lions Club
c/o Larry Guth, President
Sarasota, FL

Dear Larry,

On behalf of our team, I would like to thank the Lions Club for supporting us and being our team sponsor the past year. A new season is about to begin and we hope you would consider helping us again.

During the past season we finished ranked as the #3 team in the State of Florida for 12 year olds. We qualified to play for the National Championship in Minneapolis, Minnesota this past July, where we played teams from all over the country and finished in 8th place. I have enclosed a picture taken in Minnesota of our team last month. The uniforms the boys are wearing in the picture were paid for by your club.

As you know, we are a "travel team" that represents Sarasota and competes against teams from around the state and the country. Our boys are the very best 13 year old baseball players in Sarasota. Our team has been together since the boys were nine years old, and we have only two years left until we send them to high school.

We spent over $13,000.00 last year to run the team. We have a professional hitting coach that we pay $100.00 a week to. We have to pay tournament fees, registration fees, insurance, umpire fees, as well as baseballs and equipment for the players. The parents' fees cover about $5,000.00 of these expenses. We cannot charge them more because many are from very modest means. The Sarasota Lions Club sponsored our team for $2,500.00 last year, and we did various fundraisers to cover the rest.

The Sarasota Lions Club has been our only sponsor for the past two years. We have the Lions Club logo prominently featured on our team banner and on T-Shirts worn by the players and parents. We hope you will consider continuing to sponsor us again this year for the same amount. Thank you again for your support.

Very Truly Yours,
RON FILIPKOWSKI
Meteors Head Coach

Probably the most effective way to raise money is through team fundraisers. I have always insisted that the parents who are non-coaches play the lead role in organizing, managing, and participating in fundraisers. It is their responsibility as part of the team to contribute in a meaningful way and it will also make them feel like an important contributor to its success.

The most important participants in fundraisers, however, are the *players*. There is a sense of entitlement that many young people have these days, and I think it is very rewarding and beneficial to have the players wash cars or sell raffle tickets to help their parents out. They learn valuable life lessons that used to be taught routinely to our youth, but are overlooked by too many parents in modern society.

The most lucrative fundraiser is hosting a travelball tournament at your home park. However, that is an extremely difficult and complicated proposition that should not even be attempted by a new team. My teams hosted our first tournament in our sixth season. That was the first time I really felt I knew the ropes enough to even attempt it.

We have hosted a tournament every single season since, and we usually make a profit of around $10,000.00 that pays for almost all of the expenses of our team. The final chapter of this book outlines in detail how to host a tournament as a team fundraiser.

Other less complicated fundraisers are car washes, raffles, selling magazine subscriptions, golf tournaments, and running a concession at home games. I suggest designating two or three parents as your team "fundraising committee" and make them responsible for initiating and managing all fundraisers. You must insist on *full participation* from all your parents and players.

There will always be a few who consistently find reasons why they are unable to participate in fundraisers. After all, they are doing this to play baseball not wash cars, and they just don't grasp the concept of self-sacrifice. Many times these are parents who are well-off financially and would rather everybody write a check and pay dues rather than do fundraisers.

Try to persuade them to see the bigger picture. However, if they continue to be a problem in this area, and you aren't willing to lose a player over it, allow them to write a check equal to the pro rata share raised by each parent at the fundraisers. This will go a long way to satisfy everybody as much as you can.

Uniforms and Equipment

This is an area where you can keep your budget limited or you can spend a great deal. I have noticed over the years that the nicest and most expensive uniforms are worn by teams at the younger age groups. It is common at the 9-12 age groups to see double tackle-twill jerseys, double-piped pants, wool hats with embroidered logos and names on back– uniforms that any major leaguer would be proud to wear! By 13/14U you see cotton or poly t-shirts, ironed-on logo or name, and cotton hats.

A full uniform of top quality like the one I described would be $150-$200 per player. If you elected to go with a simple, inexpensive ensemble, you can get away with $50-$75 per player. That can make a big difference in your team budget when you multiply that by 10-15 players.

I think there are two reasons why younger/newer teams have nicer, more expensive uniforms. First, the excitement of having a new team leads coaches to want to go "all out" to have the best and coolest uniforms. Coaches want the players to feel like they are part of something special, and young kids love looking good in sharp uniform.

The other reason is that I have actually seen coaches use expensive uniforms as recruiting tools. One coach in our area used to show up at ten year olds' doorsteps will a full uniform with the child's name and number on the jersey and batting helmet. Some of these players were on other teams and were in the middle of their seasons. He thought that he could dangle some "eye candy" in front of the kids and lure them onto his team. You know what, in some cases I'm sorry to say it actually worked!

By the time kids get to the 13/14U age, they don't choose teams because of the color or style of their uniforms, so expensive uniforms no longer work as a recruiting tool. The kids at this age just want something lightweight and comfortable. As long as the uniform fits, is comfortable and has their number on it, they are generally happy. At this point you will also be tired of shelling out $2,000 in team funds for uniforms each season and will be more than happy to pay a bill for $750 a year for more practical attire.

I suggest you also buy your uniforms from a local vendor. The internet is a great and convenient tool to shop and buy some things at a good price. However, I recommend you use the internet to purchase only your bats, helmets, and equipment.

Almost every team I have seen that ordered uniforms off a website lived to regret it. Although sizing is supposed to be consistent between the different manufacturers, it certainly is not when it comes to baseball uniforms. If you have a problem with a size, or a number or a name misspelled, a local vendor can provide a quick and easy fix. Also, parents will often want to be able to buy "spare parts" like extra pants, socks, hats, etc., that match those of the team, and if they have a local store to go to, it makes things a lot easier. Some kids go through three pants a season and others one– so you don't need to buy three for the whole team. Have the parents of the aggressive sliders buy their own extra pants!

Most of your equipment can be purchased on the internet through reliable websites. Buy only one set of catcher's gear for the team because most catchers will buy their own personal gear anyway. Get your batting helmets and one or two "team bats" online.

List some good links on your team website to your favorite companies for baseball gear so your parents can find things easily. My favorite site for equipment is www.baseballwarehouse.com and I have always bought bats at www.justbats.com.

Team Mom/Hotel Booker

You should designate one parent who is not a coach to handle booking hotel reservations for the team when you travel. On my first team we called this our "Team Mom" but on the second team it was a dad, so we just called him our "Hotel Booker" or "travel agent."

This person should contact the hotel and ask for the "group reservations" department. You should be able to negotiate a more favorable rate this way. Generally, the hotels will allow you to "block" a number of rooms under the group rate; then each parent can contact the hotel individually to provide the credit card number for their room.

CHAPTER 6:
TEAM WEBSITE AND
PROMOTION

Do not underestimate the importance of a good team website. Most travelball teams have no website at all, and I think that is a huge mistake. Websites are important for so many reasons, and I will outline the most important ones in this chapter. I have used my team websites to communicate to parents and players, explain our team philosophy, provide links to tournaments and places to buy equipment, chronicle our team history, post statistics, team photos and articles about games and tournaments. If you want to visit our team websites for examples, go to:

www.eteamz.com/meteorsbaseball

and

www.eteamz.com/manasotameteors

Team websites can be extremely valuable for team morale and recruitment of players. Your players get pumped up when you praise them in an article about a game or tournament. They can link it to their friends, girlfriends or girlfriends they are trying to recruit! Players and parents can also see the "big picture" of your team– its history and purpose. It can show where you have been, what you have done, and how you have improved each season.

When you are trying to recruit a player, you can send his parent a link to your website so they can read in detail everything about the history of your team, your accomplishments and philosophy. I know that the Meteors websites have played important contributions to our recruitment of quality players. If you have a good team website, players and parents from other teams will visit it routinely to read it. Having people interested in your program and players is always positive. During our first two years, we had over 14,000 hits on our team website! These weren't all from our 14 players and parents.

You can create your own website domain and use your own template, but I think this is difficult and unnecessary since there are excellent servers designed specifically for baseball teams that are easy to use and inexpensive. There are many services available that you can use for less than $100.00 a year. I think the two best are www.eteamz.com and www.leaguelineup.com. Just follow the relatively simple instructions to create and maintain your own team website simply and at low cost.

Team Philosophy

Create a section on your website where people can click a link to a section that outlines the philosophy of your program. It does not have to be as lengthy or detailed as the one I have, but you should put in writing where you are coming from for the benefit of your parents and the parents of players you hope to recruit. As I have said in another chapter, communication with parents is extremely important and this part of a team website can be the foundation of your social contract with them.

I have ten sections in my website section called, "Meteors Philosophy." I have a few paragraphs in each section explaining my philosophy in that area. In "Program Purpose" I outline that we are an elite national program and explain what that is. In "The Players" I list the kind of players we want and what is expected of them. I lay out the ground rules for the parents in "The Parents." In "The Schedule" I explain the type of events we will be playing. Under "Playing Time and Positions" I let the parents and players know exactly where I stand in the area that is probably of the most interest to them at all times. In "Pitchers" I explain how we choose and handle our pitchers. In "Umpires and Tournament Officials" I let the players, parents and coaches know how I expect each to behave at events. "Loyalty" states that we are loyal to our players and expect that in return. In "The Coaches" I detail the duties of the manager and assistant coaches. Finally, I have a section called "Fun" that tries to put things in perspective and remind everybody that it is really important to have fun and that is what we strive to do at every event.

Team History

I think it is important for team morale to keep track of each season and the progress you make as a team as time goes on. I have a separate section where I write a few pages at the end of each season listing highlights, contributions of individual players, and a little about our prospects for the upcoming season.

On the main section of our website I list our win-loss record for each season, our tournament accomplishments, and list each team that we have played since our first day as a program. This demonstrates how we improved each season and the level and diversity of the competition we have played.

Articles on Tournaments and Games

It takes time and a little effort to produce them, but the kids, parents and relatives really look forward to reading the short articles we write each Monday about the previous weekend's games. These articles also allow grandparents and other relatives outside your state or area to follow the team and read about their favorite player.

My one suggestion for these articles is to keep them 100% positive. I have seen a lot of head coaches use their websites to rant about tournament officials, umpires, opposing teams and coaches when they feel they lost unfairly that weekend. To me, that is a really dumb thing to do with a kids' baseball website.

If you have a criticism of somebody, talk to them in person, call them, send them an email or keep it to yourself. Keep your kids and your parents out of it and keep it off your website. The purpose of a team website is to promote your program and players, not tear others down.

Statistics

This is a controversial topic where you will get a lot of different opinions from experienced coaches. I keep and post statistics each week to our players and parents. They are the only people who have access to them. I know many other coaches who keep statistics but do not disseminate them to anybody other than themselves or their coaching staff. I would estimate, however, that most travelball teams do not keep any statistics at all for their team, and I think that is a mistake.

Some coaches say they don't keep or publish statistics of players because they don't want to hurt the feelings of the players who would be at the bottom of most categories. This is silly and is another example of how we worry excessively about artificially promoting "self-esteem."

First of all, kids know when they are struggling and their name at the bottom of the stat sheet never comes as a surprise to players. Secondly, baseball is a game of failure and players need to face their shortcomings and tackle them head on, not hide from them. That is one of the main reasons I publish stats to the players – to motive them to do better and pass the guys ahead of them in each category.

The other reason I publish statistics is to be very exact in measuring the performance of the players for the parents. Players and coaches are far more realistic than parents – they know who the team leaders are in each category without even looking at the stat sheet.

However, it is a truism in youth sports that parents always see their child as at least 50% better than they are in reality. If you did not keep and publish stats, I would be willing to bet you that half of the parents on your team think their child is leading the team in hitting.

That is why, at the top of our stat sheet it says, "Meteors Reality Check." Parents are often shocked to find their son's batting average is .150 points lower than they thought! It is a natural tendency of parents to overlook the bad things and highlight the good things about their child. But, when you are having a discussion about playing time with a parent, it is very helpful for you to have accurate stats available. I have found that teams who publish stats to the parents get far less gripes from them about playing time.

The two most important stats to me that I put at the top of the "Reality Check" are "Innings Played" and "Plate Appearances." As far as I am concerned, these are *my* stats – stats a head coach should be graded on and held accountable for. The numbers in these categories are never going to be equal across the board, but I look for a fair balance and want to show the parents that I am paying attention to the opportunities I give each player to develop. I devote an entire chapter to the issue of playing time later in the book because that is the most difficult issue you will handle as a head coach.

Promotion

Travelball players are rarely recognized in local newspapers, publications or television. It is common for rec-ball leagues to have articles written about their games and tournaments in the local paper, and their All-Star tournaments receive extensive coverage. Travelball players, however, usually toil in obscurity.

I have always felt bad about the fact that my players' accomplishments were never recognized by the newspaper but far less talented players would get feature articles because they hit a few fly balls over a 200' fence in a rec-league tournament.

I have spoken to several newspaper sports editors about this issue, and they each told me that the reason they do not cover travelball is because the only people in the community who care about a particular travelball team are the parents of the players on that team. They argue that they are in the business of selling newspapers, and a travelball team has no mass appeal or interest to a broad section of the community. The city you live in may have 1,000 families involved in Little League, but there are only a dozen on an individual travelball team. This is the frustrating reality of the newspaper business.

Despite this, I do everything I can to promote my players and get them the recognition they deserve, and you should too. Send articles, highlights and updates into national travelball websites like www.travelballselect.com. If you win a tournament, send your team picture with names to the local newspapers and sometimes they will print it even though they aren't willing to write a story. Your kids will be getting a lot more recognition than the others when they finally hit high school, but do as much as you can to get them recognized for their accomplishments before that.

CHAPTER 7:
REGISTERING WITH AND CHOOSING SANCTIONING ORGANIZATIONS

The explosion in popularity of travel baseball in the United States has led to the creation and growth of a number of organizations that sanction travel baseball "leagues" or host tournaments. Registering with these organizations is usually inexpensive and simple.

If you are going to play doubleheaders or non-tournament games against other travelball teams, it is beneficial if you are both registered with the same sanctioning organization, because if there is an injury during that game you will usually be covered by their insurance policy.

Many of these organizations encourage "league play" where you make your own schedule and self-report the game results to the organization. That organization then keeps track of and posts all the game results on their central website. Many times "standings" or "rankings" are kept to determine future tournament seeding or to award champions of the league for that season.

Most of the sanctioning organizations, however, do not even attempt to run leagues. As travelball has gotten popular, more and more teams are electing not to play league games and are playing strictly tournaments.

This is especially true of elite national programs and strong regional teams. That is why a large number of organizations only host and run tournaments each year. Another reason is that, while league play is more structured and often beneficial to community based programs, there is not much profit in it for sanctioning organizations. With entry and gate fees, concessions, T-Shirts, etc., tournaments are the big money makers for these organizations that are, first and foremost, businesses.

The largest sanctioning organizations for youth travelball in the United States are the United States Specialty Sports Association (USSSA) and the Amateur Athletic Union (AAU). USSSA and AAU have thousands of teams participate every year. USSSA and AAU have league play, host local and national tournaments, provide insurance, and operate in all fifty states. Their two major national events – the USSSA World Series and the AAU National Championship –are among the most popular events in the country each year and provide separate divisions for each level of program.

Triple Crown is an organization based out of Colorado that hosts tournaments around the country. Their tournaments are very professional and they are known for pitching rules that are somewhat restrictive. I have always enjoyed Triple Crown events because of these pitching rules. They force teams to use a variety of pitchers and don't allow teams built around one or two big pitchers to advance very far.

Other organizations that host tournaments and/or sanction league play are the American Amateur Baseball Congress (AABC), the IBC Baseball League, the American Amateur Youth Baseball Alliance (AAYBA), Travel Ball Select (TBS), the United States Travel Baseball Association (USTBA), and the Cooperstown Dreams Park. This list is by no means all-inclusive. There are many other smaller organizations around the country and new ones forming every year.

Here are the websites where you can find each of these organizations to see if they have league play or tournaments in your area:

USSSA

www.usssa.com

AAU

www.aaubaseball.org

www.sunshinebaseball.net

TRIPLE CROWN

www.triplecrownsports.com

AABC

www.aabc.us

IBC

www.ibcbaseball.com

AAYBA

www.aayba.com

TBS

www.travelballselect.com

USTBA

www.ustba.org

COOPERSTOWN

www.cooperstowndreamspark.com

CHAPTER 8:
<u>BUILDING A SCHEDULE</u>

One of the truly wonderful things about travelball is that you get to make your own schedule. You decide who you play, which events to play, which organizations to sign up with, and when you want to play. I call this chapter "building" a schedule because that is the way I think you should approach it. You should start out with the major tournaments and events you want to play during your upcoming season, then build your practices and league games around those events.

An elite national program schedule is likely to be 100% tournaments, and if you have this kind of team you should be looking for the best competition in any given week. When I build my schedule I start out with the three best tournaments in the country in terms of format and level of competition.

We are blessed to play in Florida, where many of these events take place. However, I always commit to play 2 or 3 tournaments outside Florida so that my program and players get exposed nationally and get to face other elite teams from around the country. There are a lot of programs who claim that they are elite national powers, but they are unwilling to leave their home state or region to take on the "big boys." If you want your team to be considered one of the best in the country, you need to go out and play the best wherever you may find them.

The most difficult tournaments in the country are the USSSA Elite World Series at Disney's Wide World of Sports in Orlando, Florida, the Battle in The South in Knoxville, Tennessee, the AAU National Championship in various locations, Travel Ball Select Tournament of Champions in Atlanta, Georgia, and the USSSA Florida, California, Georgia and Texas Super NITs. There are a lot of other outstanding and difficult events around the country that sometimes rival those listed above, but these tournaments are consistently the best. An elite national program will typically play at least 2 or 3 of these tournaments each year and play 2 or 3 tournaments a month during the entire season.

A strong regional team should play 1 or 2 tournaments and 1 or 2 weekend doubleheaders a month, with at least one weekend completely off or dedicated to practices only. They should look to play at least one of the major national events to expose their players to the best of the best in difficult formats. They should not shy away from playing in smaller events where there may be one or two elite national teams signed up.

This will give you a chance to put your ace on the mound and take a shot at knocking off a big-time team. This gives your players confidence in themselves and in the direction of your program. If you have this kind of program, you should always sign up for the upper divisions of tournaments, sometimes called "Division I," "Majors" or "Elite."

Community based programs should sign up for a few tournaments each season and should participate in the "Division II" or "AAA" divisions where they will face teams that are similar in talent and ability to them. Most of the schedule for these teams will consist of league games, which are usually doubleheaders on Saturday or Sunday against other community based competition. It is rare for these programs to travel too far outside their area to play, although a trip to Disney, Myrtle Beach, Steamboat Springs, Cooperstown, or another vacation spot for one major event a year can be a great bonding experience for your players and parents.

I did not mention Cooperstown Dreams Park in the category of elite events only because it is primarily restricted to 10U and 12U teams. However, it is such a special place and wonderful event that it deserves to be mentioned in a category by itself. I have coached in over 250 tournaments all over the country, and I can say without a doubt that the Cooperstown Dreams Park 12U tournament is the most fun. It is necessary to put a deposit down and sign up well in advance, so I suggest you start planning your trip at least a year in advance. Sometimes it is possible to get a spot within a year of the summer of your 12U year, but that has become more difficult each year as this tournament has gained popularity.

Cooperstown Dreams Park is so special it is difficult to describe. The coaches live in a barracks with their players and eat together in a mess tent. No parents are allowed inside the "Players and Coaches Only" area. There are 102 teams from just about every state in the country each week. The final two teams get to play in the Championship Game inside the stadium in front of the players and parents from the other 100 teams.

My team was lucky enough to play in the Championship Game when we went. We lost that game, but it was so fantastic to play in that stadium in front of all those people that most of us were still on Cloud Nine even after losing. During this week, every team is going to play at least six games against teams from multiple states. I highly recommend this event for your team. It is a lot of preparation, time and money, but it is worth every penny.

CHAPTER 9:
<u>THE FIRST DAY</u>

The first day of practice is very important because you want to set the tone right up front that you are in charge, explain in detail how the team is going to be run, and let the parents and players know what is expected of them.

You should spend at least an hour having a team meeting with all players and parents before you even take the field for the first time. You must *insist* that all the players and parents attend this meeting. You should also request that any relatives or family friends that are going to routinely attend games come to this meeting as well. A lot of what you have to say applies equally to them, and they can disrupt your team and games as much as anyone else.

Do not plan to have a whole lot of baseball planned for this first day. The meeting where policies and ground rules are discussed is far more important than grounders and fly balls.

Laying Down the Ground Rules

There are two things I do during this team meeting to establish my rules and policies for the players, parents and relatives. First, I give a speech and take questions from the players and parents after each point is covered. Next, I pass out written "contracts" for players and parents to sign and also put in writing what I pledge to them. I actually have had a couple of parents quit my team after they heard some of these policies. That is not a bad thing– it is better for them to leave the first day rather than a month into the season. If they disagree that strongly with something you believe in, you are not going to want them on the team anyway.

The following is an outline of my "First Day" speech to my second Meteors team. I strongly suggest you take your time and cover your own policies on these topics with your team. You may choose to add or subtract from what I said to my team, but I spent a lot of time putting this talk together before I gave it and I think I covered all the essentials.

Startup Team Speech

EXCITED TO DO THIS – HAPPY EVERONE CAME OUT

WHY PLAY TRAVELBALL?

POORLY-RUN TRAVELBALL TEAM CAN BE A MISERABLE EXPERIENCE

WELL-RUN TRAVELBALL TEAM = CLOSE FAMILY OF BROTHERS

INTRODUCE COACHES AND EXPLAIN THEIR ROLES

MY BACKGROUND

SCHEDULE – PRACTICES AND GAMES

RECRUITING NEW PLAYERS

GOALS THIS YEAR

EMAILS AND TEAM WEBSITE

STATISTICS

LANDSCAPE OF TRAVEL BASEBALL IN FLORIDA

PLAYING OTHER SPORTS

LITTLE LEAGUE / REC BALL

DON'T CARE HOW GOOD YOU ARE NOW

PEDRO SANTANA STORY

I AM AN EFFORT COACH

I AM AN ATTITUDE COACH

PROFESSIONALISM IN EVERYTHING WE DO

1). WARM-UP

2). TAKING THE FIELD

3). APPEARANCE

4). BEHAVIOR

UMPIRES

1). DELETE WORD FROM YOU VOCABULARY

2). TREATMENT TOWARDS

NEVER START A SENTENCE WITH:

"CAN I PLAY …"

"WHEN AM I …"

"BUT MY DAD TOLD ME …"

"IN LITTLE LEAGUE …"

"BUT THAT'S HOW I …"

PARENTS NEED TO LEAVE THEIR SONS ALONE

EVERYTHING MUST BE FUNDAMENTALLY CORRECT ALL THE TIME

WHY WE PLACE HUGE EMPHASIS ON FUNDAMENTALS:

    1).   YOU CAN ONLY "CHEAT THE GAME" SO LONG

    2).   BIG FIELD BASEBALL

    3).   INJURIES

THE PROCESS IS MORE IMPORTANT THAN THE RESULT

WHY HOME RUNS ARE EVIL

EQUIPMENT

PLAYING TIME

POSITIONS

    1).   I WILL PUT YOU WHERE YOU SHOULD BE

    2).   CATCHERS

    3).   EVERYONE WILL LEARN AT LEAST ONE INFIELD AND ONE OUTFIELD POSITION

PITCHERS

    1).   PITCH COUNT

    2).   WE WILL DEVELOP A STAFF

Many of the things in this speech outline are covered in detail in other chapters of this book. For those topics, I will not spend a lot of time explaining them here. I only wanted to place them here to make the point that these are things that should be explained to parents. As I said earlier, communication is critical to keep a team together over the long term. You may have a lot of reasons why you do things, but if you keep them in your head the parents and players will not understand corrective actions you take and will get angry for no reason. That is why I think it is critical to let everybody know where you stand, in detail, right from the very first day. The following is an explanation of each point in my "First Day" speech.

Excited to Do This; Happy Everybody Came Out

It is important to get your players and parents excited and motivated to be a part of your team. You want them to know that you are also very excited and that this is not some chore for you or that you are doing it because you were "drafted." This is the case with many rec-ball coaches, and it shows in their lack of preparation and effort. You should also express your gratitude to the parents and relatives who took the time to show up at the meeting and listen to what you have to say.

Why Play Travelball?

You should sell your parents on the reasons why the sacrifice of time and money to play on your team is worth it. Explain to them that baseball is a "skill game" unlike other sports that are primarily "athlete games." Kids can play football or basketball for the first time in their lives at the high school level and excel. That is not the case with skill sports like baseball, golf or tennis. Skill sports are perfected with repetition and good competition at the early ages.

A Poorly-Run Team Can Be A Miserable Experience

Many of the players you recruited will have just left other travelball teams where it was not fun and they did not get any benefits. They might be giving travelball one last shot with your team, but one or both parents may have already decided travelball is a bad idea and that all teams are the same.

You may also have parents who have heard "horror stories" about travelball from rec-ball parents, and they are unsure if they have made a wise decision. Many rec-ball parents have kids who tried out for and did not make travelball teams, or were on teams and got cut or did not play much. They will try and talk the parents of good players out of playing travelball because of their own jealousy or spite. You have got to overcome this prejudice with some of your parents.

Well-Run Travelball Team – Close Family of Brothers

I explain that if you are part of a travelball program that is managed well, there is no better experience in youth sports. The boys will practice and play together year after year. They will stay in the same hotels, share hotel rooms, and sleep over each other's houses. They will become more than best friends– in many cases they will become like brothers. This is one of the best things about travelball teams that stay together for the long term.

Introduce Coaches and Explain Their Roles

Introduce each one of your assistant coaches and explain to everyone the duties and responsibilities you have assigned each of them. Parents will want to know which coach to talk to about their son's play at shortstop, his hitting, or his pitching.

My Background

Parents are entrusting their children to you to teach them not only the game of baseball, but life lessons as well. I let them know a little about my background that is relevant to coaching baseball. Some examples are that I tell them that I served in the Marine Corps, and a lot of the principles I use come from things I learned as a Marine. I also explain to them that I was the lead instructor at our local Police Academy, so I have training and experience in teaching and motivating students. Tell them the experiences in your life that make you a good coach as well as your background in baseball as a player or coach. Have your assistant coaches briefly do this as well.

Schedule – Practices and Games

I give the parents our complete preseason practice schedule before the first team meeting, but it is customary to hand out the game/tournament schedule for the season at this first practice. That is also a motivator for the parents to attend, because they are always anxious to receive the game schedule. Many coaches "play it by ear" and do not plan and make a schedule for the full season before it begins. They take it a week or a month at a time and decide things at the last minute. This drives parents crazy. Parents need to make arrangements often far in advance with their work schedules as well as the activities of their other siblings. Put out the full schedule for the season in writing as soon as you can.

Recruiting New Players

This is where I tell the team that it is my sincere desire that we keep every player we have on the team now up until high school and I hope that every player will develop into a great ballplayer and stay on the team until then. However, I explain that if that occurs, we will be the first travelball team in the history of the United States to achieve that! You are *always* going to lose players for dozens of different reasons. Sometimes it is your decision, sometimes theirs. Hopefully, for the sake of your program, your turnover will only be 2 or 3 players a year.

You should explain to the parents that you have a responsibility as the leader of the program to keep your eyes open at all times for potential new players and may invite them out to a practice or game from time to time to give them a look in case you have a future opening.

Goals This Year

This is something you should talk about not only in this first speech to your team but at the first practice for each successive season. Rarely should your goals be focused on wins and losses. Set a few realistic team goals for your team to strive for. Examples could be to finish with a winning record, make the "Final Four" in all your tournaments, have all your players return for next season, etc.

Emails and Team Website

Explain that you consider communication very important and that you will send out emails to parents to keep them updated on the schedule and your plan for each upcoming event. Also direct them to your new team website and explain the things you will be posting there.

Statistics

I explain that I keep team stats and why it is my policy to do that. I also state that I believe accurate stats are useful to a coach in deciding who starts, the batting order, etc., but also I am aware that stats do not always tell the full story about how productive a player is. I tell them that stats will be sent to the parents email only, and that they can chose to share them with their son if they wish.

Landscape of Travel Baseball in Florida

This can be adapted to your home state. I go over the different organizations in our state and talk about some of the teams in our area. I explain where I think we stack up against the other programs in our area and our state so that they go into each season with their eyes open and know what to expect.

Playing Other Sports

In Florida, we are blessed to be able to play baseball year-round because of the weather, and most travelball players in this state do.

Many travelball coaches discourage playing other sports because they want the full attention and commitment of their players.

I disagree with that. If a player has a desire to play football, soccer, basketball or some other sport, I allow him the freedom to do that. In many cases, the athletic movements and training in those sports will benefit them in baseball. This is particularly true of basketball, which develops a lot of the same "core" muscles that are critical in baseball. However, during the Spring I insist that my players only play baseball because we build a very heavy schedule that season and that is the time when baseball should be their priority.

Little League / Rec Ball

Many parents and players love rec-ball leagues for a variety of reasons. You may participate in rec-ball as a coach as well. Most travelball coaches of elite national teams do not permit their players to play in rec-ball leagues for many reasons. Some simply want full commitment from the players to their program. Others feel that the disparity of competition hinders players' development at the elite national level. Some don't like the way their pitchers are handled by their rec-ball coaches. There are a lot of different reasons that I have heard over the years.

I have never prohibited my players from playing rec-ball up until age twelve, even though my personal preference is that they not do it. If you have a strict rule against it, you are going to lose a lot of really good players who will not agree to come onto your team if they have to give up rec-ball All-Stars. Also, many times their dad is the coach of their rec-ball team and he may enjoy coaching in those leagues and want to continue doing it. Although I have never disallowed it, I try to have the kind of program and build the kind of schedule where the parents will not feel it is necessary to play rec-ball.

Don't Care How Good You Are Now

I explain to the players that they are on my team not for how good they are now but how good they can become. If you have recruited some great athletes who are really raw as baseball players, they are going to struggle in practices and games at first.

You do not want them to get discouraged and quit, and you also want to let them know that you are not concerned about their failures at this point in your program. Give them the peace of mind to know that that they can fail and as long as they are trying hard to get better you will stick with them.

This is when I tell the story of Pedro Santana. I recruited Pedro when he was 11 years old onto my first Meteors team. At that time, he was not a great player and had played on a very weak team that did not play good competition.

I wanted Pedro on my team because of his *potential*. I saw that he was a great athlete with tremendous baseball tools who could develop into a great player in the right environment. His first season with us he was in over his head and his batting average was .000. However, I saw he was worked hard, had a good attitude and a desire to be great. The problem was just that he was not used to the level of competition we played and had to make adjustments. The next season he batted over .400 and consistently became one of the leaders of our team in every offensively category for the next four years.

I Am An Effort Coach

I like players who go all-out all the time and never take pitches off. Make it clear that you recognize players who give maximum effort in every practice and game. Explain that you will be loyal to players when they struggle as long as they are trying their best.

I Am An Attitude Coach

There is a way I want my players to carry themselves on the field. I have talked to a lot of pro and college scouts and high school coaches about what they look for when they evaluate a player. One of the first things that they always mention is attitude. I go over how I expect my players to act and have them sign a written contract about their conduct.

Tom Hanks, in the movie *A League of Their Own*, famously remarked, "There's no crying in baseball!" Yet kids, especially at the younger levels, will often run back to the dugout bawling after striking out or making an error.

You have got to get this out of their system as early as you possibly can. I ask them who their favorite Major League player is. Then I ask when was the last time they saw this player cry after making a mistake or an out. It helps make the point a little bit, but for some kids it is just a maturity issue that goes away in time.

Professionalism In Everything We Do

I explain to the players that I consider everything they do while they are wearing the Meteors uniform to be a reflection on me and my coaching staff. Also, opposing teams will watch them before a game to try and determine how tough an opponent you are going to be. If you look sharp before a game warming up, and carry yourself like a winner, you will have an advantage over them before the game even starts. If you look like a sloppy mob, it will have the opposite effect and give your opponent confidence.

I insist on a crisp and organized pregame warm-up. When we warm up before a game, we do everything together and do not begin until all the players have arrived at a game. This policy ensures that parents will do everything they can to be on time, because the entire team will be sitting on their hands waiting for the last player to arrive.

Finally, the players' uniforms should be as crisp and sharp as their pregame warm-up. Make sure their shirts are tucked in, they are not wearing jewelry and their hats are worn properly. Tell them if they want to see an example of how a player should look and carry himself in uniform, watch the best player in baseball, Albert Pujols.

Umpires

There is a sign on the wall of our hitting coaches' gym that says, "Don't Tell Me About the Umpire!" When players come in for their weekly lesson, he will ask them about each of their at-bats that week.

What is he looking for is the pitches they hit, their location, their approach, and the result. Sometimes, however, a student will complain that he had a poor at-bat because the umpire made a bad call on a particular pitch. No coach ever wants to hear that. I have an entire chapter on this topic later in the book, but generally what I tell players is to delete the word "umpire" from their vocabulary because there is no reason they should ever need to use that word again.

Never Start a Sentence With…

This is where I explain some of the phrases that players are not allowed to begin sentences with when they come up to talk to me during a practice or game. They or their parents may talk to me about some of these issues *between* practices or games, but never during. I explain the reason is that for every practice or game we have a game plan and have a pretty good idea what we are going to do at various times. We do not need "suggestions" from the players. When they break this rule and ask these things I usually reply that I am not a radio station and therefore I do not take requests.

Usually, these statements or requests go something like this: "Can I play shortstop next inning?" "When am I going in the game?" "My dad told me not to do that?" "In little league we don't do that." Or, my personal favorite, "But that's how I've always done it!" If you have half a dozen kids peppering you with these questions during every game or practice, it will drive you crazy. Don't let the inmates take over the asylum!

Parents Need To Leave Their Sons Alone

Explain to the parents that the coaching staff is very good and it is important that they allow the coaches to do their job. Try to also communicate that it is not helpful to the player to have his parent constantly shout instructions to him. Parents can talk to their son after the game or practice as much as they want, but they must leave them alone when you are trying to run the team.

Everything Must Be Fundamentally Correct All the Time

Players are going to come to your team with a lot of bad habits in different aspects of the game. Explain to them that just because they have always done things a certain way– such as field a ground ball with one hand– that they are not going to be allowed to do that on your team. Explain to them that you are going to insist that everything be done in a fundamentally perfect way all the time and you are never going to permit cutting corners when it comes to technique.

Why We Place A Huge Emphasis on Fundamentals

Many players can have success at the youth level despite the fact that their fundamentals are poor. Great athletic ability and a lower level of competition can mask or hide deficiencies a player has in his game.

It is difficult to tell a kid who is batting .500 that his swing is terrible. Usually, he will look at you like you are crazy. But, I explain in this speech that you can only "cheat the game" so long and sooner or later poor fundamentals will come back to haunt you. The more repetitions you take with bad habits, the more difficult it becomes to fix them. That is why you must insist that the changes be made at an early age.

When a player is forced make fundamental changes to his game, the initial results are often worse before improvement is tangibly seen. Tell them you expect that and that they should stick with your plan and not get discouraged. They will sometimes want to go back to their "old way" because it worked for them in the past, but you must resist that. You must convince them that in the long run proper fundamentals will benefit them and allow them to be successful when they get older and the level of competition increases dramatically.

Players with poor fundamentals often pay the price when they move to the "big fields" at 13U and 14U. A physically strong player with a poor swing can hit a pop-up over a 200' fence at 9-12U and be a hero. However, when he goes to the big fields, that "home run" is now just a blooper in the shallow outfield. The small fields can often reward poor fundamentals, and the big fields are like cold water being dumped over these players' heads. The purpose of travelball is to prepare you for high school, not to help you be a legend at twelve. I also explain that poor fundamentals can lead to injury– especially bad throwing mechanics.

The Process Is More Important Than The Result

This can be a difficult concept for players and parents to understand, but once it is explained to them it makes perfect sense. In other sports, if you as an individual player do everything correctly, the result will be positive. In golf, if you make a good putt, the ball goes in the hole. If you make a good shot in basketball, the ball goes in the net. If you swim or run the fastest, you win the race.

This is not always the case in baseball, and that is one of the most frustrating parts of the game. That is why baseball is often called a "game of failure." However, this is also one of the things that makes baseball an intriguing game to play, coach and watch as a fan.

In baseball, a hitter can sit on a good pitch, make a perfect swing, and crush a line drive. The problem is that sometimes those line drives get hit right at a defensive player, or a defender makes a spectacular play. A pitcher can make a perfect pitch exactly where it is called and a hitter will sometimes still hammer it out of the ballpark. This is frustrating for professional baseball players, and can often bring young players to tears. These players have done everything they were instructed and planned to do, but the end result was failure.

Conversely, a batter may have a horrible swing and hit a ball well out of the strike zone and it bloops in for hit in front of an outfielder. A pitcher may miss his spot by two feet, but the batter still swings and misses at it to strike out. A fielder may jump out of the way of a hard ground ball, wildly stick his glove out, close his eyes, and still luckily field the ball and make an out. In these cases, these players did everything the wrong way, yet the result was successful.

That is why it is important for your coaches, players and parents to understand that in baseball, it is the *process* that matters, *not the result*. Explain that you are not going to congratulate them for making a play or getting a hit if they did it the wrong way. That is simply because the baseball gods will catch up with them and they won't necessarily be so lucky the next time. Also explain that you will praise them when they do everything right but still make an out or an error.

Try to make them understand that it important in this game to focus on *how* the game is played, not the end result. I have often heard parents say, "I don't understand why the coach is telling him not to do that– he still made the play." Try to explain that this is not the right approach for a parent to take and you need them as your ally to reinforce what you are trying to teach.

Why Home Runs Are Evil

Most youth fields for 12U and younger have fences that are 200 feet. That is because this is the distance most rec-ball leagues like Little League have used for a hundred years. Two things in recent years, however, have made these fence distances obsolete and have distorted the game at these age groups. Bat technology is the biggest reason. The first aluminum bats were not even approved for use in youth baseball until the 1970s, and those were often heavy and not well made.

The bats of today are insane. They are made of titanium and other alloys that are super-hard and able to be stretched very thin. This allows for lighter weights, more bat speed, bigger barrels and more "pop." Elite players as young as ten now hit "home runs" on these fields regularly and by age twelve these fields become a joke for elite players. I avoided playing tournaments on 200' fields our entire 12U year and I think our players really benefited from that.

The only tournament my Meteors team played with 200'fences during our 12U season was at Cooperstown Dreams Park at the end of the year. During our first ten games at Cooperstown, we had twelve different players hit a combined 43 home runs! It really was silly and is not the style of baseball I want to play. What should have been routine pop ups in many cases were going out of the ballpark and the parents cheered the whole thing on because they naturally got caught up in the "home run derby." I was just glad we hadn't played on those size fields all year, because I realize the bad habits that would have been created.

No coach or parent of a twelve-year-old should ever celebrate a 210' fly ball hit with a composite titanium alloy bat. That is not much of an accomplishment as far as I am concerned. These hits are all outs in baseball games played on regulation-sized fields. When players are rewarded for hitting pop ups, that is not a good thing. Emphasize with your parents you do not focus on "home runs." Explain that you would rather see a line drive base hit than a 210' pop up for a home run, and the reasons why that is so.

Equipment

Let the parents know that you will purchase a set of catcher's gear for the team as well as a couple of "team bats" of various sizes. Tell them where you are purchasing uniforms so they can visit that store and buy things of their own to match what the team wears. You can also provide them some websites where they can purchase quality equipment at reasonable prices.

Playing Time

I tell the parents and players that I go out of my way to strike a balance between individual player development and team success. It is important to give all of the players on your roster a chance to get better. However, when you participate in a tournament, the more games you win the more you play. My approach is that "a rising tide lifts all boats" and that team success leads to more opportunities to develop players.

Positions

It is very important to be firm and clear about this point. I explain that I will ask each player which position he wants or likes to play. I will also ask him where he has played in the past. I will take that into *consideration*, but that is not the determining factor in where they will ultimately end up. Most of the players you recruit will have been the shortstops on their rec-ball teams or on teams coached by their dads. That does not mean they are capable of being a great shortstop on an elite team.

Make it clear that you as the head coach will make the decision on where each child plays and that you will make this decision based on the physical tools of the player and the needs of the team. I also explain that I like to have three players slotted at each position and I have each player practice and play at least one outfield and one infield position.

Outfield gets a bad rap in youth baseball. I try to disabuse parents and players of the notion that only weak players play the outfield. In rec-ball leagues, that is usually the case because many hitters are not capable of hitting the ball out of the infield, so there is not much action for the outfielders.

I try to dispel that by explaining that high school coaches really value players who have both infield and outfield skills and they are far more likely to find a spot on the team or in the starting lineup if they can play multiple positions well. Also, I point out to them that in any given year the majority of the players in Major League Baseball who make the most money are outfielders!

Pitchers

The purpose of travelball is to give kids a future in the game, not to take it away from them. I explain that I am very protective of all my pitchers' arms and would rather lose a game than have a young player throw too many pitches or throw pitches that are unhealthy. I tell them that pitchers will be kept on strict pitch counts and that they may have to come out of a game even though they are pitching well.

Because of that, I also explain that I do not believe a travelball team should be built around one or two "workhorse" pitchers and that we will develop a "staff" of at least six pitchers that we will use each weekend.

Written Commitments and Obligations

To place further emphasis on certain important points of the speech, I pass out written "contracts" to the players and the parents and have them sign them at this first practice meeting. If there ever becomes a dispute about a team policy, I can pull out the agreement they signed and show it to them in black-and-white.

To be fair, I also give the parents a "Coaches Pledge" where my commitments to them are put in writing. These contracts and pledges make clear that we have obligations and responsibilities to each other to make our team successful and develop our players. Here are the samples of these agreements I hand out:

METEORS PLAYERS CODE OF CONDUCT

1.   I WILL NEVER USE THE WORDS "UMPIRE" OR "BLUE" AND I WILL NEVER SHOW THE UMPIRE DISAPPROVAL OVER A CALL.
2.   I WILL NEVER BLAME A TEAMMATE FOR ANYTHING.
3.   I WILL NEVER ASK TO PLAY A CERTAIN POSITION DURING A GAME.
4.   I WILL NEVER ASK WHEN I AM GOING INTO A GAME WHILE I AM ON THE BENCH.
5.   I WILL NEVER THROW MY GLOVE, HELMET OR OTHER EQUIPMENT ON THE GROUND.
6.   I WILL ALWAYS RUN ONTO AND OFF THE FIELD.
7.   I WILL NOT CRY, STOMP MY FEET OR POUT IF I STRIKE OUT, MAKE AN OUT OR MAKE AN ERROR.
8.   I WILL GIVE MAXIMUM EFFORT AT ALL TIMES ON THE FIELD BY SLIDING ON CLOSE PLAYS, RUNNING OUT ALL HITS AND HUSTLING TO BACK UP MY TEAMMATES.

_____

SIGNATURE OF PLAYER

METEORS PARENTS CODE OF CONDUCT

1. I WILL ONLY GIVE ENCOURAGEMENT TO MY SON DURING GAMES.
2. UNDER NO CIRCUMSTANCES WILL I INSTRUCT OR SHOUT INSTRUCTIONS TO MY SON DURING GAMES. IF I THINK IT IS NECESSARY TO ASSIST MY SON IN CERTAIN ASPECTS OF THE GAME, I WILL WAIT UNTIL AFTER THE GAME.
3. I WILL NOT ENTER THE DUGOUT OR FIELD AREA WHILE A GAME IS GOING ON FOR ANY REASON. I WILL ALSO KEEP SIBLINGS AND RELATIVES OUT OF THESE AREAS.
4. I UNDERSTAND THAT THE COACHES ARE TRYING TO PUT MY SON IN POSITIONS THAT FIT HIS PHYSICAL ABILITIES. IF I THINK MY SON SHOULD BE PLAYING A DIFFERENT POSITION, I WILL GIVE THE COACHES MY THOUGHTS IN A CALM MANNER AFTER A GAME (BUT **NOT** AT THE FIELD IMMEDIATELY FOLLOWING A GAME).
5. THE EXACT SAME POLICY IN #4 APPLIES TO PLAYING TIME.
6. I WILL ENSURE THAT MY SON COMES TO THE BALLPARK READY TO PLAY. THAT MEANS THAT I WILL DO MY BEST TO MAKE SURE HE (1) HAS HIS EQUIPMENT AND CLOTHING, (2) IS HYDRATED AND FED, (3) IS ON TIME, AND (4) HAS NOT STAYED UP ALL NIGHT AND HAS NOT BEEN OUTSIDE PLAYING FOOTBALL/SOCCER/ETC EARLIER THAT DAY.
7. I WILL NOT COMPLAIN, HECKLE OR SHOW DISAPPROVAL TO AN UMPIRE DURING A GAME. I UNDERSTAND THAT IT IS THE COACHES JOB TO HANDLE THE UMPIRES.
8. I WILL DO MY BEST TO BE ACTIVE IN ALL TEAM FUNDRAISING ACTIVITIES AND WILL NOT MAKE THE COACHES REPEATEDLY ASK ME TO PAY MY TEAM DUES.
9. ALTHOUGH MY PRIMARY CONCERN IS MY OWN CHILD, I WILL ENDEAVOR NOT TO OUTWARDLY DEMONSTRATE THIS. I KNOW I CAN DO THIS BEST BY CHEERING ON HIS TEAM AND TEAMMATES AS MUCH AS I CHEER ON MY OWN SON.

METEORS COACH'S PLEDGE
TO PLAYERS AND PARENTS

1. THIS WILL NOT BE A "DADDYBALL" TEAM. NO PLAYER WILL BE GIVEN ANY PREFERENTIAL TREATMENT WHATSOEVER ON PLAYING TIME OR POSITIONS BECAUSE HIS FATHER IS A COACH.
2. THERE WILL BE NO "STARS" ON THIS TEAM. ALL PLAYERS WILL BE TREATED EQUALLY REGARDLESS OF ABILITY.
3. EACH PLAYER WILL PLAY AT LEAST 9 INNINGS OF EACH 12 INNING DOUBLEHEADER.
4. EACH PLAYER WILL RECEIVE A SUBSTANTIAL AMOUNT OF PLAYING TIME IN EACH TOURNAMENT.
5. EACH PLAYER WILL PLAY MULTIPLE POSITIONS THROUGHOUT THE SEASON.
6. ALL PLAYERS WILL PLAY THE OUTFIELD.
7. ALL PLAYERS WILL SPEND TIME ON THE BENCH CHEERING ON THEIR TEAMMATES.
8. PLEDGES 4-7 APPLY TO ALL EVENTS **EXCEPT** THE STATE CHAMPIONSHIP TOURNAMENT.
9. PITCHERS WILL BE KEPT ON STRICT PITCH COUNTS AND WILL NOT BE ABUSED. NO CURVEBALLS WILL BE THROWN UNTIL THEY ARE OLDER AND NO PITCHER WILL EVER BE PERMITTED TO LEARN OR THROW A SLIDER.

CHAPTER 10:
<u>PRACTICES</u>

Great practices are critical to a successful travelball team. So many coaches have no idea how to run an outstanding youth baseball practice that develops the skill level of their players and the team as a whole. I have spent a lot of time over the years studying the practice programs of excellent professional and college baseball coaches and coaches from other sports. I then tried to adapt the principles I liked best and seemed most suited to the youth level. I have seen many players leave their travelball teams because the practices were boring or uninspired. Don't ever let that happen to your team.

Bill Walsh Philosophy

Hall of Fame National Football League Coach Bill Walsh, who won two Superbowls with the San Francisco 49ers, developed an innovative practice philosophy in the late 1970s that I think ideal for youth baseball. At that time, football practices at the college and professional level were marathon affairs that lasted several hours and were mentally and physically grueling.

Walsh believed that the majority of these practices were too long and that there was too much wasted time where players stood around waiting for their turn to do a drill. He developed a program that consisted of short, intense practices where the players were in constant motion from beginning to end. He believed players developed best with quality time in practice, not quantity, and that the difficulty of a training program should not be determined by the number of hours spent on the practice field.

I think this philosophy is the perfect approach to take in youth baseball practices. Kids have short attention spans and quickly lose interest and focus if they are not kept busy. When an individual player stands around waiting to do something at a practice, he is not getting better and will tune out.

The other reason why short, intense practices are good for the youth level is that you often only have a limited amount of field time available because you share the field with other teams. If you have shorter practices, field time will never become an issue. However, if you want to design a practice that takes more field time than you have been allotted, have your players arrive thirty minutes early and warm up and stretch on the side *before* you even set foot on the field. That way, you do not have to waste a single minute of your field time warming up.

I have watched a lot of travelball and rec-ball coaches conduct practices. It is common to see a coach on the pitcher's mound throwing to a batter, eight kids in the field playing defense, and a couple of kids waiting on deck to hit. This is a horrible practice, but one which is repeated for millions of hours by thousands of youth baseball coaches all over the country every year.

I will often pull a coach or parent aside and tell them to watch an individual player such as the second baseman or the right fielder for thirty minutes while this practice is being conducted. During that half hour, the player may get to field a couple of fly balls and a couple of grounders. He spends the rest of the time standing around while the coach throws a few bad pitches, the batters swing and miss a few times, or other players field a batted ball. 99% of the time he is on the practice field during this drill he is standing around doing *nothing*.

When I design a practice, I try to ensure that every player is doing something 90% of the time. The other 10% of the time they are catching their breath or getting a drink of water. Players never get bored or lose interest because they don't have time to. My practices are rarely ever more than two hours, but my players get more swings, ground balls and fly balls than players on other teams get in a month of practices. To run practices like this you need to spend some time thinking and planning them and you need at least three other coaches to help you. The more help you have from coaches and parents, the more you can do. Even a dad who knows nothing about baseball can be assigned the task of feeding balls into a pitching machine.

My goal is to have my players leave every practice completely exhausted and invigorated at the same time. I often have parents tell me that my players fell asleep in the car on the way home from practice. I love hearing things like that!

Coaches' Responsibilities

As the head coach, you make the practice schedule, design the practices and are normally the person responsible for leading the practices. You should actively involve all of your assistant coaches in each practice and draft other parents who are not coaches to help you if you need an extra set of hands. Try to get the practice schedule to your assistant coaches in advance of practices via email.

I did not always do this early on, and I found that it really aggravated my assistant coaches when they didn't know their assignment until they arrived at the field. Their frustration is something that makes perfect sense to me now– they want to be as prepared for practice as you are. If you are going to have a certain coach work with pitchers on their pickoff moves, he might want to take some time that day to think through his approach and teaching techniques. If he is working with a lefty, he may want to spend some time studying some of the different great lefty pickoff moves, such as Andy Pettite's. Be considerate of your assistant coaches, keep them informed of your practice plan, and they will do a better job for you.

Once you give a coach an assignment like working in the bullpen with the pitchers or in the batting cages with hitters, don't hover over them and micromanage what they are doing. Trust them and allow them some freedom to teach things in a way that is comfortable to them. You can always take a peek over at what they are doing or walk by, and you can talk to them after practice if there was something you disagreed with. However, you should not "show up" your assistant coaches in front of the players and parents by correcting or criticizing something they are doing during practice.

Individual Skill Development versus Team Drills

When you break down a baseball game, at any level, the vast majority of the game is hitting and pitching. These are individual skills that require one-on-one instruction and practice. If you break down most games, pitch by pitch, they are roughly 40% pitching, 40% hitting, 10% base running and 10% defense. Nevertheless, the overwhelming amount of time spent in youth baseball practices is devoted to team defense. I would estimate that most youth practices consist of 70% team defense, 20% hitting, 10% pitching and 0% base running.

I think the over-emphasis on defense is because team defense is the easiest thing for a single coach to work on in practice. Practices that largely emphasize defense require the least amount of planning, preparation and effort. They also require the least amount of help and input from assistant coaches.

When you view the game of baseball as largely an *individual* skill sport conducted within the framework of a team, you can recalibrate how you spend the bulk of your practice time. The emphasis of your practices should be on individual skills– hitting, pitching and playing each defensive position.

That is not to say team defense and plays like outfield relays are not important and should be ignored. I would just emphasize that these plays should make up a small percentage of your overall practice program.

I generally follow a pattern when designing practices of starting together, breaking apart, and ending together. We warm up as a team and start with a team drill. Then we break out into "stations" where the players spend most of the practice working on individual skills in small groups with assistant coaches. Finally, we come back together to work on another team drill.

Training Camp

Before each season begins, you should take out a piece of paper and list the things you want to work on in a "Preseason Training Camp." This can be a very long list if you have a lot of deficiencies or are a new team, or it can be a short one if you have been together for a long time and do many things well already.

Once you have compiled this list, you then make your practice schedule and figure out how many days you have available until the season begins. Then you design each practice by plugging in the areas you have listed on your sheet into each practice until you have covered all of them over the course of your entire training camp. Some things you may want to repeat multiple times if you think you need more work on them than others.

The following is a list of some things you may consider working on during your preseason practices:

BUNTING

HIT AND RUN PLAY

SLASH BUNT

LEADOFFS AND SECONDARY LEADS

SAFETY SQUEEZE PLAY

SUICIDE SQUEEZE PLAY

FIRST AND THIRD PLAYS

FIRST AND THIRD DEFENSES

TAG PLAYS

BASESTEALING

READING PITCHERS

DELAYED STEALS

PICKOFF PLAYS

OUTFIELD CUT PLAYS

DO OR DIE PLAYS

RUNDOWNS

INFIELD POPUPS

This list does not include the many individual skills you can work on when you break out into stations. At the conclusion of this chapter is a list of the drills I have found useful at the youth level as well as an explanation of each drill. This list also does not include strength, speed, conditioning and flexibility training. That is so important to a successful program that I have an entire chapter devoted to it. A conditioning component should be included in every practice.

Ideally, you should practice for two months before the start of each season. However, weather constraints and field availability may restrict you to just a few weeks. I have included below an example of the "Preseason Practice Schedule" for my 14U Meteors team for the Fall 2007 season. As you can see, we had less than five weeks until the start of our season, and I tried to incorporate as much as I could into those five weeks. I am also a big believer in rest to keep the players' bodies and minds fresh and healthy. In this schedule we practiced four days a week and had a day rest in between each field practice.

110

FALL 2007 PRESEASON
METEORS PRACTICE SCHEDULE

DATE	PRACTICE	LOCATION
TUES, 7/24	A	LAKEWOOD
THUR, 7/26	D	LAKEWOOD
FRI, 7/27	H	SCOTT & TED'S GYM
SUN, 7/29	C	LAKEWOOD
TUES, 7/31	E	LAKEWOOD
THUR, 8/2	F	LAKEWOOD
FRI, 8/3	H	SCOTT & TED'S GYM
SUN, 8/5	E	LAKEWOOD
TUES, 8/7	D	LAKEWOOD
THUR, 8/9	F	LAKEWOOD
FRI, 8/10	H	SCOTT & TED'S GYM
SUN, 8/12	I	LAKEWOOD
TUES, 8/14	E	LAKEWOOD
THUR, 8/16	G	LAKEWOOD
FRI, 8/17	H	SCOTT & TED'S GYM
SUN, 8/19	I	LAKEWOOD
TUES, 8/21	E	LAKEWOOD
THUR, 8/23	F	LAKEWOOD

This schedule was emailed to all the parents, players and assistant coaches one week before we started the practices. Note that each practice is assigned a letter– I attached to the schedule a broad outline of each practice by letter. All of my players and coaches knew exactly what we were going to work on in each practice for the entire preseason, and each of the areas I wanted to work on were addressed. The following is the outline of each practice and my explanation of each:

PRACTICE A

:10 INTRODUCE NEW PLAYERS / TALK ABOUT TEAM RULES AND POLICIES

:10 RUN AND STRETCH

:10 TIMED SPRINTS

:20 THROWING WARM-UP TO LONG TOSS

:20 INFIELD

:20 METEORS MENTAL APPROACH AT THE PLATE

:20 CRUCIBLE WORKOUT

Since this was our first practice of the season, I introduced the two new players and quickly reviewed some of the team rules and policies outlined in more detail in Chapter 9.

Timed Sprints

After the players get loose and stretch out, I conduct timed sprints. A stopwatch is one of the best motivators you can have at practice. All players are competitive, and when we run the bases I time them and call out their run times so that they and their teammates hear the time. Competitions always break out between players of similar speed. They will go all out to beat each other every time they run. Just pulling out a stopwatch guarantees you will receive maximum effort every time. I have my players line up and, one at a time, run from first base to third in timed sprints. After each one they return to the end of the line and repeat this three times each. The players then line up at home and run from home to first base three times. Then we return to home plate and they must run all the way around the bases twice, one player at a time.

This is a fantastic workout and a great way to start a spirited practice. After each practice I average the run times for each player at each distance and place them in ranking order on a sheet. I then email the rankings to the players, which serves as a motivator for the next practice. Players will try to beat their own "records" and their teammates each time they set foot on the practice field.

Throw Warm-up

We then begin our throw warm up to long toss. We begin throwing on one knee for five minutes, then stand up and throw without moving the feet for five minutes, then throw normally, incrementally increasing the distance by moving apart a few feet each couple of throws. The "one-knee" and "no legs" drills allow players to work on good throwing mechanics.

Taking Infield

There are hundreds of ways teams can take infield. I have adopted the infield drill that I observed at a University of Tampa practice. I found it maximizes the number of balls each infielder gets to field in a short amount of time and incorporates plays to first and double-plays. To take infield this way, you will need a total of five parents/coaches. This infield drill is broken up into two separate "rotations," and is followed by three more groundball drills in succession.

On the next pages there are diagrams of each rotation and an explanation for how each drill is conducted:

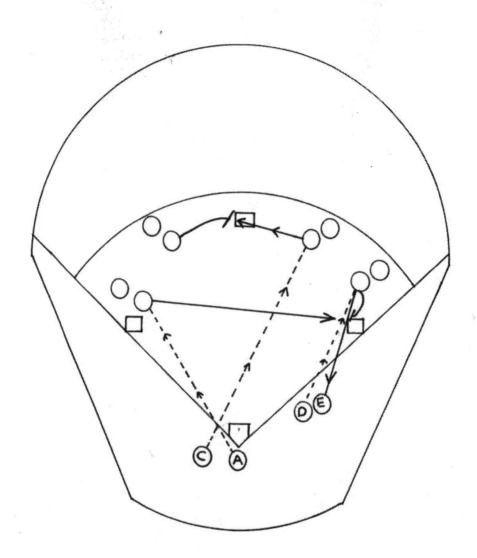

GROUND BALL ROTATION I

In this rotation the third basemen are at normal depth, the middle infielders are at double-play depth and the first basemen are playing back and in the hole. Coach D hits a ground ball to a first baseman playing deep. The first baseman fields the ball and throws to Coach E. He immediately runs over to the first base bag and prepares to receive a throw from a third baseman. After he receives a throw from third base he drops the ball in a bucket and returns to the end of the first basemen line.

Coach A simultaneously hits ground balls to the third baseman who fields the ball and throws to first base. Coach A must begin a few seconds after Coach D hits his first ball. Coach C hits balls alternately and randomly to either the shortstops or second basemen. The middle infielders simulate turning a double play by receiving the throw at the bag from the other fielder and bluffing the throw to first. The player bluffing the throw then drops the ball in the bucket and goes to the end of the other middle infield line. I have the middle infielders alternate positions after each ball they field because I like them to work at both positions.

After seven minutes of groundballs with Rotation I, each player should have fielded dozens of balls and all the players should have been in constant motion. Make sure that the players and coaches never stop in the middle of the drill because everything is synchronized together. If a player misses a ball he must just let it go and continue on to the next place he is supposed to go. At the end of Rotation I, coaches stop hitting and buckets of balls are collected so that you can begin the second rotation.

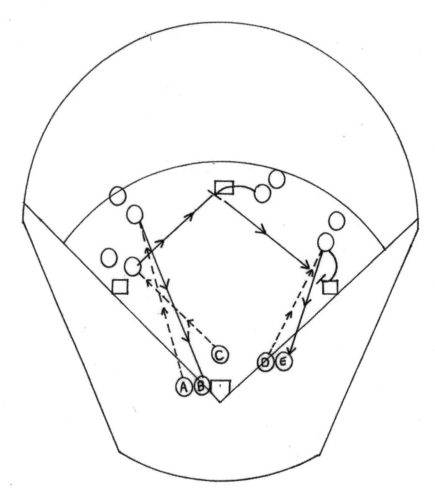

GROUND BALL ROTATION II

In this rotation the first basemen remain in the same position playing deep and in the hole. Second basemen play at double play depth close to the bag. Shortstops play very deep in the hole. Third basemen play shallow at double-play depth. Coach D starts the drill again with a ground ball to the first baseman who fields the ball and throws to Coach E. After the first baseman makes this throw he runs to the bag and receives a throw from the second baseman who is turning a double play. The first baseman then tosses the ball in the bucket and returns to the end of his line.

Coach A hits ground balls at the same time to the shortstops. The shortstops field the ball and throw it to Coach B. After the shortstop makes this throw he runs to the end of the second baseman line. Coach

116

C hits balls to the third baseman who throws to the second baseman covering second. The second baseman breaks to the bag when grounders are hit to the third baseman and turns a double-play by catching the ball and throwing it to first. The second baseman then runs to the end of the shortstop line. This rotation should also last about seven minutes.

The balls are then quickly collected, and I call out "high hoppers!" The players all go to standard infield positions. The coach then throws the ball high enough in the air to the second baseman who has to charge, field the ball and make a good throw to first. The coach's throws it should be made so that they hit the ground a few feet before the breaking infielder is able to get to it. You then throw a ball to shortstop, then third, and repeat the process. After each player fields the ball he returns to the end of his line.

You can keep this drill moving very fast by making your next throw just as a player is feeling your previous throw. This means that your first basemen are catching the throws and quickly moving to the end of their line while the next one rushes to take his place at the bag. The throws should be coming in quick succession by the infielders and the first baseman should be alert and constantly moving. I run a "high hopper" drill for about two minutes.

I then call out "slow rollers!" Follow the exact same procedure with this drill except instead of throwing the ball in the air at an infielder you roll them on the ground. In both of these drills you want to emphasize to your infielders that they must "surround the ball" so that their momentum is going towards first base as much as possible and they are not throwing across their body. When the players do not do this drill correctly and try to make an off-balance throw I yell out, "Stop trying to make *SportsCenter*!" It gets the point across in a humorous way. I tell them that when somebody pays them millions of dollars to play baseball, they can field the ball that way. Until then, they have to be fundamentally correct. I do two minutes of slow rollers.

In the final infield drill I call out "infield in" and we work on a play that can be critical late in a tight ballgame. The players move inside the baseline and must charge each groundball and fire the ball home. We then have the catcher field the ball and throw to first to add turning a home-to-first double-play into the drill. This is another fast-moving drill where you want to hit the balls quickly one right after the other. To avoid wasting time between drills, I have my catchers run to the dugout and put shin guards on while we are doing the "slow rollers" so they are ready to go as soon as we start the "infield in" drill.

This entire process of taking groundballs—two rotations, high hoppers, slow rollers, and infield-in home-to-first double-plays—should take a total of twenty minutes and should never stop for more than a few seconds to transition from one drill to the next. Each player will get to make a lot of plays and field many different kinds of groundballs. It is a fast, athletic drill that includes not only groundballs and throwing but a lot of running. Your players will be tired when you finish this and will need a break of a few minutes to get a drink of water and catch their breath.

After we finish infield and have a break, in this practice we had a "skull session" or talk about our mental approach at the plate. I don't normally like to use up practice time talking, but since this was our first practice of the season I wanted to review a mental aspect of the game I think is extremely important.

An intelligent plan and approach for a hitter at the plate is as important, if not more so, than a good swing. However, many programs spend thousands of dollars on swing mechanics and hitting baseballs, but never spend any time talking about the mental approach at the plate. There have been a lot of books and instructional videos produced by great professional hitting coaches on swing mechanics, but far less on this aspect of hitting.

On the Meteors we constantly stress *plate discipline*. Coaches describe this in a variety of ways – "don't try and turn a bad pitch into a good hit," etc.. The bottom line is that you want your players to hit good pitches – fastballs in the middle of the strike zone – whenever possible.

Most young players want to hit, not walk. Many of their parents do not want them to walk either, and will tell them to "be aggressive." Being aggressive is not a bad trait in sports, but for hitting a baseball "aggressive" can often be equated with "stupid." Our approach is simple – we only swing at fastballs unless we have two strikes. When it is early in the count or we are ahead in the count, we are locked in to a very small strike zone – about the size of the diameter of a coffee can. When we have two strikes on us, our strike zone is about four inches larger than the actual strike zone.

If you can get your players to follow this simple approach, you will have a lot of success on offense. Young hitters should be taught to look for fastballs in the heart of the plate. They should not swing at any off-speed pitches unless they are fooled or are protecting the plate with two strikes. Hitters who are overly "aggressive" will learn that, as they get older, pitchers will *never* throw them a good pitch to hit during any of their at-bats. Pitchers only throw good pitches to hit when they are forced to by a patient hitter. Also, if you have an entire team of patient hitters, you will ring up the pitch count of the opposing pitcher and chase him from the game in the middle innings. Plate discipline is something that is only achieved through a constant emphasis and reinforcement on your part.

Finally, at the end of the practice we begin our "Crucible Workout." I designed this program to be a very intense strength, speed, flexibility and conditioning workout for young players. I do not have my players begin "Crucible Workouts" until the 11U year. I explain this workout in detail and how I developed it in Chapter 11.

PRACTICE B

:20   RUN, STRETCH AND THROW WARM-UP TO LONG TOSS

:10   TIMED SPRINTS

:20   INFIELD

1:00   TWO STATIONS (30 MINUTES EACH)

Rotation I:

      I.   GROUP 1 – HOLDING RUNNERS AND PICKOFFS

:20   CRUCIBLE WORKOUT

In this practice the team is divided into two groups after we are finished taking infield. Two coaches – the pitching coach and coach primarily responsible for coaching the defense – work the station on "Holding Runners and Pickoffs." The coaches who generally work on the offensive side will handle the station on "Leadoffs and Reading Pitchers."

Holding Runners and Pickoffs

You want to divide your team equally by position. In other words, have a few pitchers in each group, a catcher with each, a first baseman, etc., so that you have equal representation of position players with each group. The pitching coach should spend the first few minutes with Group 1, talking about how a pitcher should hold runners close to prevent them from stealing. Then two pitchers alternate on the mound while the rest of the players get gloves and take defensive positions on the base or bases you are working on. One coach works with the pitchers on their pickoff moves while the other works with the infielders on tag plays after they catch the throws from the pitchers. After fifteen minutes you can switch within the group and put two defensive players on the mound and let the two pitchers that were making pickoff throws to go to the bases for tag plays.

Leadoffs and Reading Pitchers

Meanwhile, Group 2 goes to the outfield or to bases not being used by Group 1 to work on "Leadoffs and Reading Pitchers." Most travelball organizations do not begin to allow base runners to leadoff until at least 10-11U. It is obvious to me that base running is the part of the game most neglected by youth level coaches. So many players take leads that are too short and their footwork is sloppy. Many players also never learn how to properly read pitchers' pickoff moves, so they are afraid to take a sufficient lead because they are just guessing what the pitcher is going to do with each pitch.

A proper lead should be at least two cross-over steps, followed by two shuffle steps. A cross-over step is basically what you do when you are walking, except it is done in a little more athletic fashion. A runner can use a cross-over step when he is very close to the bag because he can easily get back. When he is two cross-over steps out from the bag, he must use a shuffle step. A shuffle-step is when you place one foot next to the other. The base runner must also be careful to never cross his feet when taking a shuffle step.

I line up the players on the outfield baseline and make each of them execute a proper lead in this manner several times until they all do it exactly right. A coach then simulates a pitcher either making a pickoff move or going home with a pitch. Base runners should be taught to focus on the right heel of right handed pitchers. If the right heel is raised as the pitcher's first move, he must throw to first. If the first move is with the left heel, then he must come home with a pitch.

Left-handed pitchers are more difficult to read and that is why it is harder to steal second base with a lefty on the mound. Players must focus on the left shoulder. If this shoulder goes forward, then the pitcher's momentum is committed to making a pitch home. If the left shoulder moves away from the base runner, then he is likely making a pickoff throw to first. Base runners get in trouble with lefties when they watch their head or eyes. Left handed pitchers will often use head movement to deceive the runners at first and you should instruct your runners to completely ignore any movement of the pitcher's head and eyes. A coach should simulate different kinds of pickoff moves from both the right and the left side during the time allotted for this drill. The coach should randomly alternate between going home and making a pickoff to make it as close to a game situation as possible.

The most difficult pickoff move for a runner to read when he is at second base is the "inside move." This is when it appears that he is making a pitch because his front leg is lifted first. However, once the knee is raised the pitcher spins on his back leg and makes a pickoff throw to second. The ability of a pitcher to make an "inside move" forces base runners at second to wait a little longer before they are able to get their "secondary lead" or make a break to steal third.

After thirty minutes at each station, the two groups then trade places. Group 1 moves over to the base running station and Group 2 goes to the infield to practice making pickoff moves and tags.

PRACTICE C

:20   RUN, STRETCH, THROW TO LONG TOSS

:10   TIMED SPRINTS

:20   INFIELD

:20   FLYBALL DRILLS

:20   OUTFIELD SAFETY AND DO OR DIE PLAYS

:20   CRUCIBLE WORKOUT

:10   CROSS COUNTRY RUN

Fly Ball Drills

In this practice the emphasis is on the outfield with a very heavy conditioning component. There are a number of ways to work on fly balls. I like drills that ensure that players get a lot of reps and get to field a variety of all the plays an outfielder will be asked to make. The worst outfield drill is a single coach standing at home plate hitting fly balls to the outfield with the entire team in a line fielding them one at a time.

This involves too much standing around and not enough reps for each player. If you break the team into groups and involve multiple coaches, the players will be moving almost all the time and get to field a lot more balls in the same amount of time.

I like to use pitching machines or have coaches throw to a variety of angles in drills that are sometimes called "football tosses" because they are similar to a quarterback throwing to a wide receiver who is running a pass pattern. Catching a fly ball or line drive on the run is a very difficult play at the youth level – especially at the younger age groups. Each direction of movement has its own challenges for both right handed and left handed outfielders. Hit, toss or shoot balls from a pitching machine to the players' left and right randomly so that they have to make running catches. Then do the same with balls directly over their head and in front of them. If you break your team up into two groups, and have two coaches tossing or hitting balls in each of these four directions, your players will get a lot of balls and get to make a variety of different plays.

You also do not want to slow these fly ball drills down by having players make throws. The objective of this drill is to field as many fly balls as possible, not work on outfield throwing. Just place a bucket with each group and have the players toss balls in the bucket after they field a ball and return to their line.

Up until the 12U age, I always put extra emphasis on bloopers – shallow fly balls hit in front of an outfielder. There are two reasons for that. First, these are the most difficult hits for young players to read and make plays on. They often fool an inexperienced outfielder because he sees a full swing and the ball coming at him. Seasoned players see where and how the ball comes off the bat and are also able to read the sound different hits make and know where the ball is going. This is not the case at the younger ages, except for a small percentage of really gifted kids. The second reason is that the majority of hits into the outfield at the younger ages will be bloopers. For every ball hit over your outfielders' heads, five will be hit in front of them. These are the two reasons why I always spend a little extra time on bloopers.

"Do or Die" and "Safety Plays"

"Do or die" outfield plays are base hits into the outfield where the player must field the ball quickly and immediately throw the ball in to a cutoff man or a base in the infield. Teach your players to run to ball at full speed, then "break down" by taking several small steps to slow down and get lower to the ground to field the ball. The ball should be played just outside the glove-side foot, then the player "crow-hops" to get momentum for a strong, accurate throw.

Outfield "safety plays" occur when the defender comes to a complete stop and kneels down on one knee to field the ball. Outfielders should be taught that "do or die" plays should only be used when there is a play on the bases. Otherwise, the outfielder should us the "safety" play to ensure that he does not unnecessarily give up an extra base by allowing the ball to get past him.

Cross-Country Run

At the end of this practice I incorporate a "Cross-Country Run." This is a distance run of usually about a mile. Many coaches have their players run multiple laps around the field, but I try to do something to break up the monotony of that and make it more interesting to the players with the "cross-country" aspect of it. Design a course for them to run that starts on the field but continues away from the field to surrounding areas, then return to finish at the field. You should also have them change into running shoes – it is not healthy for them to run this distance in baseball cleats. Finally, as with all the other runs, this one should be timed with a stopwatch to insure the players give maximum effort.

PRACTICE D

:20   RUN, STRETCH, THROW

:10   TIMED SPRINTS

:20   INFIELD FOREHAND AND BACKHAND PLAYS

:15   INFIELD POPUP DRILLS

:15   OUTFIELD CUT PLAYS

:15   FULL DEFENSE SCENARIOS

:20   CRUCIBLE WORKOUT

Just as it is important to design drills for your outfielders to make plays moving in all directions, you should do the same with the infield. In the infield part of this practice I break the team into two groups. Although both groups will be doing exactly the same thing, separating them allows for twice the number of reps for each player. The players form two lines – one group at shortstop and the other at the second baseman position. Two coaches work with each group – one coach to roll balls and the other to catch throws from the players.

Backhand and Forehand Groundballs

I think it is better to roll balls from a short distance in these drills than hit them. That is because the emphasis is on proper footwork and hand position, and I think the degree of difficulty for fielding each ball should be minimized as much as possible so fielders can concentrate on their feet and hands.

In the forehand drill you simulate an infielder moving to his glove side, fielding a ball while moving, and making a solid throw to first. The shortstop group should line up on the baseline on the left side of the infield. A coach stands near the pitchers mound and rolls balls to the area between third base and shortstop. The player must field the ball and make a short throw to the other coach who is standing between the pitcher's mound and second base.

Again, you are more concerned about technique, so it is not necessary to have the player make a full throw. In this drill you emphasize to the players that they should take an extra step after fielding the ball to make a shoulder turn towards the base they are throwing to. The other group of infielders does exactly the same forehand drill, except they begin near the second base bag and the coach receiving the throws from this group is near the first base line.

125

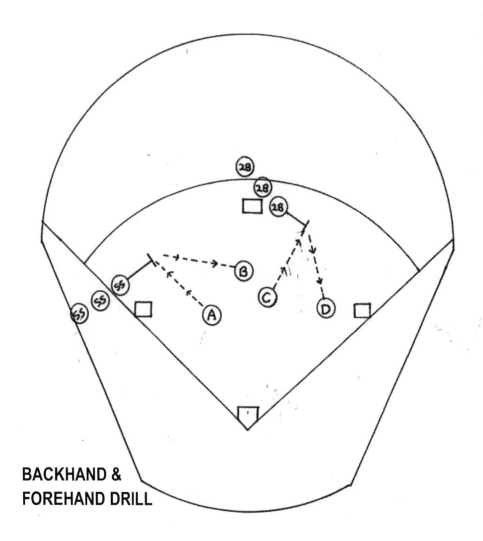

**BACKHAND &
FOREHAND DRILL**

Backhand plays are the most difficult for infielders at all levels of baseball. There are a few fundamental points that you should work on when you rolls balls to the backhand side of the infielder groups. First, they should drop their back leg (the one closest to the outfield) to get low to the ground rather than trying to bend at the waist. Second, they should field the ball just off the front toe of their front leg. Third, they should roll the elbow of their glove arm towards the outfield so that the glove is at a 45 degree angle when the ball reaches it. Finally, they should be forced to take one extra step after fielding the ball in order to plant their right foot and make a solid throw. Young players see major leaguers make throws on backhand plays while falling backwards off their left foot. Derek Jeter is famous for this play. However, this is exceptionally difficult for a young player to pull off and you should insist on the extra step to avoid giving away extra bases on a throwing error.

Infield Popups

When I work on infield popup drills, I like to use a tennis racket and tennis balls for two reasons. First, it is easier to place the ball just about exactly where you want to every time, and the location and the height of the ball is the main concern in this drill. Second, a tennis ball must be fielded with perfect form or it will pop out of a baseball glove.

Many young players move their gloves up towards the ball at the very last second in order to catch it. The correct way to field a pop up is the opposite – pulling the ball into your body by moving the glove towards you as you catch the ball. You can still get away with fielding a pop up incorrectly most of the time when you catch a baseball. However, with a tennis ball it is virtually impossible. Players who field pop ups incorrectly will get so frustrated trying to catch tennis balls. This drill will illustrate the point that they are doing something wrong and need to make an adjustment.

The primary emphasis on the infield pop up drill is to have the proper infielder make the play by "calling off" the other infielders and making the catch. Infielders colliding or balls dropping on the ground between three players is a very unpleasant experience that happens too often at the youth level. That is why this must be practiced more often for the younger ages.

The best way to explain the proper approach is to use cones to divide in the infield up into four triangles and explain that each triangle has an infielder who is "the boss" or "in charge" of fielding pop ups in that triangle. Tell players to take charge of their triangle and call the ball loudly with authority. You should also make sure that when other infielders are called off, they get out of the way so they are not in the peripheral vision of the fielder who is making the play.

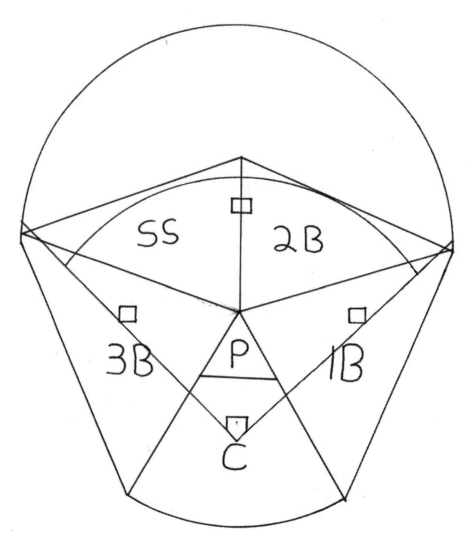

INFIELD POP-UP ZONES

Outfield Cut Plays

The outfield cut play drill is not done with a full team defense in place. This drill is done with a small group of players at each outfield position, a relay or cutoff man in the infield and a catcher.

You can have one coach alternate hitting to different outfielders and they field the ball and execute a good relay to the plate or another base with the infielder.

The most common mistake cutoff men make is that they fail to put their body in the right position to catch and throw. Too often they go to spot and stay there, no matter where the throw is from the outfielder.

Cutoff men will often get lazy and are content to catch the ball on a short hop, at their knees or to their backhand side. You must preach to them constantly to move their feet and work hard to get in position to field the ball in the air, chest high.

Cutoff men at the youth level must also be told not to "show their number to the catcher" by squaring up their back to the catcher when they receive the throw from the outfield. They should "blade" their body and catch the ball off to their glove side so that they can make a faster and more accurate relay throw to the plate.

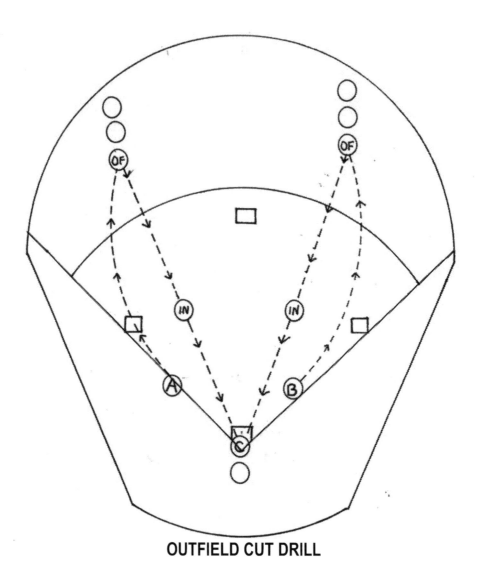

OUTFIELD CUT DRILL

Full Defense Scenarios

"Full defense scenarios" is when you put all your defensive drills together and work on everything in a total package. You put a full defense in place with nine defensive players. Extra players can alternate at certain positions. A coach stands at home plate and calls out a scenario, "Runner on first!" or "Bases loaded!" then hits the ball to a random spot in the infield or outfield where the defense must execute the proper play. After each play you can instruct players who make physical or mental errors. Every ten plays or so you can rotate your players to new positions and continue with the drill.

PRACTICE E

:20   RUN, STRETCH AND THROW

:10   TIMED SPRINTS

:20   INFIELD

1:00   THREE STATIONS (20 MINUTES EACH)

ROTATION I:

GROUP 1 - BULLPEN (PITCHERS AND CATCHERS)

GROUP 2 - HITTING STATIONS

GROUP 3 - CATCHER DRILLS

ROTATION II:

GROUP 1 - FIRST AND THIRD BASE

GROUP 2 - BULLPEN

GROUP 3 - HITTING STATIONS

ROTATION III:

GROUP 1 - HITTING STATIONS

GROUP 2 - MIDDLE INFIELD

GROUP 3 - BULLPEN

:20   CRUCIBLE WORKOUT

This is one of my favorite practices and is a great practice to do on a night once a week after your season begins because you can cover a wide variety of game-specific skills with your players. The focus of this practice is clearly individual skill development over team drills and requires a minimum of three coaches. In this practice each player will work on individual drills for his primary defensive position, have a session as a bullpen pitcher or catcher, and go through multiple hitting

131

stations. Every major component of the game except base running is covered in this practice.

After you finish infield, the team is broken up into three groups. You should know who will be in each group before you begin practice. In this practice, Group 1 should be your corner infielders, Group 2 should be your middle infielders and Group 3 should be your catchers. Of course, you are going to have a few players who may play both catcher and first base, or third base and shortstop. Just try and group the players with the positions they play the most often. Each group should have at least 1-2 pitchers, and you should have a minimum of three players in each group.

Bullpen

The pitching coach will be in charge of the bullpen. Hopefully, your field complex has a bullpen or at least a rubber and a plate off to the side of the field. Any player on your team can serve as a "bullpen catcher," so just take any non-pitcher in this group and have him get catcher's gear on. You don't need this player to be a good catcher, just a body to receive the ball from your pitcher who is the one getting the work. The pitching coach has plenty of time here to work with two pitchers on mechanics, off-speed pitches, pickoff moves, whatever is needed for the individuals he is instructing. This is also a good time for the pitching coach to talk to his pitchers one-on-one about their last outing – things they did well, mistakes they made, etc.

Batting Cages

The hitting coach will be in charge of the hitting station. At least three different "stations" should be set up in or near the batting cages so that none of the players waste time standing around waiting to hit. Ideally, a couple of parents or an extra coach will be here with the hitting coach because this is the most labor intensive station. You can choose from a large variety of hitting drills at the end of this chapter or any that you prefer. It is always good to have a coach throwing live batting practice as one of the stations. A pitching machine throwing hard is always a good option as well because it can be manned by a parent who does not even know have to anything about baseball because he is essentially just feeding balls into the machine.

Individual Position Drills

The individual defensive position stations are extremely valuable for your players. I have found that my players get more out of these 20 minute sessions than out of multiple hours in team defensive drills. These sessions give your defensive coach an opportunity to work with the catchers, middle infielders and corner infielders in small groups on a wide variety of things. Each one may be strong in one area and not another, so you can work with them on the things that require special attention. In the twenty minutes allotted I will usually spend five minutes each on four separate catcher drills with the catchers, and four drills specifically for the infielders at their primary position. Again, I have given you several choices of drills for each position to choose from at the end of this chapter.

PRACTICE F

:20 RUN, STRETCH AND THROW

:10 TIMED SPRINTS

:30 BASE RUNNING SITUATIONAL PLAYS

  1. TAG PLAYS

  2. ON SECOND WITH NO FORCE

  3. READING THE DEFENSE

  4. SCORING FROM 3RD WITH LESS THAN 2 OUTS

  5. SAFETY SQUEEZE

  6. SUICIDE SQUEEZE

  7. STEALING HOME

:10 DELAYED-BLUFF STEAL PLAY

:10   FIRST AND THIRD OFFENSIVE PLAYS

:20   FIRST AND THIRD DEFENSIVE PLAYS

:20   CRUCIBLE WORKOUT

This practice is all about base running. When it comes to base running, I am somewhat of a fanatic. I explain to players that they are going to make physical errors from time to time – miss a groundball, make a bad throw, take a bad swing – these things are part of the game at even the highest level. However, base running mistakes should *never* happen and there are no excuses for them. Some aspects of baseball require God-given talent to perform at a high level. However, it takes no natural talent to be a great base runner. The only traits necessary is for a player to be aggressive, alert and give 100% effort.

You can encourage aggressiveness by not being hard on a player who makes a mistake by being *too* aggressive on the bases. If he is trying to take an extra base when he should not have, correct him gently but also tell him you like his hustle. The only time you should really get on a player is for making base running mistakes that are not aggressive enough, or when he is not paying attention. You should never tolerate that because this is the one aspect of the game where there is no excuse for making mistakes. I tell my players that the only thing I expect from them on the base paths is absolute perfection.

In the "situational plays" part of this practice we go over plays that happen frequently in youth games. Many of these plays have to be modified or completely thrown out at the high school level, but they work well and frequently make the difference in close 9U-14U travelball games. Base running accounts for a higher percentage of runs for each year you go down in youth baseball. We practice each one of these "situational plays" for about five minutes. The concepts are easy to grasp for even young players if the plays are broken down and taught individually.

Tagging Up

When we work on "tag plays" I teach players not to watch the ball when they tag up. I want them to listen to the base coach and go when told to. I have them at the base in an athletic position with their head down ready to go. There are two reasons why I insist they not watch the catch. The first is that kids get "jumpy" and will sometimes get too anxious and leave early. The second is that opposing youth coaches almost *always* appeal every single tag play – even the ones that are not remotely close. It is an incredibly aggravating part of the youth game to me – for some reason there is always at least one parent or coach on the opposing team who is certain the base runner left the bag early. On deep fly balls where I know the player is going to score easily, I will wait a full second before sending the runner. The other teams still appeal even that!

Runner on Second, No Force

The next play is one that works often at the lower ages but rarely ever works by high school. We place runners at second base and work on the situation when there is nobody on first base and a groundball is hit to the left side of the infield. The players read the play by the defender and decide whether they can advance to third base after the fielder makes a throw to first. You should have coaches playing third base and shortstop, and tell them to do different things randomly. Sometimes they should field the ball cleanly and throw to first right away. Sometimes they should check the runner at second then throw to first. Sometimes they should fake a throw to first then quickly turn to second to try to pick off the runner.

Base runners should be taught that they can advance more off the bag the further the hit is away from them. If the ground ball is hit to the third baseman, they can safely get a lot further off the bag then if it is hit to shortstop. They should also be taught that if they are far enough off the bag and can advance to third on the throw, they should try and do it. If they are forced to remain close to second base by an alert fielder who checks them back, then they have to stay.

Reading the Defense

In "Reading the Defense" we talk about how it is the players' responsibility to take a look at where each outfielder is playing before every pitch. A good base coach will also do this, but if a player is aware of the position of the outfielders he will often know as soon as his teammate hits the ball if it is going to be a base hit or caught. If he notices that the right fielder is playing way off the line, he can break without hesitation if the hitter hits a ball down the line.

Too often young base runners execute their own version of "hit and run" – they wait for the ball to hit the ground in the outfield before they run to the next base. If they "read the defense" they will be rolling to the next base before the ball even clears the infield.

Scoring from Third With Less Than Two Outs

Next we work on scoring from third base on a groundball when there are less than two outs. Again, players must be taught to "read the defense." If the infield in playing in, a base runner can still score on a soft grounder but must "freeze" if it is hit well to make sure it gets through to the outfield. If the infield is playing back or at normal depth, runners can generally score on any ground ball except those hit back to the pitcher or hard right at the third baseman.

In this drill a coach hits different kinds of grounders and the base runners must read the type of hit and decide whether or not to go. The base runner must be decisive and quick – if he hesitates then tries to score he will be out almost every time.

Safety Squeeze

The "safety squeeze" bunt play is very similar to the last drill where the base runner must read the defense and the bunt to decide quickly whether to try and score. A coach should hit or toss the ball to simulate different kinds of bunts, including those that are popped up to different spots. The base runner should read the bunt and score or hold at third. On this play you want your base runners to be very aggressive because you are willing to give up an out at first and don't want to do that without scoring a run. I have my runners at third get a very aggressive secondary lead and break for home right away unless the bunt is popped up or hit hard right back to the pitcher.

Suicide Squeeze

We then practice the "suicide squeeze" bunt play, although I strongly dislike using this play in a game. There are just too many variables that have to fall into place for the suicide squeeze play to be successful, so I rarely ever use it. A suicide squeeze occurs when your base runner at third base breaks for home before the pitcher delivers the pitch and the hitter must bunt the ball. If it is executed correctly and the ball is bunted on the ground in fair territory, it is impossible for the defense to prevent the runner at third from scoring. That is why the play is attractive to some coaches. However, the risks far outweigh the likelihood of success. First, the play relies on the other team's pitcher to throw a pitch that is capable of being bunted in fair territory. A pitch in the dirt or off the plate can't be bunted and will result in the runner coming down the third base line to be out at the plate or caught in a run down. A high pitch can be even worse, because pitches up in the zone often result in bunts that get popped into the air for a double play if it is caught. Then, even if you get a good pitch to bunt, if your batter misses the bunt you will also make a costly out at home. It is unwise to rely often on this many variables at the youth level of baseball. Trust your hitters to drive the run in by swinging away or use the "safety squeeze" play.

Stealing Home

Stealing home is the most exciting play in baseball. If you can pull it off it is the most psychologically damaging play to an opposing team, especially to their pitcher. I have seen experienced travelball pitchers come completely unglued after an opposing player steals home on them. Even though it is only one run, it is almost like scoring three runs for the effect it can have on your team and your opponent. I cannot emphasize enough that you must have *multiple safeguards* to protect your players if you are going to try and steal home. The base runner coming from third base will often reach the plate at the time a bat will be coming through the zone if the hitter swings. This can result in serious injury or death if a base runner is struck in the head by a swing. All players miss signs – especially those at the younger age groups. *Do not "hope" the batter received the sign* when you have a base runner steal home – you must *make absolutely sure*.

When I give the batter a sign that we are stealing home, he must give me *two* signals back to let me know he received the sign and understood it. First, he must reach up and adjust his helmet. Then he has to get into the batter's box and tap the plate with the end of his bat. Only after he shows me these two signs will I then give the signal to the runner to steal home. Our hitters then execute a "bluff bunt" to distract the pitcher and catcher as much as possible while our runner is trying to come home.

An opposing pitcher will give you the opportunity to steal home when he is pitching out of the "windup" and does not pay attention to the runner at third base. If you notice the pitcher is very slow in his delivery, tell your base runner as soon as he reaches third base to start "timing" the pitcher. That is my signal to him that we are going to consider stealing home the next pitch. Your base runner then watches the pitcher closely to see when he makes his "first move" to begin the windup. On the next pitch, the runner gets a walking lead and breaks as soon as the pitcher makes his first move. This play works even better with a lefty pitcher because he will have his back to the base runner once he begins his windup. The base runner should run on the inside of the baseline and slide into the front part of home plate so the catcher is forced to come all the way across the plate to make the tag.

Delayed Bluff Steal

The "Delayed Bluff Steal" play is one of the key components of "First-and-Third" offensive plays. I use the terminology "delayed" and "bluff" to clearly indicate to my players how I want this play to be run. At the 11U and 12U ages, teams will rarely have their catcher throw down to second base when a runner tries to steal second with less than two outs if there is also a runner on third. That is because the runner at third will almost always be able to score easily on the throw. This is not the case at 13U and up because the bases are further apart and the defenders have stronger arms. However, when there are two outs, teams will often throw down to second because they believe they can get the final out there *before* the runner at third will be able to score. The delayed-bluff steal play is designed for that situation.

The objective of this play is to draw a throw from the catcher to second base so that the run will score from third. This is also a play that is essentially a sacrifice where you are willing to give up an out to score the run. The first word of the play, "delayed," means that the player on first will not break for second until the pitcher releases the ball to the plate. This is much later than it would be on a straight steal, and that is done intentionally to bait the catcher into throwing down because he will think he has a sure out. The second word of the play, "bluff," means that once the throw goes down to second base, the runner will stop to avoid running into a tag. The runner at third base will break for home on the throw from the catcher, so the middle infielder who received the throw at second will have to immediately decide to throw home or try and get the runner out coming from first. If the middle infielder throws home, the runner at first then advances to second easily. Otherwise, this runner tries to get in a rundown as long as possible to tie up the infielders and allow the runner at third to score.

I have seen teams run first-and-third offensive plays dozens of different ways over the years. Some teams have the runner at first break for second right away just like a straight steal. I think this is a mistake because that runner becomes vulnerable to a "double move" pickoff where the pitcher fakes a throw to third then spins to first and disengages the rubber. The problem with this is that the pitcher can often freeze the runner at third long enough to prevent him from scoring and still be able to get the runner at first out in a quick rundown. That is one of the reasons why I force my runners to "delay" their steal so they never have to worry about a "double move" by the pitcher.

Most teams also instruct the runner from first to run halfway to second base and stop, whether the catcher has thrown the ball down to second or not. I think this is a mistake, because a smart catcher will run towards this base runner to cut down the distance of his throw while the infielders move closer to the runner. The catcher can then check the runner at third to keep him close to the bag, then make a throw to an infielder.

If this play is executed well by the defense, it will be impossible for the runner at third to score, and it often results in two outs if he makes the attempt. For this reason, I teach my runners at first to break hard for second and do not stop or hesitate unless the catcher has released the throw to second *before they are halfway to the base*. If the catcher hesitates and the runner is more than halfway, the runner should change the play to a straight steal and continue to second. If the catcher tries to throw down that late, we will successfully steal second and also be able to score the run from third.

The runner at third base on this play must focus on the angle of the catcher's throw. Many catchers at the youth level will make throws that are relatively high when they are throwing down to second base. The runner at third must commit to go home *before* the ball crosses the pitcher's mound, so he must decide if the catcher is throwing down to second or making a pickoff play back to the pitcher as soon as possible. It is the third base coach's job to check the middle infielders to see if one of them is cutting in for a "trick" pickoff play behind the mound. The base runner should only watch the catcher and the angle of his throw.

First and Third Defensive Plays

If you use four different defenses when an opposing team has runners on first and third, and you are unpredictable about which one you will use, you can prevent the other team from stealing or induce them to make critical outs if you execute the plays properly. You can either have a numerical or other sign that you call out, or have your catcher call time and signal the infield on the play you are going to run. It is also important for the outfielders to be alert to the defense you call because they should back up the place you are throwing to.

Deception is very important in your first and third defensive plays. Each one of the four plays should look identical at the time the ball leaves the hand of your catcher. This is similar to a football team that runs multiple plays out of the same formation.

In the "one" play we have the catcher throw the ball back to the pitcher, the "two" play goes to second, the "three" play to third, and the "four" play goes to the second baseman who cuts in behind the pitcher's mound. The catcher must make each of his throws on the 1, 2 and 4 play look the same – they must all have the same velocity and height. In the "three" play, the catcher acts as if he is throwing to second but at the very last instant he turns and throws to third base to try and catch the runner breaking early.

In the "one" play the pitcher catches the ball and immediately looks to third to pick the runner off. If the runner at third has stayed tight to the bag, the pitcher should then turn to the runner breaking from first to try and get him out. It is important for the pitcher to get the ball into the hands of an infielder as soon as possible because he has his back to the runner at third at this point and is not in good position to if he breaks for home.

Once an infielder has the ball, he can check the runner at third while he attempts to make the out on the base runner at first. If the base runner has broken for home when the pitcher receives the ball from the catcher, the runner will normally stop halfway and attempt to get back to third. The pitcher must not make a quick throw home if this happens – it is important for him to run directly at the base runner to make him commit to third or home before making a throw.

The "two" play is the most basic because you are just trying to get the out at second and are willing to trade a run for an out by allowing the runner from third to score if he breaks right away. However, a little deception may freeze this runner long enough to allow you to get the out at second and still pin the runner at third.

On each of the four plays, the second baseman breaks in behind the pitchers' mound between the rubber and second base. On this play, the pitcher acts like he is going to catch the ball as the throw goes past him. The second baseman does the same. Both of these players then bluff a turn to third to fake a pick off of this runner. If the throw from the catcher is low and hard and these two fielders do a good job selling the fake, the runner at third will not break for home even though the throw goes to second base.

The "four" play is when the second baseman cutting behind the mound intercepts the throw from the catcher to second and immediately tries to catch the runner at third either breaking for home or too far off the bag. This is the most effective play if you are desperate to get the runner at third and are willing to concede a stolen base at second.

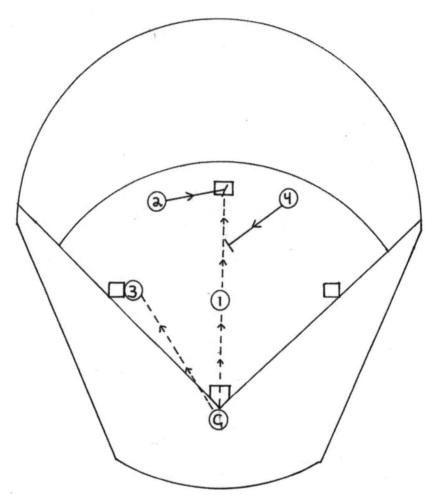

FIRST & THIRD DEFENSIVE PLAYS

When I practice first and third offense, I usually have the coaches play catcher, pitcher, second base, shortstop and third. Half of the team lines up to run, one at a time, the delayed-bluff steal at first and the other half line up to run the plays at third. Once a player takes a turn at first he goes to the end of the line of base runners at third, and the runners at third go to the end of the line at first. The coaches vary their plays to give the base runners different looks. I then have the players run through the defensive plays with no base runners. After most of the team has a full understanding of the plays on both sides of the ball, I then allow them to do it "live" by dividing the team in half with players on offense and defense. The players in the infield get together at the mound and "huddle up" before each play. The catcher calls the play in the huddle so that the base runners do not know what is coming.

PRACTICE G

:20   RUN, STRETCH AND THROW

:20   INFIELD

:15   FLYBALLS

:20   SITUATIONAL PLAYS WITH FULL DEFENSE IN PLACE

:30   LIVE STEALING WITH PITCHER, CATCHER AND INFIELDERS

:20   BUNTING AND BUNT DEFENSES

:20   CRUCIBLE WORKOUT

Live Stealing With Pitcher, Catcher and Infielders

Stealing bases and the ability to stop an opponent's running game is one of the big differences between elite teams and those that struggle. In this drill we divide the team in half. One group works as runners and they attempt to alternately steal second and third base. They are able to practice leadoffs, reading the pitcher, getting a good jump and sliding. The other group should have one or two pitchers, two catchers and at least two infielders to receive throws. The pitchers should take turns on the mound and throw at least ten pitches each. Catchers should alternate every other pitch because throwing out base stealers with catcher's gear on is difficult and stressful on the arm.

First, the base runners line up at first base to prepare to steal second. Pitchers must throw ten pitches home, but are also allowed to make three random pickoff throws over to first during this sequence of pitches. The pitchers are allowed to choose when to use each of their three pickoffs, so that the base runners will not know when he is going to pitch or throw over to first. There should be a defensive player to receive pickoff throws at first and at least one middle infielder to receive throws from the catcher at second. After each pitcher has thrown ten pitches, the base runners then move to second and the same cycle is repeated with steals of third base. After this rotation is completed, the groups trade places so the defenders can work on base stealing and the runners can work on the defensive side.

Bunting and Bunt Defenses

This is organized identically to the base stealing drill – the team is divided in half with one group on offense and the other defense, then both groups change sides. One group works on bunting and also runs the bases. They should stay in the batter's box until they are able to bunt a ball successfully, then run to first. Even if the bunter makes an out at first, he should remain on the base as a runner while the next player bunts. This should continue with each successive bunter so that the defense is presented with different scenarios as each batter comes to the plate.

Each bunter should practice bunting for a hit and sacrifice bunting. When there is nobody on base or the hitter is bunting for a hit, he generally will "show bunt" late and will not fully "square around" with his feet. This is another area of the game where I encourage "aggressive, intelligent" play by allowing my players to attempt to bunt for a hit whenever they want, even if a bunt is not called by the third base coach. When a sacrifice bunt is called, I expect my hitters to square around before the pitcher releases the ball to ensure that everything possible is done to execute a bunt in fair territory. Another difference between the two bunts is the objective of the hitter on where to bunt the ball. If a hitter is bunting for a hit, he wants the ball to be very close to the baseline or go foul. In other words, if he misses, he should miss foul. The sacrifice bunter is only concerned with advancing runners, so he should be trying to bunt the ball halfway between the baseline and the pitcher's mound.

Bunt defenses are very important – especially at the younger ages where bunting is extremely popular. This is another aspect of travelball I do not like. Frequent bunting at the 9-11U age groups will often help an offensive team score runs and win games. I have seen teams bunt in 20-40% of their at-bats during a game at these age groups. Remember, your ultimate objective is to *prepare your players for high school*, and the best way to do that is to allow them to swing the bat as much as possible. A high school player should be able to bunt but, unlike hitting, it is an easily acquired skill and you do not need your young players to give up dozens of at-bats a season working on it. Nevertheless, most coaches you face will be primarily concerned with winning and losing, so you need to have a good bunt defense.

We work on three basic bunt defenses. In our "one" play the first baseman charges the bunt and third baseman stays at his bag. The pitcher must field the balls bunted to the left side of the infield. The second baseman covers the first base bag because the first baseman is in for the bunt. In the "three" play, the third baseman charges the bunt and the pitcher is responsible for the right side of the infield. Finally, our "crash" play is an attempt to stop a squeeze play. This play involves both the first and third baseman charging the bunt with the second baseman covering first.

In this practice, you should rotate your players to different positions and have the defense make plays using each of your bunt defenses with live bunting and base runners. You will address an extremely important part of the youth travelball game on both sides of the ball in a relatively short amount of time.

PRACTICE H

1:30   HITTING INSTRUCTION AND CONDITIONING

(TWO ROTATIONS, 45 MINUTES EACH GROUP)

ROTATION I

GROUP 1 – INSTRUCTION AND HITTING IN CAGES

GROUP 2 – STRENGTH AND CONDITIONING

ROTATION II

GROUP 1 – INSTRUCTION AND HITTING IN CAGES

GROUP 2 – STRENGTH AND CONDITIONING

During my second year as a travelball coach, I was blessed to affiliate my team with two professional instructors – Scott Garrett and Ted Rose with the *Strike Zone Baseball Gym* in Bradenton, Florida. Scott was a catcher and played college and minor league baseball. Ted was a pitcher and also played college and minor league baseball. I believed in the principles they taught, and they are excellent communicators and highly respected by the kids they teach.

In Chapter 12, I address the issue of professional coaches providing instruction to your players in different aspects of the game through private lessons. However, in this practice we have our *entire team* receive professional instruction in hitting and catching.

The *Strike Zone* gym is a large, air conditioned hitting facility. It is always good to use a place like this because, if you have a rainy day, you may still be able to get a lot of work done if you are able to move your practice to a facility like this.

You should talk to coaches who give individual lessons in your area to see if they will agree to work with your team. They may be motivated to allow you to use their facility and provide instruction to your players for a very reasonable fee because they derive benefits from the deal as well. If they become affiliated with your team, they will be known as the hitting/pitching coaches for the best young players/team in the area. Your players' achievements on the field will become their best advertising. Also, many of your players will like the instruction they receive and will want to sign up for individual private lessons.

In this practice we set up three hitting stations in batting cages and a catcher station in a forth cage. Ted instructs each player individually on swing mechanics in one cage, while coaches throw or have players hit off a tee in the other cages. Scott works on drills with a catcher one-on-one and rotates them into the hitting stations when they are through. Each player spends about ten minutes in each cage.

Meanwhile, Group 2 is outside in the parking lot for strength and conditioning training. I begin with a timed one-mile run where they run a course down the street, around a tree and back. They I set up a "crucible" station in the parking lot where they do that for the next thirty minutes. After 45 minutes, the groups change places and the hitters go to strength and conditioning while the players working out go to hit in the cages.

PRACTICE I

:20   RUN, STRETCH AND THROW

2:00   INTRASQUAD SCRIMMAGE GAME

:10   RUNNING

I have never agreed with the concept of using up valuable practice time on "scrimmages" or practice games against other travelball teams. I want every minute of every practice to 100% benefit my team and players. When you scrimmage another team, 50% of the activity benefits the opponent and 50% benefits you.

I think part of the attraction of scrimmage games is that they are also a lazy man's practice. It takes no effort, preparation or creativity to show up on a Saturday afternoon and play a practice game against another team. Too many coaches take the path of least resistance even though that is not the best way to prepare their team for a challenging season.

Practices that closely simulate real games can be useful. However, my preference has always been to do our scrimmage games *intrasquad*. What this means is that the team is broken into groups or smaller "teams," and these teams play against each other.

In an intrasquad game, all the pitches, groundballs, fly balls, and hits benefit your team and your players. Also, you don't have to worry about another team picking up your signs, plays, and player tendencies and then passing that information on to other teams.

In my intrasquad scrimmage games, I divide my team into four groups with at least three players in each group. This ensures that when one team is hitting, the other three teams combine to form a complete defense.

The first thing I do is make sure I have my three catchers on different teams. Then I spread out my pitchers and position players to

148

try to make sure I do not have too many players in one group that play the same position.

Of course, just like using a stopwatch when running, you should always make this a competitive situation by offering some incentive to the "winning" team. I usually allow the winners to run half as much as the three losing teams after the game. You can also promise that each of the players on the winning team are guaranteed to start your next game and play the whole game.

You *must* take the time to write out this entire practice. If you do this right, you can really get a lot out of an intrasquad scrimmage game by giving your players opportunities at a variety of positions and trying different combinations in the infield to see which players work well together.

If you don't plan ahead and just try and move guys around as you go through the game, you will often have chaos. You will also have some players at certain positions too much and some at other positions not enough. Sit down and carefully write out every inning of this practice and think through exactly where you want players to play each inning.

The following is a sample intra-squad scrimmage game from my team:

TEAM 1 -   BRANDON, TYLER, ZAK

TEAM 2 -   CODY, JALEEL, VICTOR, NICK

TEAM 3 -   BRETT, ANDREW, SHAY

TEAM 4 -   ROBERT, DONOVAN, CORY

1st Inning	2nd Inning	3rd Inning	4th Inning
P-CODY	P-ZAK	P-DONOVAN	P-JALEEL
C-BRETT	C-BRETT	C-BRANDON	C-BRANDON
1-CORY	1-CORY	1-ZAK	1-ZAK
2-SHAY	2-SHAY	2-NICK	2-CODY
S-ROBERT	S-TYLER	2-ROBERT	2-TYLER
3-VICTOR	3-BRANDON	3-VICTOR	3-BRETT
L-DONOVAN	L-DONOVAN	L-JALEEL	L-SHAY
C-JALEEL	C-ROBERT	C-TYLER	C-NICK
R-ANDREW	R-ANDREW	R-CORY	R-ANDREW
HIT-TEAM 1	HIT-TEAM 2	HIT-TEAM 3	HIT-TEAM 4

5th Inning	6th Inning	7th Inning	8th Inning
P-VICTOR	P-BRETT	P-VICTOR	P-ANDREW
C-ROBERT	C-ROBERT	C-BRANDON	C-BRANDON
1-CODY	1-CODY	1-ZAK	1-ZAK
2-SHAY	2-SHAY	2-NICK	2-NICK
S-NICK	S-TYLER	S-ROBERT	S-TYLER
3-CORY	3-ZAK	3-CODY	3-BRETT
L-DONOVAN	L-BRANDON	L-JALEEL	L-VICTOR
C-JALEEL	C-DONOVAN	C-TYLER	C-JALEEL
R-ANDREW	R-ANDREW	R-CORY	C-ANDREW
HIT-TEAM 1	HIT-TEAM 2	HIT-TEAM 3	HIT-TEAM 4

9th Inning	10th Inning	11th Inning	12th Inning
P-CORY	P-BRANDON	P-CORY	P-NICK
C-BRETT	C-BRETT	C-ROBERT	C-BRANDON
1-CODY	1-CORY	1-CODY	1-JALEEL
2-SHAY	2-SHAY	2-NICK	2-CODY
S-ROBERT	S-ROBERT	S-TYLER	S-TYLER
3-VICTOR	3-ZAK	3-VICTOR	3-BRETT
L-DONOVAN	L-DONOVAN	L-DONOVAN	L-VICTOR
C-JALEEL	C-TYLER	C-JALEEL	C-SHAY
R-ANDREW	R-ANDREW	R-BRANDON	R-ANDREW
HIT-TEAM 1	HIT-TEAM 2	HIT-TEAM 3	HIT-TEAM 4

You can prevent this practice from dragging out too long by keeping the transitions between innings short. I have catchers go two innings in row to cut down on the number of times we have to wait for them to put on gear. The players should also run on and off the field as you call out their positions for the next inning.

In this scrimmage we had 11 different players pitch one inning, and one pitcher threw two. That does not mean that we intend to use 11 pitchers during the season, but these games provide an opportunity to get a look at some kids who can sometimes surprise you. You do not have to do it this way though – just have six pitchers throw two innings each if you want to use less, but make sure they go every other inning to simulate a real game.

Using the scrimmage above as an example, I will single out a random three players to demonstrate how I design these intrasquad games. Brett is a pitcher, catcher and third baseman on my team. In this scrimmage, he pitched one inning, caught four innings, and played three innings at third base. Robert is a shortstop, catcher and centerfielder. In this scrimmage he played five innings at shortstop, three innings at catcher and one inning in centerfield. Cody is a pitcher who is a utility infielder for us. In this scrimmage he pitched one inning, played second base two innings, first base three innings, and third base one inning. Of course, all players also hit with their team for three innings each, so they usually get 5-7 at bats against live pitching.

I suggest you use this scrimmage as a chance to move your players around and give them opportunities to compete with each other at multiple positions.

Meteors Olympics

Most of the most successful college and high school coaches in the country say that the most productive practice drills are the ones that closely resemble game situations and game speed. It is very difficult to have anything you do in a practice setting equal the intensity of a game.

In practice, there are no teammates depending on you to make a play or get a big hit. There is no winning and losing if you make an error or mental mistake. In short, there isn't any pressure in a normal practice, and performing under pressure in tournament games is difficult. Game speed and focus is also certainly a lot different than in practice in any sport.

Young ballplayers are competitive by nature. I have found just about every kid I coached to be highly competitive and want to win at everything, no matter what the competition was about. I noticed that in the games they would play at the team hotels on the nights after games. They invented all kinds of crazy games to play both inside and outside the hotel, and they took those games as seriously if not sometimes even more seriously than the baseball games we were there for!

Over time I learned that the kind of kids who are attracted to travel baseball are usually "Type A" personalities that are very competitive by nature and hate to lose at anything. I decided to capitalize on this competitiveness by designing a practice that would use that energy to simulate the intensity of a real tournament baseball game. I called it the "Meteors Olympics." It was a huge success and the players loved it. My players never worked harder or were more tired after a practice than they were when we would have a Meteors Olympics. They voluntarily gave twice as much effort in these practices as usual because we turned the entire practice into a series of competitions.

You should divide your team in half – one would be "Team A" and the other "Team B." *You* must pick the teams - never have two "captains" choose their own players for each team. That is very divisive and can contribute to factions or cliques developing, which is something that you should always work hard to avoid. You should also be the one to pick the teams because you want each drill to be competitive and therefore you want to make certain that each team has an equal ability level. You should make sure that each team is collectively equal in speed, arm strength and fielding ability. During the "Olympics" the teams will compete against each other in a series of exercises or drills, and the winning team for each one will be awarded a "point." At the end of the practice, the team with the most points wins the Olympic title. Here is a sample of one of our "Meteors Olympics":

METEORS OLYMPICS

CONDITIONING COURSE:

- MED BALL OVER HEAD/UNDER LEGS X 4

- MED BALL BACK TO BACK X 4

- HANDLEBAR – EACH MAN X 2

- TRIPLE SIDE BOX JUMP – EACH MAN OUT AND
  BACK X 2

- CONE RUNS

INFIELD PLAYS TO FIRST 15 X 2

INFIELD DOUBLE PLAYS 10 X 2

BASE RUNNING RELAY – ONE NO BALL, ONE WITH
BALL

3 OF / 2 CUT RELAYS 10 X 2

OF HIT BUCKET AT HOME – 5 THROWS EACH

BUNTS – 5 EACH

Med Ball Over Head Under Legs

Both teams form single file lines where each player is about two feet behind the other. The players stand directly behind each other in two straight lines. The player at the front of each line holds a medicine ball. When the coach blows the whistle, this player bends down and moves the ball between his legs to hand it to the player behind him. The player behind him bends down to grab the ball, then quickly moves the ball over and behind his head to the next player.

This process continues in alternating fashion so that the ball travels over one player's head and under the next player's legs until it reaches the last player in line. Then the direction is reversed and the ball is returned to the front. The first team to pass the ball to the end and back four times wins this competition.

Med Ball Back to Back

This is similar to the previous competition, except that this time the player holding the medicine ball rotates to his left side keeping his feet in place shoulder-width apart and hands the ball to the player behind him. The player receiving the ball then swivels to his right side and hands it to the next player. The players alternate handing the ball right and left until it reaches the end and back four times. The first team to do this wins. The ball must never be tossed – it must be handed off from one player to the next.

Handlebar Relay

In this competition, a player on each team holds the handlebar with a weight hanging from it chest-high. He must roll the handlebar until the weight touches the bar. He then releases the weight to the ground and repeats the process, then hands the bar to the next player on the team who must also do this twice. The first team that has each player perform this exercise twice is the winner.

Triple Side Box Jump

Two 1'x1'x1' boxes are set up next to each other with about three feet between them. You can time each team individually, or you can set up two rows with two boxes in each and have the teams do this as a race. The first player stands on the outside of the row of boxes with both feet together. He must keep his feet together throughout the exercise. The player must hop up onto the first box, then down between the two boxes, up onto the second box, then back to the ground on the other side. He then must return back to where he started with the same hopping motion. When this player goes out and back two times, the next player on the team then begins. The first team to have each player go out and back twice is the winner.

Cone Runs

Five to seven cones are set up in an "M" shape about ten feet apart from each other. The first player runs forward around the first cone, backwards to the next cone, forward again and so on until he has circled each cone. He then returns back in the same manner and the next player on his team begins when he reaches the end. The team that completes this course the fastest with all their players is the winner.

Infield Plays to First

Team A runs onto the field and each player takes an infield position with one on the pitcher's mound. The coach hits ground balls randomly and they must field the ball cleanly and throw to first. After fifteen grounders, that team's score will be the number of error-free plays out of fifteen. Team A then runs off the field and the next team takes infield positions and tries to beat their score. I do a rotation of fifteen grounders twice with one point awarded for each round. I also deduct one point from their grounder score if any player walks on or off the field – this is a good opportunity to emphasize that players must always run out and off the field.

155

Infield Double Plays

This is the same as the infield competition above except this time the infield must cleanly turn double plays. I usually cut the number of plays to ten on this drill because it is more time consuming than plays to first.

Base Running Relays

One team lines up behind the second base bag and the other team behind home plate. The players choose their own order of how they are going to run the relay race. When a coach blows the whistle, the first player for each team runs around the bases in a race.

As soon as the first player from each team hits the last base and *crosses in front* of the next player, the second player then runs. The first team to have each player complete a trip around the bases is the winner.

I then begin a second relay race with a medicine ball. The first runners must hold a 10 lb. medicine ball with both hands (*not* with one arm like a running back in football) when they run around the bases and then hand the ball off to the next player. They are not permitted to toss the ball – it must be handed off. The first team that has each player circle the bases with the medicine ball is the winner.

3 OF / 2 Cut Relays

Team A has three players run to the outfield positions with two players as cutoff men in the infield. A coach or another player can be the catcher if you have enough on each team. A coach hits balls into the outfield and the players must execute a clean, error-free relay home. After ten reps, Team A runs off and Team B runs on to try and beat their score. Repeat this two times and award one point for each cycle.

OF Hit Bucket Throw

Place a five gallon bucket on top of home plate. One team lines up in left field and one in right. The players make five throws each to try to hit the bucket. Add up the total number of hits and the team with the most wins. Players are permitted to hit the bucket on one or two bounces.

Bunts

Set up cones to form rectangles on the first and third base sides of the infield where a bunted ball would result in a hit. A coach pitches from the mound and the players from each team attempt five bunts each. If the ball stops inside one of the rectangles, that team scores two points. If the ball is bunted in fair territory but outside the rectangles, one point is awarded. At the end of this competition, the team with the most points in declared the winner.

You will be amazed at the level of focus and intensity of effort you get from the players when you introduce "points" and the element of competition into your practice drills. After experimenting with a variety of ways to simulate game speed in practice, I settled on this "Olympics" as the next best thing to a real tournament game.

Baseball Drills

There are thousands of different baseball drills for hitting, defense, pitching and base running. Hundreds of books and instructional videos have been on the market for years detailing drills used by high school, college and professional coaches around the country. Over the years, I have been exposed in one way or another to nearly all of them. The purpose of this section is to list the drills I think work best for the youth level and for teams without unlimited practice time and resources. I have already covered all of the base running drills I use in the "Training Camp" section, as well as several hitting and defensive drills. These are some of the additional hitting and defensive drills I recommend for travelball teams that were not addressed in the "Training Camp" section:

Hitting Drills

FOUR-CORNER BUNT DRILL – in this drill the team is divided into four groups. One group lines up at each of the four bases. Four coaches stand at the outside edge of the pitcher's mound to throw pitches simultaneously to a batter at each base who attempts to bunt the ball. After 7-8 pitches to each hitter, the next player in line steps up to the base take his turn bunting pitches from a coach. With this drill, each player could lay down dozens of bunts in a very short period of time.

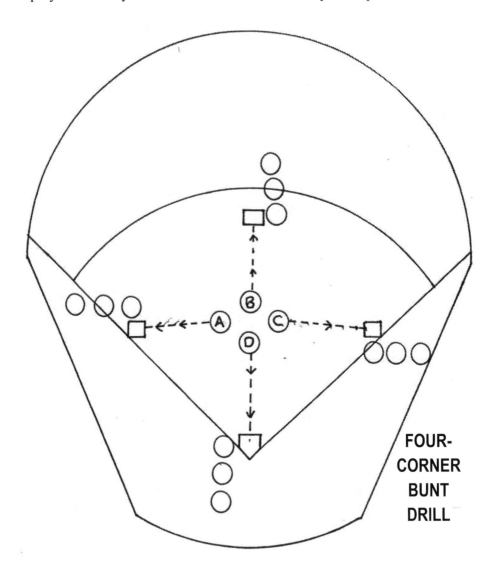

FOUR-CORNER BUNT DRILL

TEE DRILLS AT DIFFERENT PARTS OF THE ZONE – a player hits off a tee which is rotated to different locations in the strike zone.

SOFT TOSS – the hitter hits ball from a coach who flips them either from the front or side of the player.

158

ONE-KNEE SOFT TOSS – the batter has his back knee on the ground while he hits soft-toss from the coach. This can also be done with the batter using only his bottom hand on a tee-ball bat.

BROOMSTICK WITH GOLF BALLS – the batter works on hand-eye coordination by hitting whiffle golf balls with a broomstick-sized piece of wood or metal.

RAPID FIRE – the coach flips balls in quick three-baseball bursts to the hitter who must swing under control so he can quickly recoil to make his next swing.

HIT AND RUN – hitters practice "hitting behind" runners on the ground when they are stealing on the pitch.

SLASH BUNT – a good play when attempting a double steal, the hitter shows bunt early the pulls the bat back and attempts to slap the ball on the ground to shortstop or second.

HARD IN / SOFT AWAY – a soft-toss drill to simulate the way most pitching coaches like to set hitters up. A coach is about ten feet in front of hitter and tosses balls from behind an "L-Screen" with good velocity inside and softly to the outside half of the plate randomly.

Defensive Drills

PICKOFFS AT THIRD BASE OUT OF WINDUP – this is a timing play where the pitcher starts in a windup position and the third baseman plays back behind the bag. The pitcher simulates the beginning of his windup, but subtly steps off the rubber with his right foot. The third basemen then breaks hard for the bag and the pitcher spins and makes a pickoff throw to third.

CALLED PICKOFF TIMING PLAYS – most of these plays occur at second base. You can use a variety of signals and plays that are called by the coach or by the infielders. Work on the timing of your different pickoff plays so the pitcher, catcher and infielders are on the same page.

3-2, TWO OUT, INSIDE MOVE PICKOFFS – base runners are taught to run to the next base as the pitcher starts his delivery when they are in a force position and there is a 3-2 count on the batter with two outs. If there are bases loaded, have your pitcher do an "inside move" while a middle infielder breaks to second base. You can often catch the runner at second leaning towards third or starting too early.

MISSED BUNT PICKOFFS – whenever a batter misses a sacrifice bunt, an infielder should immediately break to the bag behind the base runner and the catcher should throw to this base without hesitation. It should be automatic on every missed bunt because runners will usually have a very aggressive secondary lead when a batter attempts a bunt.

PITCHER COVERING FIRST – in this drill, grounders are hit to the first basemen at different locations and the pitchers must run from the mound to cover first and receive the throw from the first basemen.

ONE-HOP TAG PLAYS – fielders run one at a time to cover a bag. A coach makes different kinds of throws – some high, some to the left, some right, some on one bounce. The players must practice fielding difficult throws and making quick tags.

RUNDOWNS – you can divide your team into two groups then switch after ten minutes. One group starts as base runners and the other as infielders. One base runner starts with a large lead at the base and the coach throws behind him and picks him off. Three infielders then start a rundown or "pickle" play, and the runner tries to force them to make as many throws as possible or safely return to a base. I make this a competition between the groups where the defense gets two points if they make an out with just one throw, one point if they get an out with more than one throw, and no points if the runner makes it back to a base safely.

OUTFIELD BLUFF-CATCH FORCE PLAYS – an outfielder who is unable to catch a blooper acts as if he is going to catch it by calling the ball and raising his hands in an attempt to keep a base runner from advancing. After the ball hits the ground he immediately picks it up and throws to a base to attempt to force out the runner.

RIGHT FIELD TO FIRST BASE PLAY – a play that is common in youth baseball is when a hitter drives a hard liner or groundball for an apparent base hit to right field, only to be thrown out at first base. Right fielders are able to play shallow at the younger ages, especially with right handed hitters up, so they will be able to throw out runners at first if they get to the ball quickly and make a strong throw. This play should be practiced just like you practice infield.

CATCHER 4-CORNER DRILL – have four catchers in shin guards and catcher's mitts play just inside the bases on the four corners of the infield. A coach stands by with extra baseballs if there is a missed throw to keep the drill moving. A player starts the drill by throwing across the diamond. That player then makes a quick throw to the catcher on his left. Each player who receives a throw from across the diamond throws to the player on his left. The player who receives a throw from his right throws across the diamond.

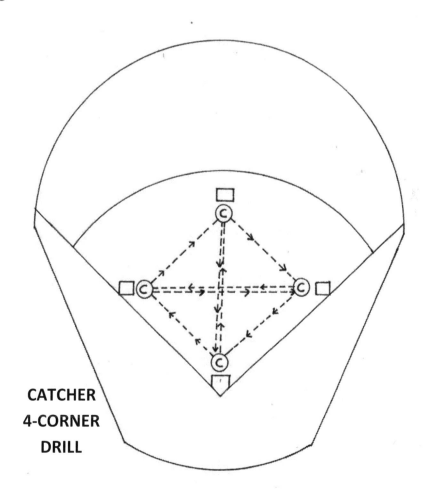

**CATCHER
4-CORNER
DRILL**

CATCHER BLOCKING – there are a variety of blocking drills you can use with your catchers. I like to start out with no glove and just work on footwork and leg positioning. After that, we add a catcher's mitt and flip baseballs. You should always flip balls lightly from fairly close range so the catcher can focus solely on technique.

CATCHER POPUPS – you can use a pitching machine, tennis racket and balls, or a bat to work on popups behind the catcher. Teach your catcher to always look straight up first and get his mask off in the same motion to find the baseball. Then the catcher should turn his back to the infield, discard the mask away from the ball, and make the catch over his head if possible with two hands.

PASSED BALL DRILLS – this is a play that happens with regularity at the youth level because of the short distance behind home plate to the backstop. A coach throws the ball into the dirt to the side of a catcher who squats behind the plate. The pitcher and catcher must not move until the ball goes behind the catcher, then the pitcher breaks for home while the catcher retrieves the ball. The catcher should "hook slide" to the side of the ball, barehand it, and pop up on one knee. He should then toss the ball *overhand* to the pitcher covering home. Pitchers must make sure to run to a spot a few feet up the third base line so they are able to make the tag before the runner reaches the plate.

SUN IN EYES CATCHES – you can hit fly balls or shoot them out of a pitching machine for this drill. Position your outfielders so that the sun is directly behind the ball when it is in the air. The player is forced to hold up his glove to shield his eyes from the sun before making the catch.

CHAPTER 11:
STRENGTH, SPEED, FLEXIBILITY AND CONDITIONING

This is the crown jewel of the Meteors training program. The biggest difference between modern baseball and the approach to the game before the 1980s is strength, speed, and flexibility training. It has become such an important part of the modern game that most professional and college players lift weights, run and train year-round. Even many high school programs today incorporate a weight training and conditioning regiment. During my third year as a travelball coach, I decided to look for a way that I could introduce my players to a baseball-specific training program that was safe for young athletes. I spent a considerable amount of time studying the programs of major league teams and talking to physicians on the kinds of exercises that would benefit but not injure kids. I adopted some of the exercises used by professional baseball players for many years and developed my own program.

I divided the exercises into four groups, based on the part of the body that is being focused on. One set was for the legs, another for the "core muscles" in the torso, a third group of exercises for the hands, wrists and arms, and the final group for shoulders and chest muscles. Many of these exercises use medicine balls, dumbbells or other weighted objects. You can adjust the weights to the size and strength of your players. The following is a list of baseball-specific exercises that are useful for players at the youth level:

Baseball Strength and Conditioning Exercises

HANDS/WRISTS/ARMS:

FOREARM BAR
HANDLEBAR
WRIST ROLLS
HANDGRIPS
INTERNAL BANDS
EXTERNAL BANDS
1-9 BOUNCE DRILL
TRICEPS KICKBACKS
LATERAL RAISES
SIDE LIFTS
SCARECROW
HAMMER WRIST FLEXION
RICE BUCKET

CORE:

RUSSIAN TWISTS
JACKKNIFE SITUPS
SIDE TO SIDES
MED BALL SITUP TOSS
SWING TURN WITH BAND
BACK TO BACKS
SIDE BURSTS
DIAGONAL UNDERHAND TOSS
LUNGE WITH A TWIST
SITTING BACKWARD TOSS

LEGS:

CONE RUN
COWBOY SQUATS
ROCKET JUMPS
HIGH KNEE JUMP
PARACHUTE SPRINTS
BOX STEP-UPS
LATERAL BOX JUMPS
FRONT BOX JUMPS
BETWEEN LEG TOSSES

CHEST AND SHOULDERS:

SHRUGS
PUSHUP BARS
CHEST PASSES
OVER SHOULDER TOSS
BENCH PRESS
MILITARY PRESS
SIDE PULLS
CURLS
MED BALL SHOT PUTS

After I found a good set of exercises to use for youth baseball players, the challenge was to find a way to incorporate them into a meaningful program that addressed all four areas of the body, yet not use up the bulk of our allotted practice time. I thought back to my training in the U. S. Marine Corps at Parris Island in boot camp. Several years ago, the Marine Corps developed something called "The Crucible," which had to be completed before a Marine could graduate from recruit training.

The Crucible was a series of difficult exercises and obstacles that had to be performed in a consecutive series. I began to think about the concept of a youth strength and conditioning program modeled after the Marines' "Crucible" that could be performed in a short, intense period of time at the end of a baseball practice. It was also created so that a lot of heavy equipment would not be needed to haul out to a practice field. Everything you need for these "crucible" workouts should be able to fit in a couple of boxes.

The program I designed was to set up twelve or more stations in a circle around the outside of the infield. Each station would contain one exercise that would be performed individually or with one partner. The stations would alternate between muscle groups, and each muscle group would be worked on equally.

For example, Station 1 might be an leg exercise, Station 2 for hands, wrists and forearms, Station 3 a core exercise, Station 4 for chest and shoulders, then the sequence would repeat three more times for a total of twelve stations. The players would spend one minute at each station, so the total workout would be an intense twelve minutes. The number of stations or the amount of time for each can be gradually increased. I started my twelve year olds with twelve, one-minute stations. By the time we finished at 14U, we used twenty stations at two minutes each for a total of 40 minutes in my dreaded "Figure 8 Crucible."

The following would be an example of a twelve-station strength, speed and conditioning "Crucible" workout:

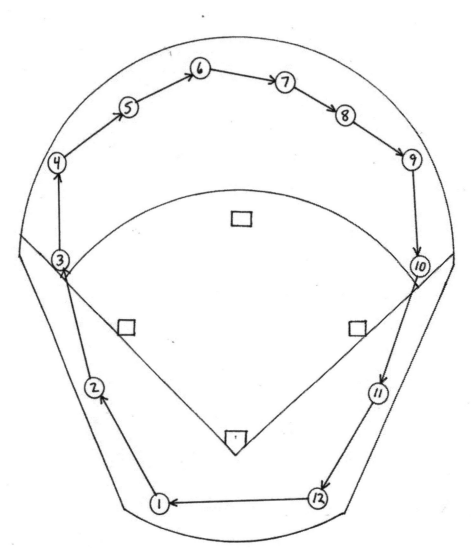

CRUCICBLE WORKOUT

Station 1:   Cowboy Squats

Station 2:   Forearm Bar

Station 3:   Jackknife Situps

Station 4:   Chest Passes

166

Station 5: Rocket Jumps

Station 6: Triceps Kickbacks

Station 7: Russian Twists

Station 8: Curls

Station 9: Lateral Box Jumps

Station 10: Hammer Wrist Flexion

Station 11: Diagonal Underhand Toss

Station 12: Lateral Raises

Some baseball programs at the youth and high school level claim they have a strength and conditioning program in place, but often their approach is utterly useless. First, all of the exercises must be baseball-specific, meaning that they are relevant to or designed for muscles that are used in baseball. They are not designed to increase muscle mass or bodybuilding. Many programs use a number of exercises that build muscle mass but are not baseball-specific.

Additionally, for a program to have any tangible results, you must work out at least three times a week for a minimum of three months. Ideally, your program should be almost year-round. Many teams will work out for a month or so before the season starts and then stop. That is worthless and those teams are better off not doing any strength and conditioning at all because they are just wasting their time. If you are going to make this part of your practice regiment, be consistent and do it over the long term. Encourage your players to work on some of these exercises at home when the team is not able to practice during certain time periods.

Your players also have to "buy into" this workout program. I have had players and parents fail to understand why we devote valuable time each practice to these workouts. If the players do not believe in it, or are lazy, they will be wasting their time. Explain to them that when it comes to working out, you get out of it what you put into it and if you don't put out maximum effort they only cheat themselves.

You also have to relate what they are doing in their workouts to what they are trying to accomplish on the field. They must understand that the exercises will help them hit the ball farther, throw harder and run the bases faster. The work they put in during this circuit training will have tangible benefits on the stat sheet, and if they understand that they will really get into it and come to love the workouts even though they are difficult.

In this Crucible workout, the stations are spread out about fifty feet apart around the outer edge of the infield or in a circle in the outfield. The equipment that is needed is placed on the ground at each location. You stand in the middle of the circle and explain the exercise for each station to your players as you point to each. If they are unclear or forget what to do, tell them that they should look ahead to the next station to see what the player in front of them is doing. Each player then goes to a station. If a station requires two players, they double up at that station. Stand in the middle of the circle with a stopwatch and whistle. When you blow the whistle, they each begin the exercise at their station simultaneously. After one minute, you blow the whistle and they must run to the next station and immediately begin the exercise there. This continues until each player has completed the entire course.

When my players were 14, they had been doing this training multiple times a week and had gradually built up the intensity of it. That year, I laid out twenty stations in a "Figure 8" shape around the entire field, and the players did two minutes at each station. We also began "track workouts" every Saturday morning of our 13U year where we ran sprints on a track at the local middle school. We ran 30, 50 and 100 meter sprints and finished with a 400 meter run. All of these were timed and I put the times in ranking order and emailed them to all the parents and players after each track workout. Although my strength, speed and conditioning program was not a picnic by any means, the players fully believed in the program by that time and all of them worked hard. They saw the results in their physiques and on the field!

The following is a detailed explanation of each baseball-specific exercise:

Hands, Wrists and Arm Exercises:

FOREARM BAR – this is a device that can be purchased from most places that sell workout equipment. The hand is place inside a loop and a bar goes over the forearm. The player flexes his wrist and resistance is given to the muscles in the forearm.

HANDLEBAR – one of the best exercises for baseball, so good I make it part of every crucible. A weighted object hangs from a small bar about two feet in length. The player holds it like a handlebar on a bicycle and rolls it up until the weight touches the bar.

WRIST ROLLS – a player holds a light dumbbell and lifts or flexes his wrist up and down.

HANDGRIPS – these can be bought in any sporting goods store and some can be adjusted for different tensions. The player squeezes these together for a good hand and forearm workout.

INTERNAL BANDS – you can buy thick workout rubber bands in any sporting goods store. These are usually color coded by the thickness of them, with the heavy bands supplying greater tension. In this exercise, a band is tied to the fence and a player stands with his side facing the fence holding the band in the hand furthest away from the fence. He goes far enough out so there is tension when the hand holding the band is in the middle of his chest. Keeping his elbow tucked at his side, he pulls the band out until his hand is straight out from his elbow.

EXTERNAL BANDS – similar to internal, except this time use a heavier band and the player begins with his arm straight out towards the fence. The band is in the hand closest to the fence. This time the band is pulled towards and into the chest.

1-9 BOUNCE DRILL – in this exercise, a one or two pound ball the size of a softball is bounced up against a wall continuously and caught by the player. His arm is in an L-shape so that his forearm and hand are like the hand on a clock with the wall being the face of the clock. The hand should only be a few inches from the wall. The player starts bouncing where 9 would be on a clock and continues until he gets to where 1 would be, then returns to 9. This is a great exercise to strengthen the muscles around the rotator cuff to prevent injury.

TRICEPS KICKBACKS – another one of my favorites. The player holds a light dumbbell in each hand and assumes the position of someone who is snow-skiing – knees and elbows bent. The player then raises the dumbbells in a backwards motion until his arms are straightened in a 45 degree angle behind him.

LATERAL RAISES – the player holds a dumbbell in each hand and lifts his arms straight out to his side to slightly less that shoulder height.

SIDE LIFTS – a light dumbbell is held in each hand. The player raises both arms straight out at a 45 degree angle from his body with his thumbs pointed towards the ground.

SCARECROW – another great injury preventing exercise for the rotator cuff and elbows. The player holds a very light dumbbell (I use three pounds) in each hand and assumes a position common in scarecrows – each arm in an L-shape but in opposite directions so one hand is pointed to the ground while the other to the sky. The player then rotates his hands up and down in a swivel motion as if to alternate the position of each hand with the elbows staying in the same spot during the entire exercise.

HAMMER WRIST FLEXION – more injury prevention for the elbow. A hammer is held in the throwing hand at the end of the handle. The arm is kept straight while the player tilts the metal part of the hammer up to a 45 degree angle keeping his hand in the same spot at his side.

RICE BUCKET – fill a five pound bucket half full with uncooked rice. There are two exercises you can perform which are great for the hitting muscles. The player can keep all of his fingers together so his hand forms a paddle. He then places his hand straight down into the rice and twists his hand "paddle" back and side to side.

In the other exercise, the player sticks his hand into the middle of the rice then moves all of his fingers and thumb straight apart wide. He then brings them back together to form a fist.

Core Exercises:

RUSSIAN TWISTS – the player assumes a "sit-up" position on his back with knees bent. However, he holds a medicine ball with both hands to his chest. He performs a sit-up and when he is upright he swivels his torso to touch the ball first to the ground on his right side, then turns to touch it on the ground to his left. He then returns to the ground. Both hands must stay on the ball at all times.

JACKKNIFE SIT-UPS – the player lays on his back with legs together and arms straight over his head. As he raises up he touches his right elbow to his left knee then returns to the ground and repeats with his left elbow to his right knee.

SIDE TO SIDES – two players stand side-by-side a few feet apart from each other. Both of them face in the same direction. A player starts with a medicine ball in both hands and swings it towards the other player to toss it to him. This player catches the ball and swings and tosses it back. The players must keep their feet in the same spot and have both hands on the ball throughout the exercise.

MED BALL SIT-UP TOSS – the player assumes a sit-up position with the knees slightly bent. A coach or another player stands at the feet of the player. The player holds a medicine ball in both hands over his right shoulder. As he raises up he tosses the ball to the coach. The coach then tosses it back to him and the player returns to the ground placing the medicine ball over his left shoulder. He then repeats the exercise.

SWING TURN WITH BAND – a heavy duty rubber band is tied to the fence and the player stands a few feet away with his side to the fence. The player holds the band with both hands at the position he would start his swing with a bat. He then executes his swing motion slowly, pulling the band away from the fence and around the front of his body.

BACK TO BACKS – two players stand back-to-back with about a foot of space between them. One player starts by holding a medicine ball with both hands in front of his body chest-high. He then rotates his torso to hand the ball to his partner who rotates in the opposite direction to receive the ball. The players continue this motion handing the ball to each other, then they reverse the direction halfway through the allotted time.

SIDE BURSTS – a player holds a medicine ball in both hands with his feet together. He then lunges with one leg out to a 45 degree angle away from where he was standing. The medicine ball is held waist high throughout this exercise. He then pushes this leg back so he returns to a standing position with his feet together. The player then repeats with the opposite leg.

DIAGONAL UNDERHAND TOSS – two players stand facing each other about three feet apart. Each player's feet are shoulder-width apart with their toes facing each other. One player starts the drill with two hands on a medicine ball at his left side. He then keeps his arms straight and swings the ball to toss it to his partner. The partner then performs the same motion to toss it back. Both players then swing and toss the ball again to the right side.

LUNGE WITH A TWIST – the player holds a medicine ball in both hands in front of him at the waist, with feet together. He then lunges straight out with the left leg so his left foot is about three feet from the right. Once he is in this position, he then twists the medicine ball first to his right, then left, then lunges back to the upright position. He then repeats with the right leg.

SITTING BACKWARD TOSS – one of my favorite core exercises. A player sits on the ground with each leg straight out in a 45 degree angle on the ground. A coach stands directly behind him a few feet away. The player bends forward until his head is close to the ground and picks up a medicine ball on the ground between his legs. He then raises his head and arms up in one motion to toss the medicine ball to the coach behind him. The motion he makes with his arms should be identical to a referee signaling "touchdown" in football. The coach then returns the ball and the player repeats the exercise.

Leg Exercises:

CONE RUN – cones are set up in a zig-zag pattern about fifteen feet apart. The player runs forward around one cone, then backwards around the next until he completes the course of 8-12 cones. Repeat until the time expires.

COWBOY SQUATS – a player stands with his feet a little more than shoulder-width apart and holds a dumbbell in each hand. He then bends his knees while keeping his back and arms straight until the weights touch the ground. Then he rises back to an upright position.

ROCKET JUMPS – the player holds a medicine ball with both hands and stands with his feet more than shoulder width apart. He then bends his knees to touch the ball on the ground. He then jumps into the air while raising the medicine ball above his head as if he is getting a rebound in basketball.

HIGH KNEE JUMPS – the player stands with his feet together with his hands in front on his chest, palms facing the ground. He then jumps with both feet, touching his knees to the palms of his hands.

PARACHUTE SPRINTS – you can now buy these small parachutes that strap easily to the waist at most sporting goods stores. The player runs 30 meter sprints with the parachute providing resistance.

LATERAL BOX JUMPS – one of the best exercises to increase speed are the various box jumps. Buy or build a sturdy, square box of wood about 12" high and 12" square. If you have two of these boxes, all of your workout equipment should be able to fit in them. In this exercise, the player stands to the side of the box with both feet together and his arms at the side. He leaps sideways up onto the box, then jumps down to the other side, keeping both feet together. Repeat back in the other direction.

BOX STEP-UPS – the player stands in front of the box and steps up one foot at a time as if running in place but up on the box.

FRONT BOX JUMPS – this is similar to the lateral box jumps except this time the player hops forward with both feet together straight up onto the box then jumps backwards to the ground landing on both feet at the same time.

BETWEEN LEG TOSSES – similar to a "granny" free throw shot in basketball. The player stands with his feet wider than shoulder width with a heavy medicine ball held between his legs with both hands. The player takes the ball back between his legs then swings his arms forward to toss the ball to a coach or partner who catches it and tosses it back. The knees must be bent because the object is to work the legs not the back and arms.

Chest and Shoulder Exercises

SHRUGS – the player stands with his feet close together with a dumbbell in each hand by his side. The player keeps his arms straight and moves his shoulders in a circular motion, first forward then backward.

PUSHUP BARS – these can be purchased in any sporting goods store, they are small handles that are raised up off the ground for pushups.

CHEST PASSES – two players stand five feet apart facing each other. One player starts with a heavy medicine ball chest high with both hands on the ball. The player then tosses the ball to his partner by bending his legs and pushing the ball forward like a "chest pass" in basketball.

OVER SHOULDER TOSS – two players again stand five feet apart facing each other. One player holds a medicine ball over his right shoulder with both hands on the side of the ball, then steps forward and tosses the ball to his partner. It is important that the player keep his hands on the *side* of the ball throughout the tossing motion – a twisting action can be harmful to the elbow. The players alternate over each shoulder.

BENCH PRESS – you can bring a small bench that folds up to use for bench press and military press exercises. The player lays on his back with a dumbbell in each hand and raises the weights from his chest straight out above him and back down.

174

MILITARY PRESS – the player sits on the weight bench and begins with a dumbbell in each hand at shoulder height. He then raises the dumbbells above his head, then back to his shoulders.

SIDE PULLS – the player stands with his left knee on the weight bench and right foot on the ground. He holds on dumbbell in his right hand and tilts his back and head forward. He then pulls the dumbbell up into his chest. After half the time has expired, the player switches to the other hand on the opposite side of the bench. The motion for this exercise is similar to reaching down and pulling the cord to start a lawnmower.

CURLS – the player stands with a dumbbell in each hand and raises then one at a time to his shoulder while keeping his elbow at his side.

MEDICINE BALL SHOT PUTS – the player holds a small medicine ball at shoulder height with one hand. He then steps forward and pushes the ball with one hand to a coach or partner who catches the ball and returns it to him.

Strength, conditioning and flexibility training has revolutionized baseball. Players at every level work out all year round – there is no off season for this aspect of the game. Even if you are not able to devote a significant amount of time to this part of the game, it is important to spend at least ten minutes of every practice on a program that addresses each of the four major muscle groups used in baseball. If you embrace this program in a serious way, you will see tangible benefits on the field in a few months.

On the Meteors we have also had a lot fewer injuries than other programs. I think this program is one of the primary reasons why our players stay healthy even though they play over a hundred games a year.

CHAPTER 12:
THROWING "THE BOOK" OUT – STRATEGY ADJUSTMENTS FOR THE YOUTH LEVEL OF BASEBALL

One of the most important things I have learned the hard way after coaching over 800 travelball games is that conventional baseball wisdom – sometimes called "The Book" – does not always apply at the youth level. When coaches, broadcasters and columnists talk about doing things "by the book" on the field, they are referring to thousands of written and unwritten rules on how to best manage and play the game. When to bunt or squeeze, to play the infield in, to steal a base, to hit and run – there are theories developed over time by coaches at the major league level that are passed down over the years and followed by coaches at all levels. However, I believe it is important to *deconstruct* the game of baseball and throw the book out in many situations at the

177

youth level. These written and unwritten rules are not always the right approach to take because the youth game is often very different than the one you see on TV.

When I say you should deconstruct the game, I mean everything about the game from the ground up. The rules permit you to place nine players in the field on defense, but only one (the catcher) is allowed to be in foul territory when a pitch is delivered. One player must have a foot on the pitcher's rubber to deliver a throw to the plate. However, there are no rules about the other seven players other than the fact that they must be in fair territory when the pitch is made. Why do we play four of these players in the infield? Why do we station two of them between first and second base and two between second and third base? Why do we put three players in the outfield? Why are they spaced evenly apart?

When you coached your first T-Ball game, you probably stationed your players in the same configuration you learned by watching and playing the game. You have probably continued to follow that pattern to the present day. In recent years, Major League teams have invested millions of dollars to study and chart hitters over a long period of time. What they learned was that conventional wisdom did not always apply to certain hitters. Some players hit the ball to the left side of the field less than 1% of the time and vice versa. Others hit the ball in a certain area when pitched a certain way, and another when pitched differently. Now, every major league team has all hitters in the major leagues thoroughly charted and they adjust the position of their infielders and outfielders accordingly. The result of this data is that teams will make radical shifts in the position of the defenders when hitters such as Jason Giambi and David Ortiz come to the plate. That is because hitters like that are either incapable of hitting the ball in a certain area or they simply refuse to try.

Most of these defensive shifts are not as radical as those deployed for Giambi and Ortiz. They are very subtle and usually go unnoticed by the casual fan. These shifts may only be a few feet to the left or right by the infielders, or twenty to thirty feet by the outfielders – not enough for television broadcasters to even mention. If you attend a major league game in person and watch closely, you will notice that nearly every infielder and outfielder changes his position on the field when a new batter comes to the plate. This is the result of many thousands of hours of scouting by their coaching staffs.

Major league hitters are obviously the best in the world. They are trained to hit the ball to any part of the field, depending on how they are being pitched. Yet, each of these hitters has tendencies that can be measured. Youth hitters have not had such extensive training and practice. It is very easy for a trained observer to watch a young player swing the bat and know exactly how to pitch him and where he is likely to hit the ball if he makes contact. Young hitters are far more likely to hit almost exclusively to one area of the field. Youth hitters that are capable of hitting to all areas of the park are exceptionally rare. In my estimation, about 5% of the travelball players in the 9/10U age groups can consistently do it, 10% at the 11/12U ages, and 30% at the 13/14U level. If such a small percentage of players are capable of hitting the ball to a particular side of the field, why would you put half of your players there?

Youth coaches learn the tendencies of opposing hitters after they face them often in games and see a pattern develop. Highly skilled and experienced coaches can watch a youth hitter swing once and know exactly where they are likely to hit the ball. You will develop this skill over time if you become a student of the game – particularly of the swing. If you pay attention to the feet, hands, front shoulder and hips of a hitter you will see quickly what he is capable of doing what he cannot do. Good coaches don't need an extensive "scouting report" – young hitters make it obvious where they are going to hit the ball as soon as they take their first swing. Experience, and study on your part, will allow you to adjust your defense if you are willing to throw out "The Book."

I also believe you should deconstruct the game in every phase. I have briefly addressed defensive positioning, but pitching, base running and offense can all be approached differently at the youth level. I think there are two big reasons why youth coaches almost never change their approach from the major league way of doing things. First, the game has been so ingrained in their heads from playing and watching it their entire lives that it becomes difficult to think creatively about it. It is just like any habit – the longer it has been practiced and repeated the more difficult it is to break. Second, youth games are usually coached by dads who did not play professional baseball. Many are insecure about their credentials in the game and do not want to look foolish by doing something that may be perceived by others as a lack of knowledge. Managers cannot be afraid of criticism from parents or other coaches for strategic moves they make during a game. This fear will stifle their ability to be creative and cause them to second-guess themselves. I will give you an example of something I did during a big tournament game that caused people to think I was either crazy or stupid.

We were playing a 12U tournament "pool game" against the North Florida Hurricanes, an elite team from Jacksonville, Florida. There were three teams in our pool, with each one playing each other. After the two pool games, the team with the best record would advance to the next round of bracket play. If two teams were tied with the same record, the next tie breaker was total runs allowed in pool play. The third tie breaker is total runs scored. Since pool games were played on a "time limit," if a game is tied at the end of six innings, the game will end in a tie. This is a very common formula in travelball tournaments. We had already played our first pool game against the weakest team in our pool and won 11-0. The Hurricanes had not played that team yet. We both knew the game against each other would decide the pool because we were equally matched teams.

In the bottom of the sixth inning, we led 9-8 and the Hurricanes were batting with the bases loaded and two outs. Their best hitter was at the plate. He was one of the top three hitters in the State of Florida at the 12U age group - we had faced him before and were hardly ever able to get him out. We had identified a big hole in the swing of the hitter batting after him, and had struck this weaker hitter out twice earlier in the game. I decided to intentionally walk in the *tying run* by giving first base to their best hitter with the bases loaded. With the score tied 9-9, we struck out the next batter for the third time and the game ended in a tie (most tournaments will allow pool games to end in ties).

I knew at the time the criticism I would take from my team's parents and coaches, opposing coaches, and observers at the ballpark. It was a move I would never have made in my early years of coaching.

However, after seven years coaching travelball, I did not care about criticism or perception. I turned to one of my assistant coaches at the time and told him that to be a good manager you can't be afraid to look like an idiot (although I used a more colorful term). I knew people were going to say, "How could you play for a tie?" "Why wouldn't you go for the win?" "What are you teaching the kids?"

What I knew at the time was that the Hurricanes now had to shutout their next opponent *and* score more than 11 runs to win our pool. That is because of the tie breaker formula in pool play. As soon as their next opponent scored one run, which they did in the second inning, we had won the pool and advanced.

My job at that point in pool play of a tournament is to advance my team to bracket play so the kids get to play more games. I thought intentionally walking in the tying run gave us the best chance to advance based on the percentages in front of me. This is something you have to learn the hard way at the youth level – you will never see that in a major league game because there are no games that end in a tie, time limits, pool play or tie breakers.

I bring up this story to emphasize that you should not take on the responsibility of manager if you are afraid of criticism or being second guessed. You have to have a very thick skin to be a baseball manager. If you don't have one, you have to learn to develop one or you should be an assistant coach who does not have to make these kinds of decisions and is therefore insulated from criticism.

I also give this example to persuade you to think creatively and deconstruct conventional wisdom so that your approach can be more dynamic and your team more successful. The following are some examples of creative offensive and defensive plays and approaches that have been successful for me at the youth level.

Creative Defenses

6 Infielders

Bunting is a hundred times more common at the youth level than it is in professional baseball. Some coaches (like me) rarely bunt except late in close games and others rely on it as a major staple of their offense.

The younger the age group, the more frequently coaches will call bunts because the defenders are not as fundamentally sound or able to make athletic plays on the move.

Many teams will also have a couple of hitters at the bottom of their lineup who are completely incapable of hitting the ball off a quality pitcher, and nobody knows that better than their own coach. If one of these weak hitters comes to the plate, you should always anticipate a bunt. If one of these hitters is up late in a close game, it is time to get creative with your defensive alignment.

When I am all but certain a hitter is going to bunt, I will pull one of my outfielders into the infield so that I have six players in the infield and two outfielders. The outfielders will play in right and left-center field. This allows me to put two infielders halfway between home plate and the corner bases to completely smother a potential bunt.

The opposing coach now has three choices: (1) He can take the bunt play off and ask a weak hitter to try and drive the ball into the outfield, (2) he can bunt the ball right into three defenders who are on top of the hitter, or (3) he can change the play to a suicide squeeze. I absolutely refuse to have my team lose a game on a bunt, so I force the opposing coach into a much lower percentage option with a creative defense.

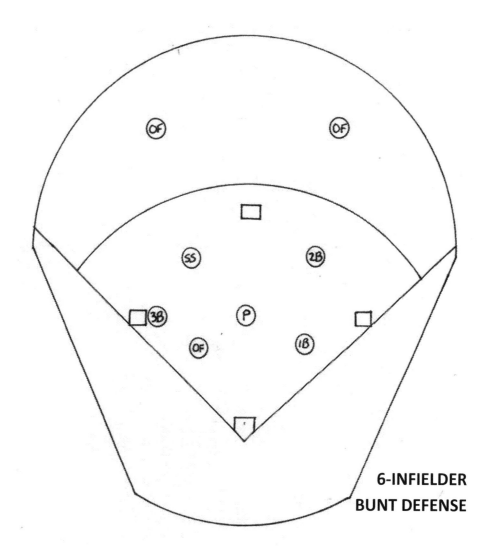

**6-INFIELDER
BUNT DEFENSE**

4 Outfielders

After you have faced certain opposing hitters a number of times you will notice that some have an exaggerated uppercut swing. This is especially true at the 11U and 12U ages where stronger players are capable of hitting home runs over shorter fences. They will alter their swings to attempt to hit home runs and are not especially interested in base hits. Players who try to hit this way rarely hit groundballs, and when they do they are almost always to the pull side. For these hitters, I have always played four outfielders and no middle infielder to the non-pull side of the infield. Before the game I discuss with my outfielders and middle infielders the one or two opposing hitters we are going to defense in this way. As soon as one of these hitters walks to the plate, the players run to their positions quickly so that the game is not delayed.

With four players evenly spaced in the outfield, it becomes very difficult for a hitter to get a hit of any kind on a line drive. If he hits a groundball to the opposite side of the middle of the infield, he will have an easy hit. However, these players are usually not capable of doing that even if they were willing to try.

Deep/Middle/Shallow

This is my standard outfield alignment for almost all opposing hitters at every age group. Our outfielder on the pull side (the leftfielder for a right handed batter), plays deep, our centerfielder plays at medium depth, and the outfielder in the opposite field plays very shallow. Therefore, instead of a standard arc-shaped alignment you see at other levels, my outfielders usually play across the field in a straight, diagonal line slanted out to the pull-side corner of the outfield.

The reason why I use this alignment is that youth hitters are almost always pull hitters. When they hit the ball to the pull side, a youth hitter usually hits the ball hard and I am willing to give up a single to the pull side but want to take away extra-base hits. Young hitters are also regularly capable of hitting the ball to centerfield, but when they do so they lose about a third of their power, so that is why I usually have my centerfielder playing "straight up."

I play my opposite field outfielder very shallow because young hitters are rarely capable of hitting the ball solidly to the opposite field. When they do hit the ball the other way, it is usually a miss-hit or a blooper. I want all bloopers to the opposite field caught and I am willing to risk an extra base hit to make sure I catch the bloopers.

You will learn through experience that ninety percent of the balls hit to the opposite field at the youth level will be bloopers or weak grounders. Additionally, if you have this outfielder stationed between the two infielders, he will be able to field ground balls through the hole and make force outs on the bases since he is playing so close to the infield.

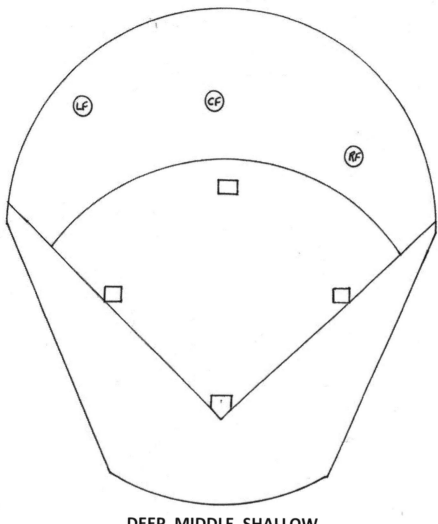

DEEP, MIDDLE, SHALLOW

Triangle Defense

This is a defense that can be used against weaker hitters at all age groups that lack power. These are typically hitters at the bottom of the order, although some teams will have these hitters in the one or two hole if they always put the ball in play and are fast. This defense is designed to smother these hitters and take away their ability to get on base.

I call out "triangles" to my outfielders to get them in proper position. They then come into the shallow part of the outfield and play behind and between the infielders. The result will be that your defenders will form three triangles and there will be virtually no open space for a player to hit ball into except over the heads of the defense. Your

185

outfielders are in a position to catch any ball in the air that is shallow and clears the infield. They are also capable of fielding grounders that make it through the infield and make force outs on the bases. It is a very frustrating defense for a weak hitter to deal with. The only way he can defeat it is to do something he is virtually incapable of – hit the ball with power into the deep part of the outfield.

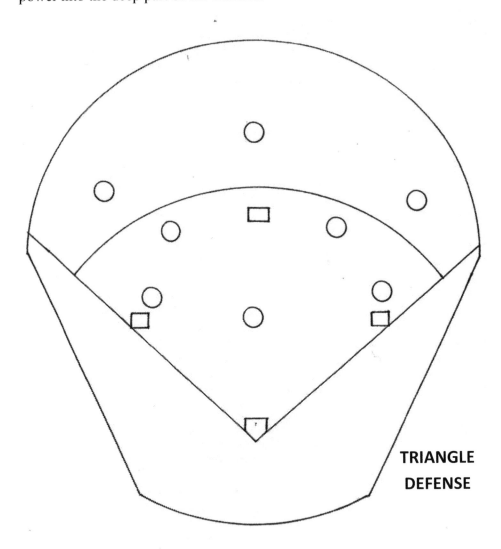

TRIANGLE DEFENSE

Shifts

Some players are completely unable to hit the ball to the opposite field. They start their swing with their hips (instead of hands), their front

186

hip clears way before the hands get through the zone and their front shoulder flies wide open before contact.

As I said before, most young hitters are pull hitters, but you still should play most hitters straight up in the infield because there will be a lot of miss-hits and bloopers the other way. However, a few hitters are so undisciplined that it is virtually impossible for them to ever hit a ball to the opposite side. For these hitters, I move my opposite field middle infielder to the pull side. For a right handed batter, I would play the third baseman close to the line, the shortstop in the hole, and the second baseman slightly to the left of the second base bag.

For each of these defenses that shift fielders to overload one side or another, four outfielders, or the triangle outfield defense, there is another positive byproduct that often results. You are giving a young hitter a look he may have never seen before staring back at him.

It certainly bothers a young hitter to see a defense out of normal position. It also presents a challenge to him to do something he is not used to doing or is not capable of doing. His parent or coach will yell out to him, "look at where they are playing you" or "there is a lot of room in right, look to go the other way!"

These players will sometimes try and do just that, and the result is usually better than if they just hit their normal way into the teeth of the shift. If your "trick" defense forces a good hitter to try and alter his swing, you have already won. The result will almost always be a blooper popup to the opposite field, a strikeout, or a grounder back to the pitcher. So, there is certainly a strong psychological impact of these unusual defenses on young hitters.

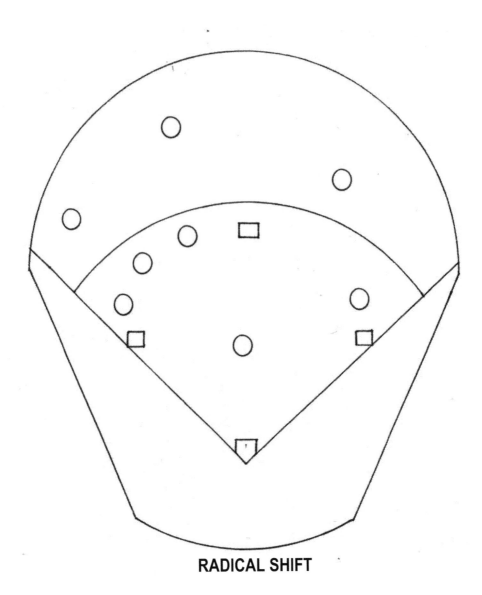

RADICAL SHIFT

Hidden Ball Tricks

I have a confession to make. Forgive me, for I have sinned. I developed my own hidden ball trick play and used it three times in tournament games. It worked twice, but I will never do it again!

The University of Miami made these kinds of plays famous in the College World Series when they faked a pickoff to first base and lured the base runner into breaking for second on what he thought was an overthrow into right field. In my earlier years of coaching I decided to

188

install a similar play, but I modified the Miami play to simplify it and adapt it to the youth level.

The Miami play worked because of the flawless execution by their players and because the noise of a large crowd and the distance of the coaches' box from first base made it difficult for the base coach to communicate with the runner. Therefore, the issue for me with using the Miami play at the youth level was that those two factors are not present at a youth baseball game.

First, there are not usually large crowds, and even where there are a lot of people watching the game, they are usually stationed between the two dugout areas behind the fence and are not near the corner bases. Second, the "boxes" for the base coaches are usually very close to the bases so that the coaches are only a few feet away from the runners on first or third. I decided that the only base a hidden ball play would work a high percentage of the time was at second base – the base furthest away from either of the two base coaches.

In our play the pitcher spins with a quick (not a hanging inside) pickoff move and throws to the shortstop who has moved to cover second. The base runner is forced to dive back to the bag with his head down. All of the players on the field and on your bench act as if there is an overthrow. The second baseman yells "get the ball!" and runs out into shallow center field. The centerfielder turns and runs straight to the fence and bends down as if to dig the ball out from up against the fence. The corner infielders also yell, "Get the ball, get the ball!" The players in the dugout yell, "Go, go, go!"

The players yelling "Go" serves two purposes. First, the base runner at second will think either his coach, parents on his team or his teammates are telling him to get up and advance to third. Second, the base coaches will usually be yelling, "No, no, no!" and that sounds similar to "Go" and it will not be clear to the runner with so many people yelling things that sound the same. When the runner gets up and leaves the bag, the shortstop immediately tags him out.

We ran this play three times at critical situations late in close games and it worked twice to help us win the game, just as it did for Miami. The reason I stopped running the play was that each time I did it

I was so embarrassed that the win did not feel the same. I felt bad for the young player we had tricked into making a critical mistake. The opposing coaches were also obviously not happy and did not appreciate losing the game by deception. I decided that, even though the play obviously works, there are some things I was not willing to do to win a baseball game and this was one of those. I am not saying that you should not use these kinds of plays or that they are inherently immoral. I just felt uncomfortable with it and decided not to use it in the future.

Pitcher Cutoff Man

Traditionally, the corner infielders act as the "cutoff men" for an outfielder's relay throw to the plate. However, when we practiced the play and used it in games it seemed inefficient and impractical on the smaller field dimensions. When my assistant coaches thought about it we realized this is another area where "The Book" should not apply to the youth level of play. The field dimensions had the outfielders so close to the infield that there was insufficient time for the corner infielders to get in the proper position to receive the throw. Also, there are a lot of moving parts in the traditional cutoff play, and young infielders rarely executed it properly in a game. We looked for a way to simplify our cutoff plays and make them more practical for the smaller fields.

In the traditional outfield relay, the pitcher would get in position to either backup home plate or third base. However, we felt that the fences behind the catcher and third base bags were so close to the fielders that backing up these fielders was not critical. We decided to have the *pitcher* serve as our cutoff man on throws from the outfield. The pitcher has to only move a few feet on the small fields to get in proper position to receive the throw. Therefore, we always had our cut man in the proper position, we kept the movement of our infielders to a minimum, and sacrificed something we felt we didn't even need. I have used my pitcher as cut man from 9U-12U on both Meteors teams for many years and I am convinced it is the best way to do it on the small fields.

Throwing Behind Runner on Missed Bunt

This is something that many high school, college and major league teams look to do on occasion, but should *always* be executed automatically at the youth level. When a coach calls for a sacrifice bunt, the base runner will usually be very aggressive on his secondary lead to try and get an extra jump to avoid being thrown out at the next base. Bunt plays are usually close, and base runners will usually anticipate that the hitter will get the bunt down and get far off their base as a result. If the hitter misses the bunt, your infielders should be taught to immediately break for the bag behind the runner and your catcher should automatically come up throwing behind the runner on every missed bunt. Even if you are not able to pick the runner off, you will cause him to be a lot more cautious when the bunt is called for again and you may be able to get the lead runner out if the hitter is able to lay down a bunt on the next pitch.

Creative Offensive Plays

Unusual Tag Plays

There are a number of plays an intelligent, aggressive young base runner can execute that would never work at the higher levels of baseball. That is because the lack of the arm strength and alertness of youth defenders and the small field dimensions create opportunities to take extra bases. One of the biggest differences between youth and adult level offense are tag plays – when a base runner is able to tag up on a ball that is caught by a defender.

One tag play we teach occurs when the first or second baseman has to run out into shallow right field or foul territory down the right field line to make a running catch. In this scenario, a base runner at second can usually tag up and make it safely to third, and a base runner at third can often tag and score.

There are three reasons why this works at the youth level. First, the defender has all of his momentum going away from the base he has to throw to, and it will take him at least three or four steps just to stop. Second, he will not expect the base runner to be tagging, so you have the

191

element of surprise and this will often delay his throw for another second. Finally, when he makes the throw it will usually be rushed, off-balance, and off-line. I teach my runners at second and third to always tag up and go when one of these defenders makes a running over-the-shoulder catch towards the outfield.

Another tag play that sometimes works is when there is a popup in foul territory halfway between home and either first or third base. Quite often the catcher, pitcher and corner infielder will all try to run and catch the ball at the same time. This will often result in home plate being wide open and uncovered for an alert runner tagging at third. Additionally, many times the fielder catching the ball will dive to make the catch and end up on the ground, or players will collide with the same result. A runner at first can tag and usually easily make second base on a foul ball caught in this area of the field by a player who ends up on the ground.

The last tag play is something I call the "Tag-Two." During our 11U-12U seasons, we played on a lot of fields that had fences 250'-300' from home plate. I noticed that the combination of good hitters capable of hitting the ball deep into the outfield, fast base runners, weak-armed outfielders and bases that were close together presented the opportunity for an aggressive base runner to sometimes take *two* bases on a tag play instead of one. If I had a fast runner on second and one of our hitters drove a ball deep, I would call out "Tag-Two" to the runner. He would tag and run outside the baseline, round third base and score. Often the defense is so surprised that they are not set up for a relay home. Also, the player making the catch knows he can't throw out the runner at third so he often just lobs the ball back into the infield, creating additional time to take the extra base.

Crazy Steals

This is a desperation play that normally only works at the youngest levels or against a very inexperienced team. The scenario for this play is when you have runners on second and third base, or the bases loaded, you have a weak hitter at the plate, and you are desperate for a run. In this play, the runner at second base breaks for third on the pitch. The third base coach then yells, "What are you doing, get back!" to make the catcher think that the runner has forgotten the count or forgot there was a runner on third. The runner then stops and slips to the ground on purpose before getting up to go back to second. The idea is for all of this to induce the catcher into throwing down to second base, which will allow your runner at third to break for home and score.

Delayed Steals

This is a play that can work sometimes at the 9U-12U age groups where the bases are close together and the players on defense are not always alert. A smart base runner can stretch his secondary lead out further on successive pitches to see if the catcher takes notice. If the catcher continues to ignore his aggressive secondary lead, and he has a tendency to lob the ball back to the pitcher, the base runner can break for the next base as soon as the ball leaves the catcher's hand. This play can be executed at any base, including home.

Dropped Third Strikes

At the youngest age groups, usually 9U and 10U, a batter cannot attempt to advance to first base if the catcher drops the third strike. However, once the rules permit it, a batter is still not able to do it if first base is already occupied by a base runner. I teach my hitters to always run hard to first on a dropped third strike – even when first base is occupied and they are already out. This deception will sometimes draw a throw to first from a young catcher and allow your other runners to advance.

Bunt/Steals

As I said earlier in this chapter, I generally do not like to call a lot of bunts for a number of reasons. The most important reason is that I want my players to learn how to swing the bat and hit, and a bunt takes away their ability to work on their hitting. However, a play that can create a lot of havoc and open holes in the defense is to call a bunt while a base runner is stealing. A bunt usually takes a defense by surprise, and infielders will often get pulled out of position when a hitter shows bunt.

The result of this will be that second or third base will often be uncovered by an infielder, and the runner will be able to steal even if the batter is not able to get a bunt down. Additionally, a the runner will often be able to take two bases on a successful bunt – the one he is stealing and another when the infielder makes a throw to first to retire the hitter.

Fake Bunt/Slash Double Steal

This is my favorite play with runners on first and second. The hitter squares to bunt very early, pulling the infielders out of position as they scramble to get in their bunt defense. Both runners then break with the pitch to steal second and third, causing further confusion for the defense. Just as the ball is about to be released by the pitcher, the batter pulls the bat back into a hitting position and attempts to slap the ball towards the center of one side of the infield. This play gives the infield three different scenarios to account for in a two to three second time span. Usually any ball hit on the ground will result in a hit. Even if the hitter misses the pitch, the runners are usually able to easily steal both bases because of the confusion created in the infield by the bluff bunt from the hitter.

CHAPTER 13:
<u>OFFENSE</u>

       I am without question an offense-oriented coach. My first priority when I recruit most players is their ability to generate runs at the plate and on the base paths. There are a number of adages in baseball – "Pitching wins championships," "Good pitching beats good hitting" etc. I agree with these principles at the higher levels of the game, and if I was a Major League General Manager I would build my team around a strong pitching staff. I also am not going to take the position that pitching is not extremely important at the youth level – is unquestionably is. However, I look to build my teams around good offensive players because it is the area of the game where natural God-given talent is a larger factor in performance, and it is also the most time-consuming to teach.

       In my experience, it is much easier to turn a good young athlete into a shortstop than it is a great hitter. Pitching and defense are areas of the game where you often see rapid improvement in skill level with proper instruction and lots of repetition. That is not the case with hitting. If you have a player who is not a good natural hitter because of poor swing mechanics, hand-eye coordination, or a fear of getting hit by a pitch, it can take *years* of hard work and *thousands* of hours of coaching to fix. Even the most dedicated coaches fail to make these players productive hitters because they are just not able to overcome their deficiencies. It is often said that the most difficult thing to do in all of sports is to hit a pitched baseball. I agree with that. If you build your team around players who are naturally gifted at hitting a baseball, you can devote a large portion of your limited practice time to the areas of the game where the learning curve is must faster.

The Swing

I am not a swing coach. This is a very technical area of the game that is best left to intensive one-on-one instruction. This is a part of the game where you have to know your limitations as a manager when it comes to time. I think of myself as a swing *facilitator*. My role is to reinforce what the players are learning from a private hitting coach or a hitting coach on my staff. The swing is an area where too many cooks can spoil the pot. A young player who is told different things from several different people will become confused, make frequent adjustments and never develop the muscle memory that is critical to great swings in all sports.

I encourage my players to seek out instruction from private, professional hitting coaches. You should find good instructors in your area who teach hitting principles and fundamentals that you are comfortable with. Then you can recommend to your parents a few coaches, and they can choose one who best fits their needs when it comes to cost, location and scheduling. It is also important for you to get to know these coaches and what they teach so that you will be on the same page and can reinforce their instruction when your players "truth it out" on the field. Good communication between a private hitting coach and a travelball coach can be extremely valuable. You can tell him each Monday about the at-bats his student had - what they did right and what they did wrong. Many players are "batting cage heroes" who look great in the gym but everything breaks down when they face live pitching. If you work as a team with your player's hitting coach, you will see positive results a lot faster.

I think the ideal set-up for young hitters is to have a private hitting instructor for one hour a week, an assistant coach in practice who strictly works on hitting and provides a lot of reps, and a head coach who can make small adjustments and reinforce what the other coaches are doing. It is also important for a hitter to hear *one voice* when he is at the plate, and that voice should be the third base coach. Too many dads shout instructions to their son as they step into the batters box. When these "tips" are added to comments from the third base coach and a hitting coach in the dugout, it results in chaos and confusion in a young hitter's head. It is tough enough to hit a pitched baseball without receiving instruction from multiple people - even worse when some of the comments conflict with each other. I make it clear that the only person who can talk to my hitters while they are at the plate is me - the third base coach.

When you speak to a hitter during or just before his at-bat, it is very important for you to (1) *keep it simple*, (2) *use positive language*, and (3) emphasize only *one thing*.

Keep It Simple

The time to give detailed swing instruction is in practice, not in games. The worst thing you can do is have a kid's head filled with tweaks and adjustments about his hands, hips, head, and feet between each pitch. You do not want your players doing a lot of thinking about these things as the ball is in the air. "See the ball, hit the ball" has always been the best mental approach for a hitter. You will often hear major leaguers on a hot streak comment that they are "seeing the ball well." This means they are not thinking about their swing - they just see it and hit it and are not making things too complicated. Although you should not try and coach the swing during an at-bat, you can provide a simple piece of advice or a comment on what you see. That is what I mean by being a hitting *facilitator* as a head coach during games.

Use Positive Language

Psychology is very important in all sports - in baseball it is critical. You don't have to have a PhD, but you should know some basic principles of positive reinforcement psychology. You can always say exactly the same thing in either a positive or a negative way. It is important that you become conscious of always using positive language when talking to a hitter at the plate. You should never put a single negative thought in a hitter's head, because hitting is a game of failure more often than not. For that reason, hitters' psyches are fragile and there is always an element of self-doubt in the best hitters every time they step into the box. The language you use from the coaching box can put your hitter in the right frame of mind to approach the at-bat.

For example, suppose the hitter you have coming up to the plate has trouble laying off high pitches. I have seen many coaches shout from the coaching box, "lay off the high ones!" or "don't chase any high pitches." This hurts the hitter in two ways. First, you have used negative language - "lay off," "don't" and therefore put negative thoughts in the player's head that remind him of his primary weakness. When you say this, his mind is likely to flash back to high pitches he struck out on and will see those swings and at-bats in his head just as he steps into the box. This is the worst possible thing for a hitter. The other problem with this is that you have just told the opposing pitching coach and pitcher what your hitter's biggest weakness is. You have alerted them to a problem he has, and you guarantee that they are going to go after this weakness early and often.

A better approach is to use positive language. Instead of discouraging the hitter not to do something, you should *encourage* him to do the opposite. This coach should tell the hitter to "look for something below the hands" or "hit a good pitch." That reminds the hitter using positive language to be disciplined and only look for a pitch in the strike zone. You give him the correct approach and encourage him not to chase high pitches without using any negative language. You also will not necessarily highlight to the opposition that your hitter is a sucker for a fastball up his eyes. If your hitter has a tendency to fly open, you should tell him "keep your front shoulder closed" instead of "don't fly open!" Instead of "stop pulling your head!" you can simply say "keep your head on it." Both things say exactly the same thing, except that one uses positive language and other negative. Be conscious of the language you use while coaching - I have often caught myself and corrected my own words from negative to positive.

Emphasize Only One Thing

Even though you are the one person allowed to talk to a hitter during his at-bat, try not to fill his head with multiple things to think about. If you give him instruction about his hands, hips and head, you will do more harm than good. Just emphasize the one thing you think is most important to keep him on task and give him a productive at-bat. When he comes to bat a couple of innings later, it is acceptable to emphasize something different, just don't talk about multiple things during the same at-bat.

Having a Plan at the Plate

The most important component of a consistently outstanding offensive team is plate discipline. A hitter can have the most beautiful swing in the world, but if he swings at bad pitches he will be an easy out far more often than he should. Disciplined hitters are tough outs. An entire lineup of disciplined hitters can wear out an opposing pitching staff. Major league and college teams are increasingly scouting and recruiting hitters who demonstrate good judgment of the strike zone - evidenced by high on-base percentages and a good walk-to-strikeout ratio.

Good young hitters want to hit. They are generally disappointed when they walk. Their parents usually feel the same way and encourage them to "be aggressive." I have seen many young hitters swing at 3-0 or 3-1 pitches out of the strike zone specifically to avoid walking. I often talk to my players and parents about the need to "buy in" to the Meteors way of doing things. Plate discipline is one of the trademarks of my teams and is something you must constantly hammer into your player's heads. It can take years of consistent emphasis by your coaching staff to achieve results in this area. You must do everything possible to reinforce what you are trying to teach when it comes to plate discipline - including using the bench. I believe the best assistant coach a manager has is made out of metal. Sitting a player down who simply refuses to follow the program can be a very effective and healthy teaching tool.

A disciplined hitter is not a player looking for walks. A disciplined hitter is a player that forces a pitcher to throw him a pitch he can hit hard. I use a variety of approaches to get my point across in this area. One thing I tell my hitters and their parents is that a pitcher will usually not throw you a good pitch to hit *unless you force him to*. If a pitcher knows he does not have to throw a certain hitter a strike to get him out, then he will not do so. That is why our approach is to have a "plan" at the plate, then stick to that plan.

Many people consider Hall of Famer Ted Williams the greatest hitter who ever lived. These same people also consider his landmark book, *The Science of Hitting*, to be one of the most enlightening books ever written about hitting. When most people reference this book, however, they talk about the part of it that deals with swing mechanics. To me, the most useful part of the book for a young hitter and a baseball coach is the chapters on the mental approach to hitting. The Williams approach is the one I have followed and the players who buy into it have reaped the benefits. It is also why my teams have consistently averaged over ten runs a game each season. There are few important parts to the Williams' mental approach to hitting:

Hit Fastballs

Curveballs and changeups look appetizing to young hitters because they can see the ball longer and in theory a slow pitch should be easier to hit than a fast one. These pitches are fools gold for young hitters. Elementary physics should tell you than an object travelling faster that comes into contact with another object will be impacted with greater force, and go farther, than a slower one. Also, pitches that are straight (like most fastballs) are easier to hit than off-speed pitches with downward or sideward movement. Our approach is not a negative one towards off-speed pitches - it is a positive one towards fastballs. It is not a passive approach, it is an intelligent, aggressive plan.

Another reason why young hitters should focus on hitting fastballs is that pitchers all the way through high school will struggle to consistently throw their off-speed pitches for strikes. It is very rare for a young pitcher to throw more than 33% of his off-speed pitches in the strike zone. Many of these pitches start out in the strike zone, but end up out of the zone when they cross the plate. Therefore, a hitter whose plan is to hit off-speed pitches will usually end up swinging at bad pitches.

When a player comes onto our team, he is told our team hitting rules. We don't take a "cookie-cutter" approach to swing mechanics, but we do insist that our hitters follow our team mental approach. One of the most important of these rules is very simple - a player is only allowed to swing at fastballs, unless he has a two-strike count. In other words, he is not allowed to swing at any curveballs or changeups unless he is forced to by the count.

Sometimes a hitter will get fooled and swing at a pitch early in the count that he thought was a fastball. This happens and is forgiven as long as the player acknowledges he got fooled and works hard to recognize the release point and spin of the ball for that pitcher's off-speed pitches. Of course, when the hitter has two strikes on him he must avoid striking out looking at all costs and has to swing at any pitch close to the strike zone. Also, we will sometimes change this rule by the third or forth inning if the opposing pitcher proves to us that he is able to command those pitches and throw them for strikes over 50% of the time.

I highly recommend the "fastball-only" approach for all youth baseball teams and hitters. If you decide to implement this policy, you must consistently reinforce it and insist that your hitters follow it. If a player will not listen to you and consistently ignores this rule, you must bench him until he realizes that you take this approach very seriously. It will only benefit him in the long run.

All Strikes Are Not Created Equal

All hitters have certain pitches that they are able hit harder and more consistently than others because of their location. A pitch that clips the lower, outside edge of the strike zone may be a much tougher one to handle that one right down the center of the plate. Both pitches are strikes, but they are certainly not equal in the mind of a hitter.

There is a great exhibit at the Baseball Hall of Fame in Cooperstown, New York that illustrates this point. It was created by Ted Williams, and is a large board the size of a normal strike zone with baseballs nailed to it to cover every inch of the zone. Painted on each ball was the number that represented the batting average he had when he hit a pitch in that exact part of the strike zone. It invariably showed that when he hit a pitch in the middle of the strike zone his average was higher. In many cases, his average was .100-.150 points higher when he swung at certain strikes over others. That is why not all strikes are equal and a smart hitter will let certain strikes go unless he is forced to swing at them.

We ask each one of our hitters what part of the strike zone is their favorite area to hit a fastball. Divide the strike zone into nine equal-sized sections.

Ask them to pick their two favorite sections. Every hitter will pick the box in the center, but some will chose high, some low, some inside and some outside as their second favorite. Our hitters are instructed to look to hit only fastballs in one of those two boxes, unless they are forced to protect the entire zone because they have two strikes on them.

If a hitter is able to only swing at fastballs in this third of the strike zone, he will be a highly disciplined and productive hitter with a great plan at the plate. A hitter should never "give in" to a pitcher early in the count or when ahead in the count. Do not hit the pitches your opponent wants you to hit. Make him throw you the pitches you can hit and hit with power. If your hitters are focused on a zone the size of the average dinner plate, and are able to ignore the rest, they will become a pitcher's worst nightmare.

Being patient and getting ahead in the count will force an opposing pitcher to throw more fastballs and more pitches generally in the heart of the strike zone. Getting ahead and hitting good pitches is what a disciplined mental approach is all about. The following shows the batting average of Major League hitters in 2009 when they hit a pitch at a certain count:

0-0	.262
1-0	.278
2-0	.293

3-0	.288
0-1	.232
1-1	.246
2-1	.263
3-1	.286
0-2	.174
1-2	.186
2-2	.203
3-2	.233

Protecting the Strike Zone

I will often ask my hitters the following: When you have two strikes on you, what is the strike zone? Many newer members of the team will begin to describe an area from the knees to the letters, shaped in a rectangle, the width of the plate. Almost every answer they will give is wrong. The correct answer is that the strike zone is whatever the home plate umpire says it is. More specifically, what he has established as his strike zone in that game and/or previous games. This is a part of the game where the players can really help each other out – even the ones not in the game.

It is against my baseball religion for one of my hitters to strike out looking. While I preach patience and discipline at the plate with less than two strikes, I want my hitters to go to other extreme with two strikes, expanding the pitches they will swing at outside the normal strike zone. A lot of players may end up having to swing at a pitch slightly off the plate that is very difficult to hit hard somewhere. That is perfectly acceptable with two strikes. When a hitter has two strikes, his job is to put a ball in play and make something happen. A soft ground ball may result in an error. A blooper may fall in for a hit. A ball in play can also advance a runner and even drive in a run. However, a strikeout accomplishes nothing.

This proves that not all outs are created equal either. There is such a thing as a productive out. When a hitter fights off a tough two strike pitch, puts a ball in play, and moves base runners, that is a productive out. It is important for coaches and teammates to come out and congratulate a hitter who makes a productive out. Young players will be dejected and feel sorry for themselves after making an out. Try to explain to them that when they openly show displeasure after helping the team, they are being selfish. Being part of a team means scoring runs, and while a base hit may help his batting average, there are lots of ways for teams to score runs other than base hits. If you are consistent, after a while your players will buy into this important "team hitting" concept.

When a hitter expands his zone because of two strikes, he will also draw more walks than a player taking pitches looking for a walk. This seems a paradox, but it makes perfect sense when you see how at-bats play out hundreds of times with these two categories of hitters. A hitter who is excessively selective with two strikes will often get called out on a close pitch – even one slightly out of the strike zone. That is because many youth umpires tend to expand their strike zone with two strikes.

There are many theories on why this happens with youth-level umpires, and I have a couple of my own. First, a lot of umpires at this level are former youth coaches. They have taught the same principle of being aggressive with two strikes to their players and their own sons. Therefore, they will punish a young hitter who does not follow that approach to teach him a lesson. In effect, they are "coaching" the hitter to take a better approach at the plate. A young player can learn a lot from a good umpire during a game. I have never had a problem with an umpire who expands his zone a little with two strikes because it is consistent with what I am teaching.

Another reason why I think umpires expand their zone with two strikes is something I call a "lack of intent to swing." When I umpired, I often told both head coaches before the game that if I believed a player was looking for a walk, then he was not likely to get one. An umpire can tell when a young player is just in the box to try and draw a walk, and will often expand his zone when that is the case to encourage the hitter to be more aggressive. If a hitter has at least swung at *one* of the pitches he

204

has seen before two strikes, an umpire will usually give him the benefit of the doubt. However, if he has looked at two pitches right down the middle, you can rest assured anything close is going to be called a strike.

Major League teams now actually *scout umpires*. They have advance scouts study videotapes of them and prepare thick briefing books on each umpire for their managers and players to study. They spend this time and money for a reason - each umpire has tendencies and a hitter or pitcher who understands them will have an advantage. Texas Rangers Manager Ron Washington described this in a 2010 interview:

"We do have their tendencies in the dugout on the wall. The name of the umpire and his tendencies, what they call and what part of the zone they call strikes."

The second reason why aggressive two-strike hitters tend to draw walks is that they will often foul off multiple pitches just out of the zone. This is another way a team with a solid mental plan at the plate can really wear out and aggravate an opposing pitcher. It is hard enough for a young pitcher to place a ball on the corner of the plate or just slightly outside the zone. When a hitter then fouls that pitch off for what would have been the third strike, it can really bother a young pitcher. When a hitter can do it multiple times in the same at-bat, it can result in the pitcher coming unglued, and make mistakes to the hitters that follow. That is why I often use the word "battle" to my hitters who have two strikes. That is the mentality I want them to have with two strikes. With less than two strikes "discipline" is the mindset, but with two strikes I want them to battle. Find a way to get on base or move runners, whatever it takes. It is very common for a pitcher who has just made a quality strike-three pitch that was fouled off to make a mistake in the middle of the zone or walk the hitter on the next pitch. I am convinced that occurs because of mental frustration on the part of the pitcher.

I have already argued that the hitter should create his own small strike zone when he has less than two strikes. He should decide the small area that he will attack. However, when the hitter has two strikes, the mental approach is that the strike zone is the province of the individual plate umpire working your game. Note that it is *never* the strike zone in the rule book. That is for fools. Baseball is a game of human error and human judgment. Until we allow computers to call balls and strikes – like you sometimes see a "K-zone" when watching MLB games on television – a hitter should never think that the zone is the one in the rule book.

Each individual umpire – especially those at the youth level, have their own strike zone that is peculiar to them. It is important for you as coaches to learn it, but even more important for your players. Most youth umpires have a lower zone than the one in the book. I have no problem with that because a lower pitch is easier to hit that a high one. Most will give young pitchers a ball off the plate away, but very few will do the same on inside pitches. Again, I have no problem with that because a ball inside off the plate is extremely difficult for a young hitter to handle. Your hitters, when they are on deck, in the dugout, and playing defense, should pay close attention to how the umpire is calling balls and strikes. All of your players should know the tendencies of the umpire by the start of the third inning, and should share that information with each other.

I am always amused when my pitcher or catcher comes back to the dugout fuming after being called out looking during their at-bat by the home plate umpire. When I asked them what happened, they will often grumble that the pitch was not a strike. I explain to them that they, of all the players on the field, have absolutely no excuse for striking out looking because they have seen the umpire's strike zone from a better vantage point than any of the other players and should know his tendencies very early in the game. They are also going to want to get that same call when they go back onto the field defensively. That is why I tell my pitchers and catchers that it is a *good thing* the umpires called them out on a pitch off the plate. They should learn from that and work that same spot to opposing hitters.

Intelligent, Aggressive Base Running

I insist that *all* of my players become *great* base runners. Anything less than "great" is unacceptable. It is the only area of the game where my only expectation is perfection. I tell my players this right up front so that it is very clear to them that I will not tolerate any corners being cut when it comes to this part of the game. There is one simple reason for this – anyone can become a great base runner simply with focus and effort. While a player may work extremely hard and do his best to become a great pitcher or hitter, his natural talent and ability establish the limits of how far he can go. Also, a hitter or pitcher's success is often at the mercy of the ability of the opponent he faces. A hitter can have three excellent at-bats, but face a great pitcher and end his day 0-3. However, a great base runner should never have a bad game or a slump while running the bases.

A great base runner is one who is alert, focused, aggressive, intelligent and gives maximum effort every single second. I demand this from all my players. There is no faster way to my bench for a player than base running stupidity or lack of effort. These things are inexcusable and you should never compromise or accept less that greatness when it comes to base running. A player with great natural speed has the capability to have a bigger impact on the bases than slower players. However, the other qualities I described above are more important than speed when defining the ability of a base runner.

Unfortunately, I had to learn this lesson the hard way. You may have figured out by now that I tend to be on the creative side and am not afraid to experiment or turn into a "mad scientist" while coaching. That is because I realized early on that youth baseball is not always governed by the rules, written and unwritten, that Major League teams played by. One of my hair-brained ideas came during my second year as a travelball coach. The tournament we were playing in used High School Federation Rules where teams were permitted a "courtesy runner" for the pitcher and catcher. Most travelball tournaments have this rule to keep the game moving. This rule allows you to have a player on your bench run for your pitcher and/or catcher if he gets on base. I decided to recruit a kid who was a future track star – unquestionably one of the fastest kids in our area. The only problem was that he had never played baseball. No problem in my mind, I would take him aside for an hour before the tournament, go over a few basic things, and he would be off and running!

That weekend was when I learned that being a great base runner is not about being fast. Although I had covered a lot of basic principles of base running with him, and he understood them, I failed to fully appreciate how complicated base running can be and how many different scenarios can pop up when a player makes a trip around the bases.

Sometimes we take certain things for granted after we have been around the game for a long time – when to run, how fast, and how far are concepts that are not grasped overnight by a fast kid new to the game. This player tried very hard, did everything I asked him to do, and ran himself into an out every time I put him on the bases that weekend. It was a lesson I learned the hard way that you should not repeat.

There are so many things to learn and study to become a great base runner that you could devote and entire book – or at least several chapters – just to this subject alone. There are some excellent books written by college coaches that are dedicated almost exclusively to this subject. I think college coaches are the best sources for base running instruction because it is something emphasized more at the college level than the pros today – where home runs are the primary way to generate offense. I am not going to dedicate a lot of space in this book to the subject, but I do want to outline some basic concepts of our "intelligent, aggressive" approach to base running.

Intelligent

There is aggressive, and there is aggressive-stupid. Your players should constantly attack the opposing defense by always looking to take an extra base, but there are few things more destructive to an offense than outs made on the base paths. You should allow your players a lot of freedom to do what they want on the bases. However, with freedom comes responsibility.

I have always allowed my players to attempt to steal a base whenever they saw an opportunity to do so. I adopted this approach because it encourages players to be alert and pay attention to the opposing pitcher and catcher, and because a player may pick up a tendency or pattern from an opponent that you have not. If that happens, you want him to attack that and not wait until the next time he gets on base after receiving permission from a coach. A player who decides to steal a base on his own does not have to be successful, but he has to be able to justify it with sound reasoning, good execution and it must have been done at the appropriate time.

For example, suppose your leadoff batter draws a walk. The pitcher then goes to a 3-0 count on the next batter. The runner then tries to steal second on the next pitch, and is throw out or (worse), picked off. This is aggressive-stupid. Your runner has just bailed out a pitcher who is struggling, and it is highly likely with a 3-0 count he would have ended up on second without attempting to steal. Next, suppose you have runners at first and second with nobody out and your best hitter at the plate. The runner at second takes off for third and is thrown out. Your odds of scoring that inning just went from 90% to 30%.

"The book" in baseball says to never make the first or last out at third. Although this is a sound principle in theory, I do not think you should be that restrictive or absolute at the youth level. Many opponents will make stealing third a cakewalk because of the way they are holding your runners on second, or because the catcher gives away the fact that an off-speed pitch is coming with careless signs. Your base runner should not be afraid to ever steal third in these situations just because of the number of outs. However, you must emphasize to your players that if they are going to try and steal third when there are zero or two outs, they *better* be right and better steal the base easily. If the steal ends up being a close play at third, your base runner has made a mistake whether he is safe or out.

First and foremost, an intelligent base runner will follow the directions and signals of the base coaches. However, if you allow your players additional freedom to read the defense and create their own opportunities to advance, you will be rewarded over the long-term with a team of great base runners that will give your opponents fits. You have got to live with mistakes when you give this kind of freedom – particularly when you first start out. But it is worth it if you handle these mistakes properly. Pull the player aside and ask him – Why did you go? What did you see? What was your thought process? Often his reasoning will be sound and after hearing what he has to say you will agree with his decision to give it a shot even though he was unsuccessful. If his reasoning is flawed, or if he can't give a reason (which happens), it gives you an opportunity to teach.

Aggressive

The best way to describe an aggressive base runner is that he forces the opposing defense to make plays. When coaching a young defense, one of the most important principles you will emphasize is not to "throw the ball around." You do not want to make extra or unnecessary throws at the youth level because a significant percentage of them will be errant. You do not want to give up extra bases on defense with stupid or careless throws.

Sloppy and careless defense at the youth level is also why it is important for an offense to be aggressive. A base runner will often jog or cruise into the next base because it looks like that base is as far as he can go based on the ball that is put in play. Although lack of effort on the bases is tolerated at the major league level, it is never acceptable in high school and college, and should be even less so at the youth level for two reasons. First, a base runner at this level should always anticipate that a player about to field a ball will make an error, even if the play looks very routine. Errors are very common at the lower levels of baseball, and your base runners should attack the bases like they *expect every fielder will make an error* every time the ball is put in play.

It is common to see a player in the major leagues hit an infield popup, toss his bat, and jog a few steps out of the batter's box with his head down. A player who does this at the youth level should be benched immediately so that he and every other player on your team will see that this will never be tolerated.

The reason for this is simple – at least ten percent of infield popups will be dropped by fielders at the youth level or fall in between fielders because of poor communication. When that popup hits the ground and your batter is thrown out at first because he is only three feet out of the batter's box, the rest of the players on the team should be justifiably upset. I have seen this a hundred times. You must create the kind of culture and discipline where this never happens on your team.

The second reason to always be aggressive on the bases is to force the opposing defense to "throw the ball around." Suppose your base runner is at second and the hitter sharply singles to left. The third base coach decides to hold the runner from scoring, and the runner sees that and jogs into third base. What is the left fielder going to do when he sees that? He is going to toss the ball to the shortstop nonchalantly, and the shortstop will walk the ball into the infield and hand it to the pitcher. Suppose that same base runner went into third base and full speed and rounded the bag hard before hitting the brakes? The left fielder would then be forced to charge the ball hard, field the ball quick and cleanly, and make a hard, accurate throw to the cutoff man or home.

There is now a lot of opportunity for a mistake to be made. He may miss or bobble the ball as he tries to scoop it up. He may make an errant or wild throw. Each of these things presents an opportunity to score a run, or at the very least allow the hitter to advance to second base. The opposing defense will not "throw the ball around" unless you force them to with aggressive base running.

The Batting Order

Putting together a batting order is both an art and a science. It is an art because you must have an appreciation for what each individual player on your team can do offensively and understand how their skills compliment the players around them. It is a science because certain basic concepts of mathematics and physics come into play.

Before I discuss how to structure a batting order, it is important to consider some potential psychological impediments to a productive, fully-functioning batting order. The obstacle I refer to is players and/or parents wanting or not wanting to hit in a certain spot in the batting order. For some players or parents, where they bat in the order is a status symbol. They want to be the "three-hole" or "clean-up" hitter because they envision themselves as the best hitter on the team, therefore they deserve to hit in that spot and anything else is a personal insult.

You cannot and must not tolerate this mentality. Make it clear to every player and parent on the team that you will decide the batting order, game to game, and week to week, without any input from the players and parents. Your decision will be based upon a variety of factors – not the least of which are production and the needs of the team – and input from a parent or player is not desired.

211

A more complicated problem is the fragile psyche of a young hitter. Players will get it in their head that they can't hit well if you place them in a certain spot in the order. I have had kids with all the physical tools and attributes of a leadoff hitter insist that they are not capable of hitting in that spot. I have also experienced this mentality with the cleanup spot. I have had players tell me that they will rake in the three-hole, but if you move them to four they will go into a deep slump.

Although there can sometimes be a rational basis for these views, the most important thing is that if a hitter *thinks* he won't be productive in a certain spot in the order, then he probably won't be because confidence is an important element of hitting. Nevertheless, I will still usually try and convince that hitter that he is being irrational or superstitious and will put him where I think he should go anyways. Sometimes that player will do well, and soon lose his fear of hitting in that spot. Other times the player will struggle, and continue to blame your lineup card for his misfortune. If that continues for a period of time I will relent and move them out of the spot simply for their own confidence.

There are four important principles to consider when putting your team's batting order together. The first is connectivity – each hitter must compliment and have a set of skills that fit together with the player in front of and behind him in the lineup. The second is the realization that every spot a hitter is moved down in the order will mean 5-20 fewer plate appearances for that player during the season. Third, you have to factor in the base running skills and abilities of each player into the equation. Finally, you must understand that each spot in the batting order will be pitched differently by most opposing teams and the player must be capable of being productive based on the way he is going to be pitched.

Connectivity

You must consider how each player will affect the other player in the order. For example, you don't want an aggressive hitter who likes to swing at the first pitch hitting behind a player who is a base stealer. That base runner needs an opportunity to work his magic, and the hitter behind him must be patient enough to let him do it. Let's say your hitter has a tendency to hit more deep fly balls than grounders. You would want that player in an RBI position in the middle of the order where his fly balls will be productive outs because they will allow fast runners on base to tag up and advance or score.

Each Spot Down In the Order = Fewer Plate Appearances

It is common for coaches at the youth level to put players at the top of the batting order who have low batting averages but high on-base percentages. I think this is a serious mistake. Although this may work for a major league team whose 3-4 hole hitters hit 30-40 home runs a year, most youth teams don't have that. You should consider that your leadoff batter may only leadoff an inning once in the entire game. He may come up two to three more times each game with runners on base and two outs. In those situations, you want a hitter in the box capable of driving in runs with a hit.

Another reason why I believe the players at the very top of the batting order should be some of your best hitters is because each spot down in the order receives, depending on the number of games you play, 5-20 fewer at-bats per season. It is a simple matter of mathematics. I want my best hitters to get the most plate appearances each season. I don't want a .250 hitter with a .450 on base percentage to get the most plate appearances. These hitters do an excellent job and can be very productive in the 8-9 spots in the order. That is where you should put them.

Factor in Base Running

Too many youth coaches only consider the hitting capabilities of a player when he is placed in the batting order. This is another big mistake. You should factor in the speed and base running ability of the player and how he fits with the players around him in the order. If you have one of your fastest players hitting behind one your slowest, you will notice at the end of the season that the fast player will have unusually low runs-scored and stolen base totals for a player of his base running ability. The simple reason for that is that you have hampered his ability to create havoc on the bases by sticking him behind a runner who clogs up the bases with his lack of speed.

Each Spot In the Order Will Be Pitched Differently

Most opposing pitchers and pitching coaches are not going to make the same sequence of pitches to a three hitter as they will to the player hitting in the 7-hole. That is why some players can be very productive hitting 6-7, but as soon as you move them up to the 3-4 spots their numbers drop precipitously. Leadoff and two-hole hitters will usually be pitched conventionally - the opponent will start then off with fastballs in the zone to get ahead, then mix in off-speed pitches and fastballs out of the zone. Hitters in the 3-5 spots in the order will often be "pitched backwards" - the opposing pitcher will start off trying to get them to chase an off-speed pitch or fastball out of the zone.

There are two reasons why hitters in the middle of the order tend to be pitched backwards. The first is that they are usually the best hitters on your team and are also normally power hitters, so the opposing pitcher is going to be very careful with them. The second reason is because many of the hitters who bat in these spots do not want to walk and are therefore very aggressive. Because of this aggressiveness, they are more likely than kids in other spots to chase a bad pitch or an off-speed pitch early in the count. Therefore, an opponent can put these hitters in a hole by feeding them junk pitches when they first come to the plate.

Since I know that this is the way hitters in the middle of the order will be pitched, I put hitters in the 3-4 hole who have good plate discipline and can lay off the junk they will see early in the count. I may end up putting a better pure hitter in the 1, 2, or 5 spots, just because I know they are not as disciplined and will get better pitches to hit early in the count.

There are a lot of theories on what kind of hitter should bat in each spot in a batting order. You can talk to a hundred different coaches and get a hundred different perspectives. My perspective is based upon the fact that I have filled out over 800 different lineup cards at the youth level, and I have a pretty good idea based upon that experience how to construct a lineup that will work at this level of ball. Here is a guideline for how you should consider setting your batting order:

LEADOFF - the leadoff batter should be a combination of an excellent contact hitter who is patient and fast. He should also be capable of bunting for a hit and should work on his bunting every practice. It is important for him to be patient because all of the other hitters on the team will watch his at-bat to see the variety of pitches an opponent has. A leadoff batter has done his job if he has made the opponent show all of his pitches during that first at-bat of the game. Base stealing is a much bigger part of the youth game that college or pro, so he must be an excellent base stealer. This should be a hitter that will score 90% of the time if he leads off an inning by reaching base. He should have both a high on-base percentage and batting average. Do not put a fast runner at this spot if he is not a good hitter, because speed is useless if you can't get on base, and this player will get the most at-bats on the team during the course of the season so he must be able to produce at the plate.

TWO-HOLE - this batter is similar to the leadoff in many respects. He should be a fast, base stealing threat able to generate offense with his speed. I believe a two-hole hitter must be the most patient hitter on the team and ideally also be the player who strikes out the fewest percentage of the time. He must be an excellent sacrifice bunter and groundball/line drive contact hitter with good bat control. His job is often to take pitches early in the count to allow the leadoff hitter to steal second. Therefore, he must be very comfortable and productive hitting behind in the count. All of his outs must be productive outs - he must move the leadoff man at least one base by putting the ball in play at least 90% of the time. You should be willing to sacrifice some batting average if this hitter has all the other attributes listed above.

THREE-HOLE - this should be your best overall hitter. This player should have the best combination of power, on-base percentage, batting average and speed on the team. In other words, if you rated every player on your roster 1-10 in each of these four categories, he would have the highest overall rating. This hitter is going to get a lot of at-bats, and many of those will be with runners in scoring position. He should also be a hitter that rarely strikes out, because he will often come up with a runner on third with less than two out and he must be capable of putting the ball in play and scoring the run.

CLEANUP - most teams will have a stereotypical four hole hitter - a big, slow, power guy who is "feast or famine" - either a home run or a strikeout. I have already argued that you should not do this at the youth level for a variety of reasons. Those kinds of hitters can be valuable, but they are better suited to the 6-7 spots. A cleanup hitter does not have to have great speed - his job is to drive in runs. He should also be a patient hitter because he is not going to see a lot of good pitches to hit in the middle of the strike zone. A cleanup hitter is lucky to get one good pitch to hit during each at-bat. He must wait for that pitch and be prepared to jump on it and drive it somewhere with power when he gets it.

FIVE HOLE HITTER - this hitter should be almost identical in characteristics to your cleanup hitter, except that he is just a notch below in ability in each area.

SIX/SEVEN HITTER - like the 4-5 hole hitters, these spots in the order are also similar, except that the six will be slightly better than the seven. This is where I put my most aggressive hitters who can really hit the ball. They will come up often with runners in scoring position and two outs. Therefore, you should not be concerned with an overly patient, bat-control guy in this spot who makes productive outs - that is not his role. He is usually not going to be called upon to simply move runners, he has to drive them in. Since the opposing pitcher has just run a gauntlet of outstanding hitters he has been careful with, he will be anxious to go back and pound the zone and get ahead early in the count with fastballs to these hitters. These are the kind of guys who are aggressive early and can really make a pitcher pay for a mistake. These are often my most productive RBI guys on the team - even more so than the 3-4 hitters because of the way they are pitched.

EIGHT/NINE HITTERS - these hitters should be annoying pests to the opposing pitcher. They must always be very patient and rarely swing at the first pitch. They should walk often or at least force the opposing pitcher to throw a minimum of five pitches to them during their at-bat. If you have solid, disciplined players in these spots who understand their role, they can be really valuable to your team. When an opposing 9-hole batter swings at the first pitch and makes an out, it makes me very happy because he has just done my team a tremendous favor. At the very least, these hitters must make an opposing pitcher work hard to get them out and must ring up his pitch count.

CHAPTER 14:
DEFENSE

Deciding Positions

Almost all players will come onto your team with the expectation that they will play a certain position. Parents of these players will often have even stronger expectations in this department. It is extremely important for you not to make any promises to a player or a parent about what position he will play on the defense. You can certainly listen to their input and you can promise to give them an *opportunity* to play a certain position, but you must never make any promises or guarantees beyond that. You should stress to parents and players that the first opportunity is given in *practices*, and that you will not put a player in a position during a game unless he demonstrates proficiency in practice first.

Depth is very important on the defense. That is because youth baseball teams typically do not have "specialists" - players who only pitch or serve as designated hitters. Unlike other levels of baseball, your pitchers will also be position players. Therefore, you must have skilled players available to take the position of that player when he goes to the mound. Ideally, most of your players will be able to play multiple positions and have no ego about exclusively playing a certain position. Travelball is also primarily tournament baseball where your team may have to play two to four games in one day. This is also different than other levels of baseball, and it is important to be able to rest your starters during these grueling days and still have your team play at a high level.

To reinforce this versatility concept with a player or a parent, I explain to them that when they get to high school, their coach is going to ask them what position they play. The worst possible answer is "first base" or "third base." This kind of an answer can be interpreted by the coach a variety of ways. He may think that you have never played another position in the past, or that you have an expectation to play only that position. That program may also have a lot of depth at that particular position, but have a need in another area. That is why I tell my players and parents that the ideal answer to that question, whenever possible, is, "Coach, I will play anywhere you want to put me." That kind of an answer is going to put a big smile on any coaches' face. Your odds of making the team and cracking the starting lineup just increased substantially.

To prepare a player to be able to give that answer to the question, he must learn to play multiple positions at the youth level. That is why I move my players around quite a bit on defense. It is good for them - makes them more marketable in the future - and is good for your team because it gives you flexibility if you have injuries, illnesses or absences. I like to develop at least three players who are capable of playing each position on my team. The starter will usually play 70% of our innings at that position, his backup will get 20% of the time and the third-stringer gets 10%. What that means for each individual player is that he usually will learn two infielder positions (except lefties) and everyone on the roster will rotate into at least one outfield position. If you adopt this system, each of your players will become proficient at three defensive positions, and some of them will also pitch. This will make them very valuable to their future high school coach, and to your team.

You should decide what position to put each player into based upon his physical tools. Most of the rest of this chapter is devoted to that subject. You should never put a player in a certain position simply

220

because he or his parent wants him to play that position. That is a recipe for disaster. If you agree to that, and your team gets eliminated repeatedly from tournaments because a player is not capable of playing his position well, you could lose your whole team. This most frequently happens with great hitters or pitchers. You want them on your team because of their ability to hit or pitch at a very high level. However, they may also insist that they will not come onto the team unless they start at a certain position - and they are not very skilled at that position. There is great temptation to agree to those terms - especially if that player is an outstanding pitcher, because pitching is a precious commodity. However, you must not give in to this temptation. You always have to think about the long-term best interests of your program, and while this may help you in your next tournament, it will be a serious problem for your team over the long term if you go down this road.

I have had a few parents insist on this kind of an arrangement with me. I politely explained to them the policy of my team and explained to them that the only thing I can promise is opportunity. Most of the time, if these parents really want to come onto your team, they will back down and agree to let you make these decisions. However, some will not agree and will walk away. Trust me, you don't want the ones who walk away after you have made them a very fair and reasonable offer. These are the kinds of parents who expect to be able to dictate to the coach where and how much their son is going to play. That is the last thing in the world you want in your program. This attitude can disrupt the chemistry of your entire team. If word gets around (and it always does) that you allowed this for one player, you will have a parent mutiny on your hands. The policies of the team apply to all players and parents, or they apply to no players and parents. If you set them aside for one, the rest will ignore them.

It is also important for you not to "pigeonhole" a player. You may have put a player at shortstop at nine years old because of his physical tools at the time, but he may not have those same tools at twelve. I have been around competitive youth sports long enough to realize how much children's physical abilities can change over time. I have seen many players who were slow at nine be one of the fastest players around at thirteen. I have seen players with weak arms at ten have powerful throwing arms at fourteen. Some kids are enormous at twelve, but are still the same size two years later. I remember dozens of kids that towered over my son at younger ages who are now several inches smaller than him. Kids all mature at different times. Some hit their "growth spurt" a lot earlier than others. You should always be aware of the changing physical abilities of your players, and should always be willing to reassess and reevaluate the positions they should be playing based on those changes.

Infield

First Basemen

All lefties on your team should work at first base - at least in practice. If you have a short, fast lefthander you may never want to put him at first base in a game, but he should at least work there in practice when you take infield because his physical tools could change as he gets older and this is the only infield position a lefty can play. I have seen a few coaches play lefties at other infield positions. When I asked them about it, they would tell me that the player is better than anybody else at the position and "gets the job done."

This is ridiculous. The reason why lefties cannot play second, shortstop or third base well is a simple matter of physics. Infield plays almost always go from left to right and a lefty will have to spin his entire body around to make throws on these plays. A ten year old lefty may have the best hands and throwing arm on the team, but the ultimate goal is to prepare him to play high school baseball. A lefty is *never* going to play shortstop in high school, so don't do him a disservice by putting him there at a young age just because you think it can help you win a ballgame at 10U.

There are some things in life that can't be taught - either you are born with certain abilities or you are not. I have come to the conclusion that "soft hands" - the ability to field a fast moving ball on a short hop quickly and easily - is one of those innate skills. Soft hands are just like speed - you can improve it marginally with technique and practice, but there is only so far you can go before God-given ability limits you. I want my first basemen and shortstops to be players who naturally have soft hands.

It is easy to see which players have it. All you have to do is hit or throw several balls to a fielder that he has to field on a short-hop - where the ball hits the ground just in front on his glove. Certain players just have a natural feel for how the ball is going to come off the ground based upon the angle and speed of the ball. These are the kinds of players you want in these two positions, where soft hands are critical. A first baseman with soft hands who is able to field errant throws in the dirt from the other infielders is worth his weight in gold. At the higher levels of baseball, the ability to dig out a ball in the dirt is a given. At the youth level it is a rarity and if you have a first baseman who can do it consistently, he will become the best friend of your shortstops and third basemen.

Your first basemen can be your least athletic players, and many teams put their slowest player who does not have great feet at first base. I would be cautious about doing that because the first baseman touches the ball in the youth game a lot where bunting is more common. If you have a slow player with limited athleticism who is on your team for hit bat or pitching, first base can be a popular place to "hide" him on defense, but up until you reach 13U I would rather have him in right field. Although a right fielder has more ground to cover than a first baseman, at the younger age groups it is not the case because the outfields are much smaller. The right fielder will have to make far less plays than a first baseman, so I would rather put the least athletic player there if possible.

It is also not mandatory that your first baseman have a strong or accurate arm. He is required to do the least amount of throwing on the defense, so many coaches will put a player at first base who has a weak or erratic arm. It is also beneficial to have a first baseman that is tall. Many errant throws will be high, and a tall first baseman with long arms is able to catch high throws. Many coaches will put a shorter player at first if he is good at scooping short-hops, but you also can't coach height, and a short first baseman is simply unable to reach certain throws that taller players field easily.

Second Basemen

A second baseman doesn't have to be fast, but he does have to be quick. He must be able to cover ground and do it with quick reaction time. In many ways, the qualities of a good, solid second baseman are similar to shortstop, except a second baseman can get away with having a weaker arm because most of his throws will be from a short distance. A strong arm can be useful for turning double plays, but these throws are not that far until you reach 13U. Although he does not have to have a strong arm, he should be a very accurate thrower.

Your second baseman should be extremely reliable and consistent with his glove. I have charted hundreds of youth baseball games over the years, and up through 12U, the second baseman gets more balls hit to him than any other position on the field. Since he will get the most action, he must be the most consistent and solid player on the defense.

I do not need a flashy second baseman who makes spectacular diving plays. I want that kind of athleticism from my shortstops, but I would trade that at second base for a player who is fundamentally sound and makes all the routine plays.

Your second baseman should also be a tough, gritty player who is not afraid of contact. He will be asked to turn a lot of double plays at second base, and he cannot be worried about a base runner sliding into his legs as he makes the throw. He will also receive the majority of throws from the catcher on steals of second. Again, many of these runners will be on top of him as he catches the ball, and he cannot take his eye off the throw our jump out of the way if a base runner is close. Many great second basemen are small in stature but make up for that with absolute fearlessness.

Shortstops

This is the position on the defense where "daddyball" rears its ugly head most often. A very high percentage of coaches' sons are shortstops. Sometimes it is because he is the most capable at that position and is there by merit. Most of the time, however, these players are at shortstop because their father is a coach. For some reason shortstop, like the 3-hole or cleanup hitters in the batting order, is an ego thing for parents. Parents view the shortstop as the "best" position to play and that the "best" player should be there. This is utterly foolish. The most valuable and most productive overall player on your team may be your right fielder. If you are an intelligent coach, you will put players where their defensive tools dictate, and not consider any other factors. If you have the wrong player at shortstop, you will lose a lot of games you should win. If you have your son at shortstop, and he is obviously not the best player at that position, you will not have your team for very long.

The shortstop is the captain or quarterback of the infield defense. A great shortstop, like a great leadoff hitter, is one of the most difficult things to find in youth baseball. I believe great shortstops are born with the tools and instincts for the position. Although a coach can teach good fundamentals and knowledge of how to play the position, the feel for the ball coming off the ground and the angles to take to a moving ball are innate. I have seen so many great athletes with all the physical tools of a great shortstop fail miserably despite the best coaching and thousands of repetitions in practices and games. This has convinced me that, with this position, you either have "it" or you don't. How do you know what the "it" is? Well, it is hard to describe but you will know it when you see it.

I don't think you can have a truly outstanding travelball team without a great shortstop. If I was to prioritize positions on the defense in the youth game, I would say that catcher is the most important and shortstop is second. Many excellent teams will consistently fail to reach the elite level because they lack a top notch shortstop. Until the steroid era in Major League Baseball, professional teams wanted great defensive shortstops who made every play, covered a lot of ground, and turned a great double play. The shortstops of the first hundred years of baseball were not expected to hit much or hit for power – their defense was so important that they were not expected to contribute much on offense. That changed in the 1990s with the arrival of admittedly juiced shortstops like Alex Rodriguez and Miguel Tejada, and suspected juicer Nomar Garciaparra. This new breed brought 25-40 home run power numbers to the position, and the old defensive wizards like Ozzie Smith, Dave Conception and Omar Vizquel seemed a thing of the past.

Thankfully, with the steroid era at an end, even major league baseball has seen a renewed emphasis on shortstops who play great defense.

If you have an opportunity to get a player who is a great defensive shortstop, you should not hesitate. If this player is able to be a productive hitter, you should only consider that a bonus.

A shortstop at the youth level is asked to make some very difficult plays, and it always seems like they have to handle a hot smash or a backhander in the hole late in close games. The ball always seems to find them in key spots, and you want a steady hand there. I have coached teams with great offensive shortstops who were inconsistent in the field. I have also coached teams with great defensive shortstops who were shaky at the plate. Trust me, I have learned my lesson the hard way – take defense over offense at this position!

Some of the qualities of an excellent shortstop are soft hands and excellent range. They must be both quick and fast in all directions – laterally to either side, backwards and forwards. They must have good anticipation and a feel for where the play is going to go after the ball is put in play. Leadership traits are also a plus. A vocal shortstop who moves his teammates where they are supposed to be and directs traffic can be an invaluable "coach on the field."

Your shortstops must have both a strong and accurate arm. Many of the throws they have to make will be on the move, slightly off-balance, or from a long distance. A shortstop with a weak arm is a second baseman out of position. A shortstop with an inaccurate arm is an outfielder out of position.

Third Basemen

Your third baseman should be the player most similar to the shortstop in physical tools, except that he will not have the same range laterally. However, he must have a very quick first step laterally because he is closer to the batter than any other infielder and, although he does not have to move far, he has to get to the ball quickly. He must also be quick forward to the plate because he is going to have to make plays on hitters trying to bunt their way on base. A third baseman must also be fearless – he is going to field the hottest smashes ripped right at him, and you cannot have a player afraid to take a ball off the chest as your third baseman. Finally, the third baseman must have a very strong and accurate arm. He has to make the furthest throws of any player on the defense, and if he can't make an accurate throw with a lot of juice on it then he will be a liability.

Catchers

I often refer to catchers as a "voluntary position." It is the only voluntary position on my defense. What I mean by that is that you should assign every player on the defense to a position based solely upon his physical tools and skills *except catcher*. That is not to say certain physical tools are not important at the catcher position. What I am saying is that you cannot put a player at catcher who does not want to be there. Almost every single season, at the very first practice, I pull all of my players aside before we begin and I ask them who is interested in playing catcher. I do this with no parents present because some kids will be pressured by their parents to play catcher even though they don't really want to.

Very few players will ever raise their hand to volunteer to play catcher. There is a reason for this – it is the most physically demanding position on the field. It is a position where the player gets hit, bruised and dinged more than any other player by foul balls, interference plays, wild pitches and base runners aggressively crashing into home. This is the reason why catcher's gear is often called the "tools of ignorance." There is no way I would ever play catcher in a baseball game. Most of the people who play baseball at every level agree with me and would not want to go behind the plate. That is why I call catcher a voluntary position. If you try and put a player at catcher because of his tools, and he really does not want to be there because of the physical demands of the position in games and in practice, you will regret it.

A great catcher is a tireless worker in both practices and in games. The drills that catchers have to do in practice are a lot more difficult than other positions. You cannot have a lazy player at catcher because he will be unwilling to put the time in or work on improving his skills during these difficult drills. They also must be tireless in games.

227

In tournaments you may play three to four games in a day. Your starting catcher may have to catch a lot of innings on very hot days. However, if he lets his guard down or fails to work hard on every pitch, he is going to cost your team in a critical spot. That is why you have to find high energy, high motor kids to play catcher on travelball teams. The stereotype of the big, overweight kid behind the plate you see in some movies is just not going to work in travelball tournaments.

It is also important for your catchers to be great leaders, or to learn how to be leaders. A catcher has to be decisive and take charge of the infielders on outfield relay plays. If he is a shy or quiet kid he is going to have to lose that on the field if he wants to play catcher. A catcher should also not hesitate to trot out to the mound to have a short chat with a pitcher who is struggling with his control or focus. Coaches are limited on their trips to the mound during games to talk to pitchers, catchers are not. A catcher who can help you with handling pitchers is extremely valuable at the youth level. You have to have a player with the right kind of personality who is willing to accept that responsibility.

I have talked a lot about attitude and leadership but not much about physical tools. That is because I think those traits are even more important than great tools when it comes to catchers. However, a player who can combine those abilities with great physical tools will consistently be your most valuable defensive player.

A great catcher has good hands and is an excellent *receiver of the baseball*. I use that term because I think great catchers do not catch the ball; they receive it. Some refer to this skill as framing, but I have never liked that term much. A great catcher will also have a very strong arm with a quick release. You cannot have a catcher who takes his arm all the way back in a classic pitching motion when he throws. The priority for a catcher is to get the ball out fast and have it reach the target quickly. He can have the best arm in the world, but if he takes too long to get rid of the ball it is utterly useless.

Outfielders

Left Fielders

As I have said earlier, most of the balls that are hit hard at the youth level are to the hitter's pull side. The great majority of hitters you will face will be right-handed. Therefore, most of the hard hit balls to the outfield will be hit to left field. For that reason the left fielder will, on average, have to cover more ground more often than the right fielder in youth baseball.

Your left fielder should, therefore, be the second fastest player in the outfield after the centerfielder. In addition to speed, he should also be the player who "tracks" the ball well. This means that he has a good feel for where the ball will end up shortly after it comes off the bat based on the sound and the trajectory of the ball. The left fielder should also have decent arm strength to be able to throw runners out at the plate, but does not have to have as strong of an arm as the right fielder.

Center Fielders

The center fielder should be your fastest player and best tracker of the baseball because he has the most ground to cover. You can sacrifice a strong arm for speed because a center fielder is not expected to throw out runners at the plate as often as a corner outfielder.

Right Fielders

This is where you can put your slower outfielders for the reasons stated above. A right fielder will get fewer balls hit to the outer third of the field, so he will usually have less ground to cover. However, when left handed hitters come to the plate he will have to field balls driven deep into the outfield. I will do this very rarely because it can be embarrassing to a player, but sometimes late in a close game in a critical situation I will flip-flop my right and left fielders when a lefty comes to the plate. I am just trying to get the outfielder with the most range in the spot where the ball is most likely to be hit hard. If you do this often you are going to have some very upset players and parents – justifiably so.

However, if you limit this move to only a few key spots during the course of a season, few people will object.

The right fielder should have the best arm of the three outfielders. This is because he will have to make a couple of important throws that the others are not asked to make. First, the right fielder in the youth game is able to throw base runners out at first on hard shots hit directly at him. That is because outfielders at this level are a lot closer to first base than they are in high school and above. Therefore, you want a right fielder with a rifle arm who is capable of making this throw, which will demoralize an opposing hitter who just thought he had a base hit. Secondly, the right fielder will be asked to make a long throw across the field when a runner is trying to go from first to third base on a hit. None of the other outfielders are expected to make throws of that distance.

A solid, consistent defense that fits well together can be the foundation of an outstanding travelball team. Pitch counts are very important for young pitchers. An excellent defense can help get your pitchers off the mound faster and they will be able to go deeper into games. Poor defense can also be a morale buster for the entire team. A lot of young players will be mentally finished after making a couple of bad errors, and their poor defense will affect other aspects of their game. You will be able to develop an excellent defense if you have recruited players with the right tools, put them in the positions they should be playing, and design practices to teach proper fundamentals and maximize repetitions. If you have done these three things, you will put your team in a position to win a lot of travelball games.

CHAPTER 15:
SIGNS AND SIGN STEALING

Developing Your Team Signs

At the higher levels of baseball, signs and signals are highly complex. This is appropriate because opposing teams will often spend a great deal of time, energy and resources trying to figure out or "steal" signs to gain an advantage. If you are able to decipher your opponent's signs, it will give your team a tremendous edge. During World War II, the United States was able to intercept and break the Japanese code to their naval fleets. This directly led to a decisive victory in the Battle of Midway and contributed significantly to the American victory in the Pacific Theatre. If you know what your opponent is going to do before he does it, you will be on a very uneven playing field.

At the youth level, three principles should dictate the development of the signs you use - simplicity, creative uniqueness and consistency of deception. I have seen a lot of new travelball coaches who have years of experience playing and/or coaching at the professional and college levels. Invariably, they employ a system of signs and signals nearly as complex as these professional or college teams. The basic problem with this is that you are coaching kids, and kids sometimes get confused, distracted or misread complex signs. I have seen a lot of teams lose games because a player missed a sign in a key situation. I never wanted to lose a game because of a missed sign, and that is why I always kept my signs basic and easy to understand.

Simplicity

All coaches justifiably have little tolerance for a player that misses a sign. If your signs are basic, or if you have been able to use the same signs for a long period of time, you can fairly hold a player accountable for missing one. However, if you feel it is necessary to employ a complicated set of signs, then I guarantee that your players will miss a significant percentage of them and your sign regime is partially responsible. I have seen teams unravel over this issue - even when a missed sign occurred early in a game and didn't affect the outcome. The coach gives a long, complex series of signs, a base runner or hitter misses that sign, then the coach comes unglued. The coaches' reaction then makes the player upset and puts him on the defensive. The player then makes some lame excuse for missing the sign. The coach then gets even more upset after the excuse. The player's parent either gets upset at the coach or his own son. For the next inning or two, the team and coaches are distracted and not entirely focused on what takes place after the missed sign. All of this is completely unnecessary, and you should try to have a set of signs that will almost never be missed.

Many coaches defend their relatively complex regime of signs by arguing that they are not nearly as sophisticated as professional teams. That should never be the standard of comparison. Essentially, what you are doing is the equivalent of trying to force elementary or middle school math students to take a calculus test. Your signs should not be simple *for you*, they should be simple *for kids* at the age group you are coaching. As your team gets older, you can gradually make your signs more complicated. However, if your signs are creative and unique, you may be able to keep them simple and never need to change them from year to year.

Almost all baseball signs follow a similar pattern. The signs are given by the coaches, using hand signals, and are triggered by an "indicator." An indicator is something you do with your hands - touch the bill of the cap, your nose, etc. - that tells the player that a play is on and usually the next sign that is made after the indicator tells the player what you want him to do. As I mentioned in previous chapters, I like to be creative and deconstruct the game. In the corporate world, this is called, "thinking out of the box" - challenging conventional wisdom with creativity. When I thought about employing signs for my first Meteors team, I wanted them to be very simple but also deceptive at the same time. Since almost all baseball coaches use an indicator, and use hand signals, it made sense to me that opponents trying to steal my signs would watch my hand signals to try and pick up a pattern, figure out my indicator, and then work on detecting the signs given after the indicator. If that was what they were going to look for, I was determined to never let them find it.

Creative Uniqueness

I will give you one example of a sign that I used for ten years that was simple, hardly ever missed by my players, and never stolen by opponents. I was able to accomplish this because I went against conventional wisdom and made sure the sign was both creative and unique.

Since opponents trying to steal your signs will be fixated on watching the pattern of your hand signals, I decided to give our steal sign *with my feet*. I would give a complicated and varied set of hand signals to my base runners, but all of these signs and signals were completely meaningless and they were able to ignore them. They ignored them because I gave my steal sign with the location of my feet. If my feet were apart - I kept them at least shoulder width - while I gave my hand signals, then there was no steal on. If I had my feet close together while giving signs with my hands, that was the signal to steal. In over 900 travelball games, I do not think any opponent ever picked up on my steal sign. It was so simple and basic that it was virtually impossible for my players to miss - even as young as nine years old. The reason why I was able to use the same simple, basic steal sign for so long was because it was creative, unique, and unconventional.

Consistency of Deception

A common mistake coaches make is that they only give signs when a play is on. At the higher levels of baseball, a full set of signs is given to the hitters and base runners before every single pitch - whether a play is on or not. Although this is ideal, very rarely are signs given this often at the youth level because coaches at this level are multi-tasking - giving instructions on fundamentals, attitude, etc. during games. Giving a full set of signs on every pitch just overloads the youth coach who has to deal with all of these other things during a game that a Major League manager does not have to worry about. You have to find a happy medium. Giving signs every pitch can wear you out, but only giving signs when you have a play on alerts your opponents that you are up to something even though they may not know your signs. In my experience, you can give signs 33-50% of the time and this will be consistent enough to keep your opponent guessing.

Ethics of Sign Stealing

This is one of those topics where you can ask a hundred different coaches their opinion and get a hundred different answers. College and professional teams actively, aggressively and constantly try to steal their opponent's signs. Players at these levels are equally involved in looking for this critical edge. Sign stealing is a common, accepted practice at the higher levels of baseball. When a coach on these teams thinks his signs have been compromised, his reaction is to simply change them. However, when many youth coaches think you are stealing their signs, they will often get extremely upset and lash out at the opposing player or coach suspected of doing it.

The primary reason why youth coaches get upset at their opponent when their signs are detected is not rational. The source of their dismay is frustration - at their opponent doing it, of the affect it has had on the game, and the difficulty of changing signs with young players in the middle of the game. While these are understandable reasons to be upset, they are certainly not legitimate reasons to be upset *at your opponent.*

My own philosophy on stealing signs at the youth level has evolved over the years based on experience. On the one hand, I believe sign stealing is part of the game and has been for over a hundred years. Therefore, I do not think there is anything intrinsically immoral about it. I don't think any opponent should be overly criticized for doing it as long as it was done in an ethical way (more on that in the next section). However, there is a difference between the goals and objectives of college and professional coaches versus a youth coach. The primary and virtually exclusive mission of the college and professional coach is *winning baseball games*. The primary and virtually exclusive mission of the youth coach is *developing players*. Sign stealing can become so pervasive on some teams that it actually hinders players development.

Young base runners have to learn how to read pitchers. Young hitters have to learn how to recognize pitches and adjust to the ball when it is in the air based on this acquired skill. If a coaching staff adept at stealing signs consistently feeds their hitters information before each pitch on what is coming, a hitter on that team will not learn to recognize pitches because they will not have to. A hitter who produces when he knows what pitches are coming most of the time is not very impressive. At the Major League level that does not matter - the only thing that counts is production. However, the last thing you want at the youth level is to send your hitters to high school after they have spent 4-5 years being told what pitch is coming during each at-bat. Winning is not unimportant, but in travelball developing your players should always take precedent.

Does that mean that we have never stolen signs? No, that is certainly not true. As I said, my thinking has evolved over the years on how to best balance player development with winning in the area of sign stealing. My opinion is that there are two situations where it is acceptable to steal signs at the youth level. First, I always allow *my players* to steal signs whenever they want and help their teammates out. This keeps the players mentally alert and allows them to learn a finer point of the game. My coaches and parents, however, do not actively attempt to steal the opponents' signs.

The second situation is the only one where the coaches will become involved in sign stealing. If we are very late in a close game and are having trouble with an opposing pitcher who is mixing his pitches well, I will ask my coaches to see if they can pick up their pitching signs or if the pitcher is "tipping" his pitches. We are usually able to figure out an opponent after a couple of batters and will begin to let our hitters know what is coming. I want to emphasize that no coaching staff should make this a regular practice. If you do it very sparingly and it helps you win late in a close game, that means you move to the next round and play more baseball. To me, this strikes the appropriate balance between player development and trying to win baseball games.

Detecting Sign Stealers and Peekers

It is important to be constantly aware of the possibility that your signs are being stolen by your opponents. If this has happened, and you fail to detect it quickly enough, it is highly likely your team will go down to defeat. My apathy about this, and failure to detect our pitching signs being stolen, cost my team a State Championship during my third year as a travelball coach. Once I realized months later that sign stealing had cost us that tournament, I was furious at myself and vowed that it would never happen again. To this day, I stay very aware at all times to the possibility that my opponent may have figured out our signs.

The tournament I refer to was the AAU Fall Florida 12U State Championship in 2004. My Meteors team had been together for three years and we went into that tournament clicking on all cylinders. We had won something like twenty games in a row going into the tournament and most teams considered us the favorites to win it all. In the quarterfinal game we faced a very good team, but one we had played three times that season and won all three. Although we knew it was going to be a tough game, we were pretty confident because we knew that team well, were on a roll, and had our best pitchers rested and ready. One thing we didn't account for was that their hitters would know every pitch we threw before we threw it.

We started our #2 pitcher and from the first inning he got hit hard. Our opponent continued to hit him every inning and we were forced to take him out down 4-1 in the 4th inning. It surprised us that he fared so poorly because he really had good stuff that day - he had all his pitches working and we were mixing things up pretty well. We figured that maybe our opponent just had that pitcher's number (it happens) and we went to our ace. Our offense finally got cranked up and we took the lead 5-4. Our ace then started to get knocked around and we were flabbergasted. At one point, my pitching coach threw up his hands and said, "It's as if they know what's coming!" I asked him if he thought they had stolen his signs and he said he had been watching the opposing coaches and their bench since the fourth inning and it did not appear anybody over there was paying the slightest attention to him. We lost 8-6 to a team that had absolutely no business scoring eight runs off our best pitchers. It was a loss that still bothers me to this day because I know we had the best team in the tournament and did not deserve to go home early.

I tried to move on and forget about that game as we headed into the Spring season. My pitching coach, a great guy named Rick Mullen, couldn't forget about it. Rick was certain that the other team had stolen his signs but he could not figure out how they had done it. He had even changed his signs to the catcher twice during the game and it didn't seem to matter. He started to watch that team play in the next couple of tournaments. It took him a few games, but then he figured it out. When he did and told me about it, I was incensed.

The first base coach on this team was stealing the signs and relaying them to the batters. He wasn't stealing them from the pitching coach though, he was getting them from the catcher. When there is no runner on second base, a catcher will usually put down one finger to signal the call to the pitcher. He is not concerned about giving multiple signs because no opposing player or coach should be able to see them. However, on the smaller youth fields, base coaches are a lot closer to the catcher and are not angled out to the sides as much. If a catcher was careless and had his legs too far open when giving the sign to the pitcher, a base coach may be able to peek in and see his fingers. We noticed that this base coach made it a habit to walk over next to the first base bag as the catcher was giving signs. Against opponents whose catchers were careful, he would squat or kneel close to the ground and try to peek *under* their legs! Sometimes he acted like he was tying his shoes. Other times he pretended to have a nervous habit of picking blades of grass from the ground.

To signal the hitter, he would call out the batter's name before the pitch if a fastball was coming, or his jersey number for an off-speed pitch. "Come on, Jimmy, you can do it!" "Nobody better, Jimmy." "Head on the ball, Jimmy." All of these were signals to the batter that he was about to get a fastball. Substitute his number for his name in these phrases and he was able to sit back and know he was getting an off-speed pitch. When we caught on, we confronted him and his head coach. At first, they denied it. Then they just shrugged their shoulders and said it was part of the game. I didn't think kneeling on the ground on the base coaches' box to peek under a twelve year olds legs was part of the game I knew, but rather than whine about it we decided to get even. Every single time they played a new opponent, we would wait until after the first inning, then tell the coaches of the team they were playing what was happening. They would get upset, fix the problem, then commence to hammer this team. That team did not know what to do at the plate when their umbilical cord - the sign stealing coach - was cut. At the end of the season, they had broken up and that guy never "coached" again. Guys like that never last long in travelball. Travelball is the ultimate free market where every player is a free agent every day. He was a dad with a baseball hat on - never a coach. The parents and players on this team found that out.

You have got to have at least one coach periodically watch the other team to see if they are stealing signs. You will usually only have to watch two places - coaches sitting or standing outside the dugout, and base runners leading off second base. A base runner may signal a hitter on either the pitch called or the location. Usually, this is done with some kind of hand or arm signal and is pretty obvious if you watch him. Your catcher should be taught to watch the base runner after he puts down his signs to detect any unusual movement. When a base runner at second is stealing signs or signaling location, your catcher should go out to the mound and change them instead of a coach so you are not charged with a mound visit.

To detect whether a coach on the sidelines is trying to steal your signs, simply watch him as you are giving them. If you notice a particular coach stop to stare intently at you every time you begin your signs, then you can assume he is trying to steal them. Once you have targeted a certain coach who may be trying to do this, you should then watch him to see if he pulls the players aside in the dugout to talk to them. If he has your signs, he will pull the players together to tell them how he is going to relay signals to them where they are in the batter's box. Usually this will involve calling out something to the hitter - the name and jersey number described earlier is the most popular signal I have seen. If you see a coach who has been staring at you call a huddle or if you hear a steady stream of chatter before every pitch, there is a good possibility that it is time for you to change your signs.

You also have to be aware of "peekers." Peekers are hitters who wait for the catcher to set up, then quickly glace back at him to see where he is located. A peeker usually will not turn his head - he will slyly and quickly glance back to see if the catcher is calling for a high pitch, inside or outside. You should do two things to combat a peeker. First, your catcher should not set up at the location of the pitch until the last possible instant. Second, a catcher should watch the batter's eyes when giving signs and moving to his position. If you watch a Major League game on television and are able to see the catcher close up, you will see him watching the batter's eyes every single time he gives signs and sets up.

Unfortunately, sign stealing in the youth game is not always limited to coaches and players. Parents in travelball always seem to want to find a way to contribute to the success of the team - even when they are not serving as coaches. Most of the time, their contributions are useful and constructive - running the concession stand, maintaining the website, organizing fundraisers, booking hotels, etc.. However, some parents are not satisfied with this kind of a role. They want to become part of the action, and they believe the best way to help the team is by stealing signs and signaling players from the stands.

I have seen a handful of parents on opposing teams try and do this, but let me return to my old sign-stealing friend from earlier in this section. The year after he had stolen our signs by squatting down in the base coaches' box, he was now just another dad outside the fence on one of our rival teams. My pitching coach heard a familiar voice coming from the stands that seemed to be signaling the hitters after we finished our signs. We looked around and there he was - squatting down behind the backstop peering under our catcher's legs from behind!

My old pitching coach, Rick Mullen, was a nice guy, well-liked by all, but still very competitive and wanted to win as much as anybody. Rick had moved away from our area though, and my new pitching coach was a guy named Jerry Frye. I loved Jerry and so did the kids. Jerry was a very good pitching coach, but he was a genius when it came to psychological warfare on the baseball diamond. Because of this, he was not especially well-liked by opposing coaches, and he seemed to revel in that. When Jerry realized what was happening, he waited until the sign-stealer's son came to the plate. Jerry had our catcher intentionally give our sign for a curveball so that the dad behind the fence could see it. Right on cue, the dad called out to his son their code for a curveball. We had changed our signs, of course, and threw a fastball high and inside. As the pitch came towards the plate, the batter started to move into the plate because he thought it was a curve and it was going to break over the plate. At the last instant, he realized it was a fastball and had to hit the deck to avoid being drilled in the chest. The batter came up shaken and looked at his dad. We struck him out on three pitches as his dad gave the wrong signal every time.

Between innings, Jerry walked halfway from our dugout to this dad behind the fence. I heard the first thing he said, "Are you happy, you just got your kid struck out!" "You just cost your son an at-bat!" I didn't hear the next thing he said because he lowered his voice as he pointed to his own head. When he came back to the dugout, he was grinning. I asked him what he said when he got over to this parent. He said he told him that if he caught him stealing signs again and signaling them to any player, he was going to have our pitcher throw the next pitch directly at his son's head. I am sure my eyes got big and I said, "Jerry, we can't throw at a kid's head!" He smiled again and said, "Oh, don't worry, we won't have to." I never saw that guy try and steal signs ever again.

CHAPTER 16:
LESSONS WITH PROFESSIONAL COACHES

As I have expressed earlier in this book, I am a big fan of travelball players seeking out private lessons with professional coaches. Baseball is a skill sport where one-on-one instruction is invaluable. It is virtually impossible to devote the time needed for swing and pitching mechanics in the context of team baseball practices.

Almost every community in the country now has coaches who offer private individualized instruction in hitting, pitching and even strength, speed and conditioning. You should ally yourself with these professional coaches and encourage your players to sign up with them. These lessons usually lead to improved fundamentals and benefit the individual players in your program and the team as a whole.

You should make it your business to find as many private coaches offering baseball lessons in your area as you can. Call them or introduce yourself in person to them. Tell them who you are and what you are doing with your team. These coaches realize that travelball coaches can be their best agents, and that you can be an important part of the success of their business. You should get a feel for their personality, demeanor and the substance of what they teach. They may also offer discounts to members of your team if more than one player goes to them for instruction. They may also agree to "sponsor" your team by donating money or some free lessons. If you are comfortable with them and what they teach, recommend them to your players and parents. Don't recommend anybody you haven't met though - if they are teaching something off the wall, or generally aren't nice people, you don't want to get in trouble with your parents for steering them in the wrong direction.

It is also important for you to meet these professional coaches because communication and cooperation between travelball teams and private coaches is critical. Do not talk to each other through your players or parents. What I mean is that many times a player will tell you something his private coach told him to do, and it will make no sense to you. How you react to this is very important. If you say to him or his parent, "That is totally ridiculous, I don't want you doing that," then that is how problems get started. The player or parent will then relay that back to the professional coach, and he will tell them that you don't know what you are talking about. I have seen this happen more times than I can count between youth coaches and coaches giving private lessons. The players and parents get confused and don't know who to believe. Almost every time this entire problem can be avoided with better communication directly between the coaches.

Players and parents, for some reason, *almost never* accurately relay to a coach what was told to them by another coach. They always seem to leave something out, take a comment out of context or misinterpret what was said. When a disagreement like this happens, a wise coach will always pick up the phone and call the professional coach. Invariably, after they speak directly they learn what was really said and that they have no basic disagreement after all. People use different words, terminology and examples to get the same point across. Often it is just a matter of semantics and is easily cleared up. I can't tell you how many times I had a player tell me his professional coach told him something different than I teach, only to have that coach tell me the opposite when I talk to him directly. When both of you get on the same page, you can then find the same way to communicate what you both want to the player and his parents.

A criticism of players who have had a lot of private lessons on either pitching or swing mechanics is that they are *too mechanical*. A young player who is relatively new to lessons will tend to break things down and slow down his swing or delivery to make sure his body and hands are in the correct spots at the proper times. This can look very mechanical when a young player is essentially trying too hard and really thinking about the principles his private coach has taught him.

I don't worry about that too much because it tends to go away over time. As the player gets more comfortable with what he has been taught he tends to relax, gain muscle memory, and let things flow more naturally. It is common for pitchers who go to a lot of lessons to be very slow to the plate and easy to run on for base stealers. That is because they tend to separate their hands and bring their arm back in a longer arc. Pitching coaches are primarily concerned with throwing mechanics, not holding runners. You have to work with these pitchers to help them understand that proper mechanics does not mean *mechanical* and that part of being a pitcher is to deliver the ball to the plate quickly when runners are on base. There is no reason why they have to sacrifice good mechanics for this if they are being taught and coached properly.

Do not be a "my way or the highway" coach. A lot of travelball coaches get bruised egos when they find out one of their players is getting lessons or instructions from a private coach. That is ridiculous. A very high percentage of Major League players work out with their own private coaches during the season and the off-season. If professional teams do not have a problem with it, you should not. A player who wants to work hard to put in extra time to get better in addition to your practices should be praised not discouraged. Most of the really successful travelball teams have a majority of their players get weekly lessons from professional coaches on at least one aspect of their game. That is not coincidence.

CHAPTER 17:
MANAGING PLAYING TIME

This is one of the most challenging responsibilities you have as the head coach of a travelball team. It is perhaps the leading source of tension between parents and coaches who otherwise like and respect each other. I have not only seen teams break up over this issue - I have also seen close friendships ruined. You should be very thoughtful and circumspect about how you handle playing time. All coaches have good intentions when they start out, and may have it in their heads that they are going to play everybody equally, etc.. However, most of the people who choose to take on coaching positions are competitive people, and the temptation is strong to try and win every game by having your best players on the field the overwhelming majority of time. I have found over the years that managing playing time is an art that requires thought, consistency and communication. If you handle this area well, you will have a much better chance of keeping your team intact and together over the long run.

Of course, you may intend to have a community-based team where you will play only a few small tournaments. If that is what you intend to do, you may decide to have a small roster of ten to eleven players. I have also seen travelball coaches limit their rosters to this small number of players to specifically avoid having to make tough decisions on playing time. If you have only one or two players on your bench, playing time will rarely become an issue. However, if you intend to have a 12-15 player roster like most travelball teams, it will be something you have to deal with every week.

I encourage travelball teams, especially those seeking to play primarily tournaments, to carry a larger roster of at least 12-13 players. If you want to build an elite national team that plays in the big events where you have to win 6-8 games in a weekend, you will need at least 13-15 players. Although the primary reason for needing extra players is pitching depth, these events can be very grueling and the most consistently successful teams are the ones who are able to give their starters a healthy amount of rest. In many tournaments, teams will be asked to win 3-4 games in one day, and it is extremely difficult to do that without the ability to rotate fresh players into the game to give the starters a breather. This is especially true during the hot summer months when most of the really big events occur.

Development versus Team Success

This is the great balancing act for travelball managers. It is your responsibility to give each player on your roster the opportunity to develop his skills. Practices are extremely important to development, but so are innings and plate appearances in games. You should have an idea in your mind of the number of innings in the field, on the mound, and appearances at the plate each player should fairly receive each month and for the entire season.

Notice that I did not specify the amount of playing time during a particular game or weekend event. That is because you should never box yourself in or commit to a minimum amount of playing time in a small window. A certain event one weekend may be very difficult with a lot of tight games, but you know the following weekend you will be doing something where you can even things out. You should settle on an amount of innings that you consider a baseline for the entire season, then *communicate* that to your players and parents.

My benchmark for playing time has always been based on a high school season. In Florida, high school teams play 25-30 games a season. That means a starter who plays nearly all of the time gets about 150-170 innings in the field and 70-90 plate appearances during the season. Therefore, that is my minimum goal for each player on my roster, and I explain to them before each season how much I expect each to play and why I set these benchmarks. I think it is very important for them to understand that it is not how much they play *compared to other players on the team*, what counts for their futures is how much they play overall. Parents will always want to compare how much their son plays relative to another player they view as not as talented as their son. You have to break that mindset. It is easier to overcome as time goes on and you have been together for a while, but at the younger ages this can be a persistent problem.

The other side of the coin is team success. I explain to my players and parents over and over that "a rising tide lifts all boats." The more games we win the more we play. The more runs we score results in more at-bats for everyone in the lineup. Team success can benefit everyone if you are fair.

Obviously, your team will perform at a peak level when your best nine players are on the field. However, you can't always have your best nine out there if you are going to develop all of the players on your roster. This is the great balancing act in the youth game that makes managing playing time an art. You want to try and win every game possible while being fair with playing time to everyone on your roster. It is not easy. You must always remember that you have an obligation to each player you have placed on your roster. You made a commitment to them and they have to your team. You also have an obligation to your team as a whole and very few travelball teams survive without at least some team success.

Several parents of your best players will always want to see the best nine on the field and in the lineup. They won't usually say this openly to you, but they will comment about how "the team really clicks" when all the starters are in, etc. You should just nod your head and let them know you are well aware of that. I reassure these parents that come crunch time - a big game against a tough opponent in a major event - the best nine will be on the field. However, you should explain to these parents that the role players are also important even though they may not see it. You will likely have players on your team who will have one particular skill - pitching, hitting, defense or base running - that is better than someone in your starting nine. These players can be very valuable to your team late in a big game. The parents of the top players on your team have to understand that and see the big picture. That is where communication becomes very important.

It is quite common for a travelball team to have one or two players who are outstanding pitchers but weak in other areas of the game. You want them on your team for their pitching, but these players and their parents are not going to be happy if they only pitch - especially at the younger age groups. So, if you want these outstanding pitchers, you must understand going in that when you take them on the team, you are going to have to give them enough plate appearances and innings in the field to keep them happy.

It has been my experience that the parents of these players do not necessarily expect them to be starters or full-time players. They do expect, however, for their kids to get at least enough playing time and at bats to allow them a chance to potentially develop as a position player. When you take these players onto your team, you understand this balancing act, but the parents of your best players may not. You have got to help them see the big picture and understand that great pitching is a premium and to get it at the youth level there are often tradeoffs involved.

You will also have parents who feel that everybody on the team should play equally. These are usually the parents of players who get the least amount of playing time. You have to explain to them in a tactful way that travelball is different from rec ball leagues. At all levels in every sport there are inequalities based upon athletic ability and merit. Competitive sports are survival of the fittest. In high school and college, generally the best nine players play at least 90% of the time. I have seen very good high school players get one or two at-bats for *an entire season* because a better player is starting ahead of them. That is just reality and you have to explain that to your parents, some of whom may not have ever played team sports at the high school level.

I explain to my parents that even though the playing time on our team is not going to be equal, it will be a lot *more equal* than any other team they will play on as they climb the baseball ladder. I have had parents of players who averaged 150 at-bats a season complain about playing time! Years later, their kids were getting 10-20 at-bats a season in high school and I looked pretty generous by comparison. They realized only then that competitive sports can be a tough business.

It is also important to have *everyone* on your team spend some time on the bench. This is good for team morale and character building. On many travelball teams, the best two or three players never sit on the bench. This is unhealthy because these kids tend to develop a "prima donna" attitude and feel they are better or more valuable than some of the other good players because they never sit out.

When the best players sit on the bench, and have a good attitude about it, all of the other players and parents notice it and that can really be a positive team building experience. These players should be strongly encouraged to cheer their teammates on while they are sitting. Outstanding players are usually very competitive and want to be out there all the time. You should take them aside and explain to them that when the other players are on the bench, they are always cheering them on and focusing on the game. The very least your best players can do is return the favor. When they are cheering on and encouraging your weakest players when they are on the field, it makes those players feel really good about their team and their teammates. It is your job to make sure your best players understand how important it is for them to sit out sometimes and have a good attitude about it when they do.

Playing Time in Tournaments

It is very important to let all of your parents know well in advance what your plans are when it comes to playing time for a particular event. If they know what you are thinking, they can plan accordingly and there will be a lot less friction between you. I break down each of our tournaments as either a "team priority" or an "individual development priority" event. At the beginning of each month, I send out an email letting each of our parents know what my plan is for each tournament that month.

For example, you many have a smaller, less important event during a particular month and a big State Championship tournament the same month. You should focus on team success in the big event, and play your top players most of the time, then even that out by playing the other players a lot in the smaller event. If you let the parents know what you are going to do with playing time well in advance, they can plan accordingly. They may decide to skip that event and send their son with another player's parents - especially if it is a long ways off and involves hotel rooms, etc.. They may not have relatives and friends come out to watch a particular event.

The worst thing for you is to have parents invite the grandparents out to see their son play, and that happens to be a game he is spending a big chunk of time on the bench. Not only have you wasted relatives' time (grandparents only care out watching their grandson), you have also embarrassed a set of parents who now have to explain to grandpa why their superstar son they have been telling him about is not playing. Avoid these problems with communication. They may not agree with your plan for the month, but at least they will know about it in advance and can prepare for it.

Here is an example of an email I sent out to my parents shortly before we started the summer of our 13U season where we were scheduled to play four national tournaments in three different states:

"This past weekend demonstrated the importance of a big roster. It is the reason why we have built a solid roster of 15 players. Many travelball coaches and parents would say that this is way too many players. It may be for the schedule and events they play. However, we play a lot of games so the first reason is that there are plenty of innings to go around.

"I built the big roster because we are designed to be an elite national program focused on competing in national tournaments during the hot summer months. You see what happened last week when we tried to play in 98-degree weather with only 12 of our players there. We flat out wilted by the final game. What a difference it would have made if we could have ran out six subs in the 3rd or 4th inning of each of those games! Our boys would not have been so worn out for the money games.

"If anybody didn't understand why we have such a big roster, and why I pull starters out of the game as early as I can in pool games, you got the answer last weekend. Everybody - starters and subs - have got to buy into the system and understand that this is the only way to win these big events. Pitchers have to understand that if we are counting on you to win a big game for us late on Sunday, you may not be on the field a whole lot in the early Sunday games. It is more important for the team for you to be fresh to pitch your big game than it is for you to get at-bats Sunday morning. If you are an elite pitcher, travelball is probably the last time you will ever take the field and play in a game on the same day before you will pitch in a game later.

"The players on the bench need to understand that I am not blowing smoke when I talk about how important they are to the team in these national tournaments. It is critical that I have good players I can count on to go into these games as early as possible and continue our momentum with solid play. I have total confidence in all of them. The parents of these guys know that they would be starters if they were playing on another team. But they chose to play on an elite national team. They will be better off in the long run for this choice.

"I know it is hard to sit on the bench. It is hard for parents of a starter who just went 2-2 at the plate to get pulled out to sit on the bench when he is hot. It is hard for parents of the subs who travel a long way to watch these events. But it is how an elite team is run. The reason why we have stayed together and been successful is because the parents who have been on our team a long time and the ones who come onto the team understand and buy into this system. They realize, even if not at first, that over time it is the best way to run a team like this and benefits their son over time."

251

In virtually every tournament I try and manage playing time over the course of the weekend based upon the type of game we are playing. Most tournaments start out with preliminary games or "pool" games that are often only used to determine seeding or byes for "bracket" or single-elimination play. Since a loss in these pool games will not eliminate your team from the tournament, this is a good time to play guys full time who are not going to start in bracket play.

My general policy is to play these guys almost all the time in pool games and rotate my best players onto the bench. Then, when bracket play begins, the best nine players are in the starting lineup and the other players are subbed into the game when the score is one-sided either for or against us. I may also use them in "specialty" roles like courtesy runner, defensive sub, pinch hitter or relief pitcher. I can tell you that it is a lot easier for these players and parents to deal with sitting on the bench if they have made *some* contribution to the team in a big game, even if it is limited.

Finally, there are the "daddyball" issues. The parents on your team are all going to pay extra special attention to the amount of time the coaches' kids spend on the bench - especially the head coaches' son. If you try to keep your son on the field 100% of the time for every game, you are simply not going to keep your team together. Believe me, parents know *exactly* how much the head coaches' son has played after every event. If he is taking his regular turn on the bench just like everybody else, you will not have a problem. Additionally, if a coaches' son is playing more than his production justifies, this is going to cause problems for your program.

It is difficult to be objective about your own son. However, once you accept the responsibility of being the manager, you have an obligation to try as hard as you can to be fair as possible in evaluating your own son. Keep accurate stats in all categories and rank your players. Look where your son ranks in every category and avoid making excuses for him in your own head. The other parents on your team will be very attentive to this subject. Daddyball from the head coach is the #1 cause of the breakup of travelball teams.

If you are thoughtful, fair, have a plan and communicate that plan to your players and parents, you will have far less issues regarding playing time than most teams. This is a critical part of the job as manager, perhaps the most important part. You have to evaluate yourself in this area - look at the number of innings and at-bats each of your players is getting and ask yourself constantly if you are being fair and giving everyone enough opportunities. It is competitive baseball, so the playing time is never going to be completely democratic. But it is also youth baseball, where development is the highest priority and your responsibility to each young man who plays for you is to give him every opportunity to rise to his full potential.

CHAPTER 18:
<u>PITCHERS</u>

When it comes to handling pitchers, you must always remember the reason why you decided to become a travelball coach. The purpose of travelball is to give young players a future in the game, not take it away from them. If you mishandle or abuse your pitchers, you can do a lot of damage to their ability to play the game as they get older. I know a lot of high school players who have had serious arm problems who now despise their youth coaches. They realize, now that they are older and wiser, that the innings and type of pitches they threw at a young age have caught up with them years later like a couple of hundred thousand miles on the odometer of a car.

Young players' arms – the tendons, growth plates, muscles, etc., are obviously not fully developed. I always viewed my players' arms as treasures that I have been entrusted to guard. The health of your players' arms is your responsibility and you must view it as your duty to protect them – even sometimes from themselves or their own parents. No ten or twelve year old baseball game – even a State Championship game – is worth sacrificing the long-term health of a young player.

Coaches and organizations are a lot more aware of the dangers of high pitch counts and curveballs and sliders than they were when I started coaching. Many have adopted rules to rein in coaches who get too carried away, and I have been very glad to see it. Sadly, travelball remains the "wild west" in this area where many tournaments have no pitching rules or have pitching rules so liberal that a young pitcher's arm can get severely abused. I realize it is impossible for travelball tournament directors to keep track of pitch counts during a weekend tournament where hundreds of games are played. However, I would like to see organizations have pitching limits of a maximum of six innings allowed during a weekend event up until 12U and seven innings for 13U and older. This would protect the arms of young pitchers and encourage coaches to develop a complete pitching staff rather than ride the arms of one or two players all weekend.

Uneducated coaches often ask a young pitcher how they feel in order to gauge whether a pitcher has thrown too much. This is a very foolish approach. Players are competitive and kids don't know their bodies well enough to understand the difference between fatigue and overuse. They will lie to their coaches to stay in the game even if they don't feel right. You cannot rely on this subjective approach to protect the health of your players. You should approach each season, and each month and weekend within that season, with an idea in mind of how many pitches you are going to allow your pitchers to throw.

You must keep an accurate pitch count during the games and *stick to your plan regardless of the game situation or score.* Keep reminding yourself that you are out there to give your kids a future, not take it away from them. You will earn a lot of respect from other coaches, parents and umpires, if you take a pitcher off the mound in a very tight game because he has thrown enough pitches. You not only protect your players, you also enhance your reputation as a coach and that of your program. Believe me, people will notice that and you will be rewarded. You will find that parents of pitchers getting abused on other teams will call you wanting to become part of your team. One of the best recruiting tools a travelball team can have is the character of the head coach.

The damage to a young player's arm usually does not show up until many years later. This country has had an epidemic of arm injuries and arm surgeries during the past decade to high school age players. This is completely unacceptable and sadly, the growth of travelball has been a contributing factor. However, you can play a heavy travelball schedule, play year-round, and still protect your players' arms. My teams have averaged 125 games a year and play in the Fall and Spring. In ten years I have never had a player miss a single game with an arm injury. My pitchers who have gone on to high school have never had a serious arm problem or injury. No player who has ever played for me has had arm surgery. If you do this in an intelligent way and you are careful about how you handle your players from an early age, you can play a lot of baseball and still protect your players' health.

Mechanics

There are a lot of good books and videos on how to teach proper pitching mechanics. Even if you are not the primary pitching coach for your team, I encourage all travelball coaches to read a few books or talk to experienced pitching coaches to become familiar with some basic principles and concepts of good pitching mechanics.

A young player can be a very effective pitcher and win a lot of games with poor mechanics. Coaches who are only focused on short term results will not correct or fix fundamental mechanical flaws because when you make these changes you often get worse before you get better. That is because whenever you seek to change "muscle memory" there is an adjustment period because the new action will not always feel right to the player and he will fall into and out of his mechanics. Many coaches are not willing to suffer through the growing pains that often accompany fundamental changes. Parents and players can be even less patient. You have to continue to emphasize that this is a marathon not a sprint and the long term is a lot more important than the next "big" game.

Good solid pitching mechanics make pitchers more consistent and keeps them healthy. I have often heard youth coaches say that they don't want to make changes to a pitcher's mechanics because the player has a lot of "natural movement" on his ball and that makes him a lot more effective. Although this may be true, that movement likely comes at a price that is not worth paying. Poor mechanics can often result in a ball sinking or running left or right. Some young pitchers essentially have curveball or slider action on their fastballs, and it is because of an unhealthy delivery. You can choose to have an effective pitcher at ten years old who will break down at fourteen, or you can fix his mechanics at a young age and ensure a healthy productive future.

Just like swing mechanics, there is no "one way" to pitch properly. However, there are certain basic fundamental things that all pitchers do that make them consistent strike throwers and durable. Make sure your pitchers are fundamentally sound – either by teaching them yourself if you have the expertise, or putting them in contact with an excellent pitching coach. The last thing you want to do is show up at a high school game years from now and have one of your former players walk up to you with his elbow in a sling. Keep your players healthy and productive over the long term by insisting on proper fundamentals.

Throwing Programs

Like strength, speed and conditioning, a good throwing program should be a cornerstone of the foundation of your program. Good throwing programs build arm strength and help condition the arm for a long season. You should begin each season with at least a month of throwing before you play your first game. Too many coaches are anxious to jump into playing games and scrimmages before their players are physically ready. As I said in the chapter on practices, scrimmages are a lazy-man's practice and should only be used right before the season is about to begin or as mid-season tune-ups during off weeks.

I incorporate a number of throwing drills at the beginning of every practice to help build and maintain strong, healthy arms. Each drill is designed to work on a particular part of the arm or of the throwing process. We start with a drill where we throw while kneeling on one knee. This emphasizes generating power with proper positioning of the elbow and of a good follow-through with the wrist and fingers. After five minutes of this we stand up and throw while keep both feet firmly on the ground – the "no-legs" drill. This emphasizes using the back and finishing your throw by driving the throwing shoulder over your plant knee. After five minutes of that we throw regular from a close distance.

258

These three mechanics drills last about a total of fifteen minutes, then we begin to work our way into long toss. I have my players throw about two minutes at a certain distance, then them move back about ten feet and repeat for another two minutes. Good mechanics are very important during long toss. It is perfectly acceptable for them to "crow-hop" when they throw as they get out to a long distance, and to make the throw on one bounce if they have to. However, the one thing they must not do is change the trajectory of the throw. You do not want your players throwing long toss to put a high arc on the ball because this changes the mechanics in the shoulder. You also never want your players to throw with 100% effort during long toss. Once they get far enough out where they are at 90% capacity, that is as far as they should go. Finally, once they reach this peak distance they should not stop throwing right after some reps of that length. They should make a few throws as they slowly begin to come back closer together until they finish throwing at the same distance they started from.

One pet peeve of mine that you see often with youth players and teams is that they begin throwing before any kind of warm-up or stretching. This is extremely unhealthy for the arm. It is very important for a player to run to get the blood flowing throughout the body and then to stretch the muscles out *before* they pick up a glove and ball to begin throwing. For some reason players do not like to properly *prepare to throw*, and coaches have to constantly watch them to make sure they warm up properly.

A good solid, consistent throwing program, implemented well before the start of game action and continued through the end of the season is critical. Too many teams don't put a whole lot of time or thought into throwing – one of the most important aspects of baseball. Make sure you dedicate at least 20-30 minutes of each practice just to throwing.

Pitch Counts

The most positive development in the recent history of youth baseball is the increased awareness of the importance of keeping pitch counts. Traditionally, youth leagues and travelball organizations focused their pitching rules on *innings pitched* rather than the number of pitches thrown. This is obviously because it is a lot easier for officials and coaches to count innings than pitches.

The problem with this approach is that it is possible for a pitcher to throw 100 pitches in five innings while his opponent may throw 60 in the same length of time. It is not the innings that take a toll on the arm, it is the number and type of pitches thrown. That is why it is important for you to keep track of the number of pitches your player throws, not the innings.

A number of studies and a lot of thought has been put into guidelines for the number of pitches young players should throw. Dr. James Andrews is widely considered the leading physician in the country in the area of arm injuries to athletes in baseball and football. He was a pioneer for the "Tommy John" procedure for replacing elbow tendons as well as rotator cuff procedures for injured shoulders. He has been alarmed over the past decade by the number of teenage athletes coming to his office for these major arm surgeries.

The proliferation of these injuries to young players in recent years has led him to work with other surgeons and experts in sports medicine to develop guidelines for pitch counts for youth pitchers. If you follow these guidelines and marry them with proper mechanics, your pitchers will stay healthy and be a lot more effective as they get older and develop. Here are the guidelines developed by Dr. Andrews and the board of the American Baseball Foundation that he chairs:

Suggested Pitch Counts

AGE	PITCHES / GAME
9-10	37-67
11-12	50-86
13-14	60-92
15-16	75-107
17-18	90-122

Suggested Recovery Days

(Based on number of pitches thrown)

AGE	1 DAY	2 DAYS	3 DAYS	4 DAYS
9-10	21	34	43	51
11-12	27	35	55	58
13-14	30	36	56	70
15-16	25	38	62	77
17-18	27	45	62	89

Source – USA Baseball Pitch Count Guidelines from American Sports Medicine Institute, *www.asmi.org*.

OFF-SPEED PITCHES

It is an old adage that the best pitch in baseball is a fastball. While I certainly agree with this, I would modify that by saying the best pitch in baseball is a *well-located* fastball. Off-speed pitches are only effective when the hitter is forced to process what he sees very quickly because the pitcher he is facing has good velocity on his fastball. The harder a pitcher throws, the less time a hitter has to adjust to an off-speed pitch, and timing is everything when it comes to hitting.

Even though a good fastball is the foundation of any pitcher's arsenal, you will quickly learn that in travelball you cannot get good hitters out with just a fastball, no matter how hard you throw. Many rec-ball leagues like Little League have their pitchers throw from 46' even after they have turned thirteen years old. In that type of setting, it is possible to consistently throw a plus fastball by excellent young hitters because the 46' distance is just too close for pitchers that age. When USA Baseball changed the age cutoff to May 1 from August 1 (which was a terrible decision), all youth organizations followed suit. The result is that older kids are now playing on smaller fields at closer distances.

There are several reasons why fastballs are not as effective at consistently getting hitters out in travelball as they are at other levels of baseball. One reason is that the mounds are further back from the plate than in most rec-ball leagues. Another is that travelball players are generally better and batting lineups are deeper with quality hitters. Finally, travelball players play a lot more baseball and many play year-round. This allows them to time up fastballs a lot better because they see thousands of them every year. All coaches and players learn pretty quickly that they have to develop some other pitch to show good travelball hitters to keep them off-balance.

There are several different off-speed pitches in baseball that a pitcher can learn and throw to get hitters out. They are effective because they create movement and a change of speed from the fastball to throw off hitters' timing. There is a lot of controversy surrounding certain kinds of pitches like curveballs and sliders, and you will hear a lot of different opinions about these pitches at the youth level. My views have been formed by articles I have read from pitching coaches with decades in the game, medical journals from physicians who specialize in sports medicine, and my own ten-plus years coaching young pitchers.

The Two-Seam Fastball

This isn't normally classified as on off-speed pitch, but I include it here as one alternative to a normal fastball. To achieve maximum velocity, a fastball is usually gripped across four seams. This generally results in the hardest and straightest pitch that can be located precisely. A two-seem fastball is thrown exactly the same way except the fingers only cross two seems of the baseball instead of four. This normally results in slightly less velocity and more movement that a four seem fastball. It is a safe alternative to a normal fastball and is something a young pitcher should experiment with.

Change Up

There are two different change ups that are common in baseball - the "circle change" which became popular in the 1990s and the classic "palm ball" type changeup. Both pitches are thrown with the same motion and release point as a fastball but the grip results in the ball coming out of the hand slower. Both grips result in the ball resting deeper in the palm of the hand instead of out on the fingers, creating a "drag" on the ball when it is released. I encourage all young pitchers to experiment with both change up grips and use the one that feels most comfortable to them. A change up is a great pitch for young players to learn because it is easy on the arm and can be devastating when perfected.

Knuckleballs

This is another pitch that puts very little stress on the arm so it can be a great pitch for a young player to learn as an off-speed pitch. I don't recommend that a young player use a knuckleball as a staple of his pitching arsenal though. This is a pitch that is generally used by pitchers who are unable to get hitters out because their fastball is lacking, so they resort to this pitch. A young pitcher should develop his arm and throw mostly fastballs. A twelve year old kid should not become a knuckleball "specialist" because he will not properly develop his fastball.

Curveballs

This has become a controversial pitch as more and more young pitchers are throwing them a lot - some as many as 40-50 in a single outing on national television in the Little League World Series. Some argue that if a curveball is thrown properly, it is completely safe. Others argue that a curveball should never be thrown until high school. My own perspective is somewhere in the middle.

A curveball can be a dangerous pitch to throw because it puts stress on the ligaments of the elbow. It is generally the pitch considered most responsible for "Tommy John" surgeries that replace the tendon on

263

the inside of the elbow. No single curveball throw causes this tendon to tear. It is the cumulative effect of thousands of these pitches that can cause the damage over a longer period of time. Young pitcher's tendons and ligaments are not as strong or securely attached to the muscles. His biceps, triceps and forearms muscles are also not fully developed, and these are the muscles used to stabilize and control the elbow as a curveball is thrown. Many young pitchers also have hands and fingers that are smaller, so their grip is not as stable and they aren't consistently able to release the pitch properly. These are the reasons why pitchers who throw a lot of curveballs before puberty often have their high school careers interrupted by arm surgery.

So when is it safe to start throwing a curveball? There is no hard and fast chronological number. Anybody who has worked with kids for a long period of time knows that some mature faster and at different times that others. Based on the literature and experience I would factor in a number of different things. First, I would not allow any pitcher to throw a curveball until he has pitched for at least one season at the 60'6" distance. A pitcher should not make the jump to regulation mounds while throwing a curveball. This first season is stressful enough on a pitcher's arm without trying to also snap a curve off from the increased distance. Almost every pitcher I have seen throw a steady diet of curves in their first season at regulation distance has broken down or lost velocity on their fastball by the end of the season.

Second, I would not allow any pitcher to throw a curve who has not hit puberty and *finished* the growth spurt that accompanies it. This can come at different ages for different players. A player who is hitting puberty and growing has their muscles, tendons and growth plates in a state of transition. It is simply not healthy to put extra stress on these things while they are changing so rapidly. After this time period is over, the young pitcher should at least be physically ready to *begin* to be introduced to a *properly thrown* curveball.

Do not attempt to teach a curveball unless you understand how to properly throw the pitch and grasp the mechanics of it. Do not allow another coach to teach it to your player unless he meets this criteria. Many of the pitchers who have injuries in their teen years occur because they learned to throw the curveball improperly.

Finally, do not allow the pitcher who is learning the curve to "fall in love" with it. A player who has hit puberty, finished his growth spurt, and has learned to throw the curveball property with good mechanics *in practice* should be allowed to begin to throw it in a game. However, I only allow my pitchers to throw curveballs *10% of the time or less.* It should be used to attempt to retire a batter who is a tough out and is fouling off two-strike pitches. I have seen way, way too many young pitchers make the curveball a steady part of their arsenal - throwing it 30-40% of the time. This is extremely unhealthy and any coach who calls this many curveballs during a game should be ashamed of himself. If you feel yourself falling to temptation in the heat of the battle in a "big game," remind yourself again that the purpose of travelball is to give kids a future in this game, not take it away from them.

Sliders

This is a horrible pitch for a young pitcher to learn and no player should throw it unless he is being paid to play baseball. A slider is a pitch that has sideways movement caused by the fingers sliding off the side of the baseball as the pitch is being released. It can be a devastating pitch to hitters, and equally devastating to a pitcher's health. I have seen a lot of kids throw this pitch and not even realize they are throwing a slider. It is easy to see because the spin of the ball makes it look like a pinwheel. This pitch puts the most stress on the elbow and shoulder of a pitcher and should not be taught to or thrown by kids.

Handling Pitchers in Tournaments

You must go into every tournament with a plan of who you are going to pitch each game and map it out all the way to the championship. Of course, as the immortal Mike Tyson once famously said in one of my favorite quotes, "Everybody has a plan until they get hit!" Some of the greatest disasters in warfare occurred when Generals went into a battle with a plan then failed to make adjustments to that plan when unforeseen circumstances required it. So, my general recommendation is to map out a pitching plan before each event, then be prepared to throw it out the window if necessary.

There are several things to think about when preparing your pitching plan. How many games are you likely to play? How important are the pool play games? How many days is the event? What are the capabilities of each of your pitchers? Who is likely to be the toughest opponent? What is the best matchup? Do you need a pitcher to play an important, physically demanding position when he is not pitching? You must put a lot of thought into answering each of these questions when you are putting together your pitching plan for a tournament.

Most tournaments are weekend events that take place from Friday night to Sunday. They typically begin with "pool play" - two to three games that will determine either advancement to bracket play or simply seeding for bracket play. If it is possible in a particular event to be eliminated after pool play, then those games obviously take on greater importance than pool games that are just used to reseed. In that format, every single game is "do or die" and you may have to burn your top pitchers at the very beginning. If the pool games are only used for seeding purposes, then it is more important to make sure your best pitchers are fully rested and ready when bracket play begins.

The single most common mistake made by baseball managers is the choice of which player to pitch in a certain game. I know there have been dozens of tournaments my teams have played in where I was certain we lost because the pitcher I put on the mound was the wrong choice. This is not an exact science, so you have to go with the pitcher that gives you the best chance to win based on the matchup in front of you. I have never lost sleep after a tournament loss when I started a pitcher that I truly believed gave us the best chance to win in a particular game. The only time you even run the risk of jumping off the nearest high bridge is when you hold back your best pitcher because you are saving him for the next game. If you do this and lose, then you know you were partially responsible for your team going home early, and that is tough for any coach to accept.

Does that mean you should always pitch the best pitcher you have available for each game? No, it does not. Although the most important game is the one you are about to play, you simply have to take some chances and hold back your best pitchers sometimes in youth tournaments. You will often have to win 5-7 games to win it all, and the last two will usually be the toughest opponents. So, when other coaches ask me about how I decide who to pitch in the early bracket games, I tell them to pitch the weakest pitcher you have available that will still be able to win the game. If you are facing a much weaker opponent in the first bracket game, you don't need to put your ace on the mound to win 10-0. It is far more intelligent to pitch your #4 guy and win 10-4. It is always a gamble any time you don't put your best on the field in an elimination game. But, being a baseball manager means you are taking calculated gambles all the time and not being afraid to fail.

I never fault a manager for putting his #2-#4 starter on the mound against a weaker opponent early in bracket play. However, where managers screw things up, and I have seen it hundreds of times in a lot of big events, is when this pitcher is getting hit and the manager is too slow to make a change. Everybody has a plan until they get hit, and when your guy starts getting hit you have to throw out the plan. If your pitcher gives up two or three runs in first couple of innings, usually you can come back from that if you are the superior team. However, if you wait to change pitchers until you have fallen four or five runs behind, then you are in big trouble. Your opponent will gain a lot of confidence and they will battle as hard as possible to hold onto the lead. Since youth games are also not nine innings, and most are on time limits, it is tough to come back from a big deficit no matter how good you are. That is why if you hold back your best pitcher and fall behind by more than two or three runs, you have to have a quick hook and bring your best guy on in relief. There is nothing worse than driving home from a tournament after a loss with your best pitcher rested and ready to go.

Many teams put in schedule requests with tournament directors not to play on Friday night of a weekend tournament. They may have players unavailable, parents who can't get off work early, or are simply trying to save money on the hotel bills. I never request Friday nights off because it is a huge advantage to get at least one your pool games out of the way as early as possible. I am willing to play on Friday night even if I know I may be missing one or two players for the reasons stated above. If you get a Friday night game, that will allow you to pitch your top pitchers a couple of innings in that game and they will have a full days rest before bracket play begins on Sunday. It is so much easier to set up your pitching plan with a Friday night game.

How many innings or pitches should a pitcher throw in a pool game? I use this simple formula - as many as they can go and still be 100% ready and effective when bracket play begins. Many coaches ask a different question - what are the pitching rules for the event? I think this is a very bad approach. I never look at the pitching rules until after I have my entire plan in place. One reason is because my pitchers never throw as much as travelball tournaments allow, but the main reason is because the pitching rules are not important to my standard of having every pitcher who takes the mound 100% rested and ready. If a particular event allows a pitcher to throw ten innings in the weekend, many coaches will look at that and decide to have their ace throw four innings on Saturday and six on Sunday. In other words, the maximum allowable innings in the rules dictates their pitching plan. This is insane and common.

I have never seen a pitcher go over thirty pitches in a game and still be 100% rested and ready the next day. That is why I set my limit at thirty pitches if I am asking a pitcher to throw the following day. Ideally, I try to never have a player pitch on back to back days. However, if it is necessary to do it, less than thirty pitches should be fine. If a pitcher is going on a Friday night, I will typically set a limit at 45 pitches so that he is 100% ready to go on Sunday with a full days rest. That is why the Friday night games can give you a really big advantage in a weekend event.

Let's say you are playing in a weekend tournament where you play three pool games - one on Friday night and two on Saturday. You then have to win three bracket games on Sunday to win the Championship. This is probably the most common format for a weekend travelball tournament anywhere in the country. In this scenario, I would pitch my top three pitchers two innings each in the Friday night game. My #4 and #5 pitchers would each pitch half of the toughest Saturday game and my #6 guy would pitch the other Saturday game. By doing this, I now have my top three pitchers 100% rested and ready for Sunday, and in a pinch I can get an inning or two out of my #4/5 guys in relief.

Of course, there are also other considerations that come into play when deciding your pitching plan. I always have one or two players that I am trying to develop - long term "projects." They may be players who have strong arms but are wild or have poor mechanics, or they may be left-handed and potentially valuable in the future as a setup specialist. Whenever I get a substantial lead, I run one of these guys out to the mound so they can work on things and get experience when there is no pressure. My assistant coaches and parents often hate when I do this, because a game that is going very smoothly can slow down quite a bit when your "project" starts walking guys or uncorking wild pitches. However, you have to always have the long term best interest of your program and players in mind, and games where you are way ahead or way behind are opportunities for experimentation and development. I had one player who never pitched an inning for me his first two years on the team sign a Division I baseball scholarship as a pitcher before his senior year in high school. He was a "project," and we suffered some growing pains at first, but he eventually became our #1 starter. This is not that uncommon if you are patient with talented kids.

The last thing to take into account is what you are asking a pitcher to do before and after the game that he pitches. This is the single most overlooked factor by coaches working their way through a tournament. In the Major Leagues, a starter goes every fifth day because all he does is pitch. The other four days he is either resting or preparing for his next scheduled game. In youth baseball, your top pitchers may also be your best infielders and hitters, so they may hardly ever come off the field. You must factor in how much these players are doing in the games before their next start on the mound. If one of your top pitchers is also a catcher, that is not an ideal scenario. I have had catchers who had the potential to be excellent pitchers. However, I don't like players getting behind the plate and pitching on the same day in a tournament. Both positions are very physically demanding and playing one can have a big impact on the other. Strong legs are very important to a pitcher, and catching certainly is very taxing on the legs. A catcher also has to make long, strong throws, each of which can be equivalent to a few pitches on the mound. If you are asking a player to catch a game on Sunday morning, do not expect him to be at his best when he toes the rubber that afternoon.

I explain to my top couple of pitchers that being an ace on one of my teams comes at a price. It is very likely that they will be a designated hitter or not play at all in a game that we play earlier on the same day they are scheduled to pitch. Again, my criteria is that I want every pitcher to be 100% rested and ready when he takes the mound, so if it is a really hot day and I don't need him in the lineup, there is a very good chance he will not be playing the game before he pitches.

Talk to these players about it and explain to them that with great power comes great responsibility. You are giving him the ball to play the most important position in the most important game in the tournament. They should be prepared and willing to sacrifice some playing time earlier in the day so they will be ready to be at their best when the team needs them the most. When you explain it to the player and their parents that way, they will usually understand and buy in to what you are doing. As with everything in youth baseball, communication is the key to making everything work.

Calling Pitches During a Game

Over time I have adopted two main policies in the area of calling pitches. First, I think it is very important for the coach calling pitches in a game to not be distracted with a lot of other responsibilities. The best coaches at calling pitches understand the abilities of the pitcher on the mound and are good at spotting weaknesses in swings of the opposing hitters. This coach should be very focused and immersed on handling his own player and studying each of the opposing hitters. This is time consuming and detail-oriented. The last thing this coach should be doing is trying to decide defensive or lineup substitutions and issues. I like my pitching coach to focus almost exclusively on his job, which is critical to the success of the team.

The worst games I ever coached happened when I was trying to do too much. Assistant coaches were missing for various reasons, and I stepped into their shoes to multi-task. I was deciding the lineup, defensive positions and substitutions, dealing with umpires, coaching third and calling pitches. When you do this, your mind never gets a break and you will lose focus as the game goes on and start to make mistakes. Delegation of duties to reliable assistants is absolutely critical to the successful management of any baseball team. If you try to do everything yourself you are doomed to fail.

When we are on defense, each of our coaches has a role that compliments each other and we work together to help the players as much as possible. The pitching coach calls the pitches and handles the pitcher and catcher. Another coach moves the infielders and outfielders depending on the game situation and the capabilities of the opposing batter. My role is to pay close attention to what each of them is doing and thinking so that they are on the same page. I may also make a suggestion, or if I feel strongly about something I may override what they are planning to do, but that happens very rarely. I also will help the pitching coach out by paying some attention to the other team to detect if they are actively trying to steal our signs and signals.

The second policy I have in this area is to prepare each of my catchers and pitchers to learn to call their own game. It is my goal to begin to have the players call their own game at age thirteen, then give them almost complete control of this part of the game by age fourteen. In order to do this, we will spend time with each pitcher and catcher during practices and between each inning of games, discussing with them why we called a certain pitch or why we called a sequence of pitches to a particular hitter. We will teach them how to identify weaknesses in an opposing hitter based on their position in the box, how they carry their hands, how they start their swing, their bat speed or swing trajectory, etc.. By the time they are 13-14 years old, they should be knowledgeable enough to set hitters up and call a game. A really intelligent pitcher and catcher can actually do a better job than a coach because they have a better vantage point to see and hear what is going on with the hitters, and they also have a better feel for which pitches are working well on that particular day. A pitcher knows how his own body and arm feels at a moment in time a lot better than a coach sitting on a bucket.

You should have a good pitching plan that takes into account the health of your players' arms, winning, and development of new pitchers. You should also be prepared to change the plan if it is not working and the circumstances warrant it. You should work together as a coaching staff to divide the responsibilities while you are defense and teach the players how to think and operate independently. If you do each of these things, you will keep you opponents in check and give your team a chance to win every game.

CHAPTER 19:
__MANAGING PLAYERS__

The relationship you have with your players and parents - what I refer to often as my "baseball family" - is perhaps more important to the long term success of your program than any other factor. It is certainly more important than how you manage a game or a tournament. I spend a great deal of time at the beginning of this book emphasizing the importance of recruiting the right kind of players and parents. Most of that earlier chapter had more to do with their attitude than it did the physical abilities of the players. If you are careful when you put your team together about the types of *people* you bring into your baseball family, then you will have fewer problems as you go forward. However, travelball is competitive sports involving kids, and as one veteran coach once described it to me, the only two constants in travelball are *change* and *drama*. Once the games begin, you will have plenty of both!

When I first started coaching youth baseball, I fell back on my experience in the Marine Corps. The leadership principles I learned as a young man were taught to me in boot camp at Parris Island and during my four years in the Marine Corps Infantry. Those principles had served me well in all of my endeavors later in life, and so naturally I turned to them when placed in another leadership role - coaching kids. I suppose in my early years I adopted the persona of an only slightly toned down Marine Drill Instructor. My practices were highly organized, energetic, efficient, disciplined and I ruled them with an iron hand. I would say that my players learned a lot, there was certainly no fooling around, but at the same time a lot of them became afraid of me. Looking back I wonder if they played as hard as they did out of fear of their coach as they did love of the game. Most of them stayed with me as I slowly mellowed out as the years went on. I think both they and their parents understood that I had good intentions and we were all heading in the right direction, even though the methods I chose weren't always the best.

As a result of this approach, the relationship I had with the group of players on my first travelball team was quite a bit different than those on my second team. I learned, slowly over the years, that handling kids is something that is very unique. There just aren't any books or literature you can find on the subject of how to relate and motivate kids in a competitive travel sports environment. I had to learn by trial and error, reflection, and self-criticism. Sometimes I had to learn the hard way - by making a mistake then wincing the next day when I was able to reflect on it and realize I screwed up. Hopefully this chapter can help you avoid some of these mistakes I made.

Some of you may be blessed with a mellow disposition. I think that I am and it takes a lot to excite or anger me in everyday life. However, when many of us are put in a competitive athletic situation, sometimes competing against people we do not like, the little devil on our shoulder can take possession of our senses. So many coaches "flip out" or do crazy things on the baseball field - we have seen some of these antics on ESPN's "Sportscenter" over the years from coaches at even the highest levels of the game. It is systemic to a "Type A" personality. I think this personality is what leads us to want to be coaches - we are leaders and competitive by nature. When this mixes with competitive sports, it can often lead to temporary insanity - and we do things we really regret later. Having been in that position too many times than I want to recall, it really is like an out-of-body experience where it often seems like it was not even you who did or said the things that happened.

I have noticed that the frequency of these episodes - instances where coaches "flip out" over a bad call, an opposing coach, or a stupid mistake by a player - is directly proportional to the amount of years that coach has spent working with kids in a competitive environment. As time goes on, you learn to handle things better and let things go a lot easier.

I have often said that I don't think I really became a good coach until after I had lost 100 games. What I mean by that is that it becomes a lot easier to handle things when they don't go your way as a coach once you have experienced failure and adversity enough times wearing that hat. You gain a sense of proportion and perspective. You realize that everyone connected to the game is going to make hundreds of mistakes - parents, players, umpires, and coaches - even you! Once you come to terms with that and accept that concept it becomes a lot easier to internally deal with these mistakes when they happen.

After my first year coaching my second Meteors team, the players from my first team attended an awards banquet with the players from my new team. During the dinner they had a chance to mingle with each other and talk a little. The players from the first team had just completed their freshman year of high school and were all 15 years old. The new recruits were all 11 years old.

I overheard a conversation at the next table where some of the older boys said to the younger ones, "What do you think of Coach Ron?" The younger ones replied, "Oh, Coach Ron is cool!" I looked over and saw the older boys with their mouths open and their eyes wide in amazement. There is no way any of them would have ever described me as "cool." They noticed me looking at them with a big smile on my face. They just shook their heads, and the ringleader said to me, "Coach you must be mellowing out - these guys are spoiled!" No, I thought to myself, they are just the beneficiaries of the experience we had together.

Consistently Treat Each Player Different

One of the lessons I learned after a couple of years of coaching is that you simply cannot approach and handle every kid the same. My initial approach was that the only way to be "fair" is to treat every player the same way. I suppose this concept is based on what we learn in the workplace with employer-employee relations. If you are in a leadership position in your company, and you treat your employees differently based on certain factors, you are going to be looking at a discrimination lawsuit. However, sports teams are not and have never been IBM or some other Fortune 500 company, and you can't manage athletes the same as you would an employee of a business.

Every player is going to have a different personality, and therefore have to be treated differently. As a coach, you have to find the best way to "push their buttons" - to get through to them, motivate them, encourage them to improve. I have learned that players have these "buttons" pushed in different ways depending on their personality type.

Unfortunately, some players only seem to respond to a tough, in-your-face approach. You will find that the only way you can get through to these players and get them to respond positively is to challenge them in a confrontational way. If your personality is such that you are not comfortable doing this yourself, you need to have someone on your coaching staff do it for you.

I am not saying that you have to be verbally abusive - there can be a fine line in this area and you have to get your point across in a way that is tough but not destructive. Generally these players have a personality some would call "slackers." They are not lazy, but they look for the path of least resistance and will cut corners whenever possible. These players will often make excuses for poor effort or fundamentals by telling you that they "made the play" anyway or "still got the job done." Too often the only way to get through to these guys is tough love.

Other players are guys who want to please people around them. They want to make the coach and their parents happy and are always very concerned about letting them down. The absolute worst approach you can take with these guys is to be confrontational or yell at them. If you take a confrontational approach with them they will put even more pressure on themselves and become so freaked out they will be unable to perform even though they are putting forth maximum effort. The best approach with these kids is quiet encouragement. Many of these kids lack self-esteem and I try to always be completely positive with them because I know that they already put enough pressure on themselves.

Then there are the kids who are natural born leaders. They are outgoing, gregarious, the kinds of guys who are always the life of the party. When these players are pointed in a positive direction they can be the best ally you have on the team. Leadership from players is critical to the success of all teams at any level of any sport. The other players on the team tend to gravitate towards these guys.

The flip side is that these players can also be leaders of mayhem. You cannot have a player with this kind of personality who is not on the same page with what you are trying to accomplish. A player like this can lead other guys on the team with "follower" personalities in the wrong direction, and soon half your team will be tuning you out behind your back. It is important to get these players on your side, allied with you in common purpose.

You will have to explain and reason with these players more than others by taking them aside. Where you will just have to give an order or direction to other players, these guys will want to know *why* you want them to do something in a particular way. If you refuse to explain it to them, they will rebel against you and often lead others in rebellion. If you take a few seconds to pull them aside and sell them on what you are trying to do, they will help you by persuading their teammates to get with the program.

The other type of personality that is common is the quiet, lunch-pail kids who keep their heads down and generally keep to themselves. They usually attach themselves to the one or two other players like them on the team and become inseparable. They are not usually influenced by others, so they can be your most reliable and loyal members of your organization. These players are often misunderstood - many consider them aloof, think they don't care or are not passionate about the game. It is a mistake to think this. For most of these guys, they have a fire inside them that burns as hot as any other competitor; it is just that it is not visible to those around them because they don't express it. They are often the hardest workers, but that is not always apparent because they are not flashy or vocal about the extra time they put in. You can find out exactly what they are up to only by pulling it out of them with specific questions.

These players can really get hurt and take things to heart when they are yelled at or criticized. You many not even realize how upset they are because they won't always show it because they rarely express displeasure. If you have a couple of these types of kids, it is best to pull them aside and talk to them very quietly when they are doing something wrong. They will usually hang on your every word and do exactly what you ask them to do if you do it calmly and quietly.

"Guest" Players

Many teams, especially elite ones, will pick up a few guest players from time to time for a big tournament where they expect to play a lot of games against tough competition. This is a controversial area and a lot of thought has to be put into whether you will do it, how you will do it, how it affects your other players, and how you will treat these guests.

If there is one team rule or policy that is most responsible for keeping my teams thriving and together over the years it is this: No Meteors player will EVER guest play for another team. I mean never. Some parents on my teams have tried very hard to get me to change this uncompromising rule. They have threatened to quit, tried to reason with me about what a "great opportunity" it is for their son, or just tried to sneak off and do it hoping I would not find out.

Some parents will threaten to quit or take their kids to other teams all the time as soon as something happens they don't like. Many coaches will cave in to their demands, whatever they are, to placate them and keep them. You simply cannot operate a team that way. Once you do that, they will be back two weeks later asking for more because you have shown weakness. Other parents and players will also find out and they will soon try you also. This is just a really bad road to go down.

Whenever a parent threatens to quit my team, I tell them to go right ahead. I tell them that I don't want anybody to play for me who doesn't want to be there and if they really think they can get a better deal elsewhere they should. These people almost always back down after you call their bluff. Most really don't want to leave the team, they just want you to run it the way they want it and are using a ploy they believe will persuade you. If they come back next season or a few weeks later threatening to quit a second time, I usually give them the same reply with one caveat. I explain to them that the next time they talk about quitting, they will not be given a chance to quit because they will be fired. I have done this several times, and never heard a peep out of these parents again for years.

Then you will have parents who explain to you that it is a great opportunity and "honor" for their son to play a big event with another team and that you should let them do it because you would otherwise be "denying" them this chance. While this may be true, these are people who have difficulty understanding the concept of what being part of a team or organization is all about. They only think about what is beneficial for them or their son in a particular week or weekend. They never think about the big picture or long term effects their decisions or choices have on other people.

You have to make all of your parents somehow understand that being part of a travelball team is like a marriage - it is a deep social contract that should be taken seriously by all parties. Would you allow your wife to spend the weekend in Las Vegas with John Stamos or Brad Pitt? While this may be a "great opportunity" for her for some fun and adventure, and the intention might be purely platonic, most likely this will have negative long-term affects on your marriage. This may sound like an extreme analogy, but many times the guest player situation can have a lot of parallels to a weekend in Vegas with an attractive secret admirer!

Most of the teams will bring in a guest player with the underlying intention of trying to persuade him to come onto their team on a full-time basis. Of course, they will never admit that to you or say that openly, but that is their ultimate goal. Since that is what they are trying to do, the time as a guest player becomes like a honeymoon period. The coaches on the host team will constantly praise the player, stroking his ego and that of his parents. They will make subtle hints about a spot being open on their team and half-joking tell him how good he looks in their colors. They will give him new uniforms and gear to keep - equipment, gloves, bats, etc. These guest player situations really can be like a courtship where the player and his parents are only shown the good side of a situation and are not exposed to the warts until months later.

If you explain this concern to parents of one of your players who want to guest play for another team, they will usually say that they are very loyal and that you have "nothing to worry about" because they are very happy and would never consider leaving your team. That may be true, and that may be their intention when they begin, but all human beings (especially parents of children) have egos that can be stroked and can be vulnerable to a great sales pitch. The bottom line is this – I have seen hundreds of outstanding players guest play for other teams over the past decade, and over 50% of them left the team they were playing on shortly after doing so. Unfortunately, the grass always does look greener to many parents and they will often see the new team through rose colored glasses.

Even if you could be 100% certain that a particular player who wants to guest play would not leave, if you allow him to do it a precedent is set for other players who you may not be as secure with. Here is a pattern I have seen play out countless times: An assistant coach goes to the manager and tells him that his son has an invitation to guest play in a big tournament for another team. The manager and the assistant coach are good friends, and the manager does not want to deny his friend this opportunity and he is not concerned about his friend leaving. After playing one event with the other team, that team asks the assistant coach about a couple of other players on his team to see if they are available to guest play for the next big event. How can this manager possibly say, "No" to these parents after he has just let his assistant coach do it? The answer is that he cannot. The problem he has now is that he is not as certain about these other players leaving as he is about his best friend. This is the slippery slope that guest playing can put your team on. It is the exact reason why I never allow it.

Let's talk ruthless, hardball, Machiavellian travelball recruiting where I will assume the role of a coach who cares about building his team a lot more than he cares about making friends with other coaches. You have three outstanding players on your team and I want them to come onto my team. The best possible way for me to get them is to target the son of one of your coaches. Hopefully he is the parent of one of those three players I want, but that is not a deal-breaker. I will take one weaker player on the team if I know his dad can facilitate the acquisition of the three kids I really want. Once I have convinced that coach and his son to come onto my team because it is better than the one he is on, I am going to use that coach to go after the other three players on that team that I really wanted in the first place. He has their contact information, a relationship and trust with them and their parents that I do not have. A defecting assistant coach can be a lethal recruiter. Sound rough to you? Immoral? Unethical? Unfair? Welcome to the real world of youth travel sports in America.

Encourage Freedom and Initiative

In different parts of earlier chapters I mention examples of areas where I allow my players to do things independently. They are free to try and bunt for a hit whenever they want. They can steal a base whenever they see the opportunity. My catchers and pitchers are trained to eventually call their own pitches. These policies are not only smart baseball, they are good morale boosters and inject the kind of free-wheeling spirit I want from my players. Many players who come onto my team smile when I tell them these policies. They are amazed that they are allowed to make some of their own decisions and operate independently of the coaches. You can almost see in their eyes the number of times an opportunity to be aggressive on the baseball field passed them by because they were restrained by an over-controlling coach. Encourage your players to think for themselves and act on their own when they see an opening to help the team. Not only will it make them a better player, it will become another reason why they will love the team they are on and appreciate your coaching style.

Provide a Relaxed, Fun Atmosphere

Repeat after me: "BASEBALL IS A GAME. IT IS SUPPOSED TO BE FUN. IT IS NOT WARFARE."

One morning our team walked into the dugout at ESPN's Wide World of Sports at Disney for the semi-final game of the USSSA Elite 32 World Series. The team we were playing had won the AAU National Championship the week before and was undefeated that summer. The winner would play in the Atlanta Braves Spring Training stadium for the

13U USSSA National Championship. I could tell before the game that my players and parents were a little tense.

I gathered up the players, and the first thing I said to them was the team that smiled the most would win the game. At first they looked at me a little puzzled, then they all laughed. They understood the point I was making very well. Relax! Go out and have fun and the scoreboard will take care of itself. Every game requires a certain tone to be set before it begins. For some games, you have to persuade your players to take them seriously. For games like this, persuading them to relax is the right tone for a head coach to set. (Yes, we won the game!)

It is natural to feel pressure when you play travelball tournament games. Your coaches, players and parents have invested a lot of time, effort and money to achieve a high skill level for your team in a difficult game. You want to win because if you do, you advance to the next round and get to play more games. You want your boys to succeed because you know how hard they have worked to prepare themselves. You want your team to have success so it can prosper and thrive and the people connected to it will feel good about it and return next season. You may also be playing a rival team that has beaten you before, or a team with obnoxious coaches that you don't like. Yes, there can be pressure even in youth baseball.

The great trick for all coaches is not to show your young, impressionable players that you feel pressure. You must fight to keep it inside and keep your cool as much as possible. They will feed off of you and if you are freaked out and uptight, they will be freaked out and uptight and that is not the best way to play a skill game. The term I use often and preach to myself, coaches and players is *relaxed focus*. To me, those two words are the right approach to take in youth baseball games – perhaps in all baseball games. You have to be somewhat relaxed and loose so that you are able to perform at a high level and do not allow your emotions to impair your ability. However, you can't be an emotionless cold fish either and that is where "focus" comes in. Although you maintain a calm demeanor, you are still very focused on the job at hand and focused on the details that lead to success. *Calm intensity* may be another way to express what I am trying to say. If your players are loose, but also focused on their game, they will be in the right frame of mind for a big tournament game.

One thing I have done for many years to set the right tone is to use music. I started with a bulky boom box, but technology has led me to a small, rechargeable dock for an iPod music player. I suppose this has become a trademark for my teams – all you have to do to find the field we are playing on is follow your ears. I decided to start playing music, during pregame warm-up and between innings, as a very calculated move to keep my players relaxed and loose. You may be "old school" and don't like music with baseball, but keep in mind this is not about you; it is about the kids and how to best motivate them and encourage them to play at a high level.

If you decide to use music in the dugout, you may decide to drag out your old favorite classics from the '70s and '80s. Please do not impose your personal artistic preferences on kids! Adults have been doing that for generations and for generations kids have rebelled against it. Let each one of your players give you a list of their four or five favorite songs. Get on the computer and listen to them. Almost all music services also offer songs in a "clean" version if they contain lyrics that are unsuitable for youth baseball. Get the music your players like, play it at appropriate times, and it will be a useful tool to help achieve relaxed focus.

Monitoring Player-Player Issues

Never underestimate the social aspect of travelball. Many coaches only think about whether the team fits together from a baseball perspective. They made certain they have enough middle infielders, pitchers, catchers, power, speed, etc.. However, they are often blind to whether the team fits together from a social perspective. Your players spend A LOT of time together in travelball. You play a lot of games, stay in the same hotel, practice a lot and hang out at the ballpark between games. The best case scenario is for your players to all get along and become great friends. If this doesn't happen, at the very least you want them to tolerate each other.

Many players will choose the team they play on based on where their friends are, or at least whether they like the kids on a particular team. Adults tend to only look at the baseball aspect of a team. Is this the best team? Are they good coaches? What kind of events are they going to play? Kids don't always care about that stuff, especially the younger ones. If you have a team at ages 8-11U, the most important priority for these players is to play with their friends. As they get older, they tend to factor in the baseball and competitive part of things and will leave their friends to go on a better team and make new friends.

Your concern as a coach is to monitor whether there are any serious problems between the players. The flip side of the recruiting benefit of friends wanting to play together is the fact that you may lose a very good player who is happy with you but cannot stand one of the other players on the team. Often coaches are completely oblivious to these conflicts until it is too late. I have always had a couple of players on each of my teams that I talk to about stuff like this. They are the "social butterflies" who get along with everybody, like to gossip a little, and seem to be into everybody's business. They know where every kid goes to school, who their girlfriends are, whether their parents are getting divorced, etc.. I talk to these kids from time to time to monitor whether the players are happy, if they are all getting along or if there is serious trouble brewing.

If you find out that there is a problem between two players that is festering, you have to intervene as soon as possible. You aren't trying to pick their friends -emphasize to them that you don't care whether they are even friendly to each other. However, point out to them that your job is to make sure the team plays together and gels on the field and that you will not tolerate anything that might negatively affect that. Often you will find out that one of the players is simply being a jerk to the other one and is clearly the party at fault. Explain to this player that you want him on the team and like him, but you also value the other player just as much and if he continues to bother him you are going to cut him from the team. You must monitor these player-player issues and tackle them head on as a peacemaker.

Discipline

There are a number of different options to achieve modification in the behavior of your players. Discipline should never be imposed for physical errors or mistakes. These are unintentional and simply part of a game played by fallible human beings. However, it is appropriate to impose some form of disciple for lack of hustle or effort, mental errors, or bad conduct. I would generally place the different types of discipline into three categories: verbal, physical and metal.

Verbal

You can use an elevated voice or strict, abrupt tone to get your point across. This is the most common form of discipline for coaches in any sport. As long as you don't cross the line into excessive verbal abuse, a tough tone is entirely appropriate in the athletic arena.

Physical

No, I am not talking about beatings! Many coaches prefer to make players perform difficult or taxing physical acts as punishment. Common examples in baseball are running laps or "poles" (running from foul pole to foul pole) or doing pushups or some other exercise. I rarely employ these kinds of things simply because my practices already push the players as far as I want them to go physically, and I don't want to add to their workload any more than I have planned. Also, physical punishment after a game often looks silly and embarrassing as players, friends and relatives stand there waiting while players are running poles. You may also have another game to play later and the last thing you need to do is wear out your team.

Metal

This is the method I prefer to get my point across in a way that tends to last in their memory banks. I have often said that the best assistant coach on any baseball team is made out of metal, because it is the bench. Sitting a player down or taking him out of a game is absolutely the best way to make an impression. There is nothing kids want more when they are at a game than to be on the field. When they have to sit in the dugout watching the other players play because they have done something wrong, it really hurts. It is also the punishment that is most noted by the parents, and hopefully they will reinforce what you are doing because they also want to see their son on the field.

If you are late to pregame warm-up, you don't start. It's just that simple. The parents know it and the players know it. I may insert them into the game in the third or forth inning, but they will not be in the starting lineup. This policy has always resulted in great team punctuality for the Meteors. If you make repeated mental errors in a game you will be taken out of the game. If you fail to hustle or play hard, you may be taken out of the game immediately - sometimes in the middle of an inning.

Pulling a player off the field in the middle of an inning is the ultimate indignity to inflict on a player. Reggie Jackson got into a fistfight with New York Yankees manager Billy Martin for doing that to him in the 1970s. However, I think it is a great way to get your point across if a player is just dogging it out there and really deserves it because of lack of effort or poor attitude. If I give an instruction to a player during the game and he yells back at me, he is benched before the next pitch is thrown. Once your players see that you will not tolerate lack of hustle or disrespect, they will tow the line and be better off for it. Your job is to get that stuff out of their system before they get to high school, because if they do it then they are likely to get permanently cut from the team.

On certain things, discipline should be swift, harsh and consistent. If a player throws his helmet or equipment after making an out. If he fails to run out a popup. If he doesn't slide into a base on a close play. These kinds of things should never be allowed under any circumstances. When a player does this that is a direct reflection on the head coach and his program. If one of my players does this, I take it very personally and explain to him that he has just insulted me and everyone who has worn the Meteors uniform. Whenever an opposing player does one of these foolish or disrespectful things, I will immediately look at the other coach to see what he is going to do about it. If he does nothing, I will usually have something to say to the kid because he is not only disgracing himself he is disrespecting the game.

There are two guiding principles I use when imposing one of these forms of discipline. I explain to the players that I am not doing it because I am *angry* at them and are seeking retribution for damage done to the team. The reason why I am benching them or getting on them verbally is because I want to *change their behavior*. I am trying to make them better, not hurt them. I think it is important sometimes for kids to hear that because they often will not understand that concept and think you are mad at them.

The second principle is to always give them a chance at redemption as soon as possible. Let them know that they are going to get another chance to prove that they have learned the lesson you are trying to teach. Whenever I bench a player in the middle of an inning (which I do very rarely), I fully understand how difficult and embarrassing that is for a player and for his parents in the stands. That is why whenever I do this I always try to put that player back into the same game later on so that he will hopefully end the game on a positive note (all travelball organizations allow you to re-enter starters back into a game). If their baseball weekend ended with a benching, it can leave a very harsh and bitter taste in the mouths of the player and his parents. I believe in forgiveness and redemption in everyday life, and there is no better subject for that than a young baseball player.

CHAPTER 20:
MANAGING PARENTS

When I sat down over the course of a couple of days to outline the contents of this book, I realized that this chapter was going to be the most difficult to write and perhaps the most important. Children usually become the center of a parent's universe from the time they are born. When a parent places their child in a situation where they have to compete against other children it can be an emotional and volatile situation. Parents' natural instincts are to protect and promote their children. They want them to succeed and it pains them deeply to see them fail. Slights directed towards their children, real or perceived, often produce angry reactions. Failure is often ignored, excused or blamed on others. It is also natural for a parent to believe that his child is a lot more talented and productive than he really is.

Like coaches in college and professional baseball, youth coaches have to deal with personnel issues, training and practices, game strategy, handling players, etc.. However, unlike these coaches at the higher levels of the game, travelball coaches also have to deal with the constant presence of hovering, meddling, critical, doting, or overprotective parents. Of course, not all parents will cause you headaches and issues, some will be almost invisible and let you do your job without any interference. But parents of young children who are placed in competitive athletic situations often turn into people they would not even recognize outside of that environment. There is a saying that in divorce court you often see good people at their worst. Unfortunately, the same can be said of parents at youth baseball games.

The most difficult part of being a travelball head coach is the ability to manage and handle the parent dynamic. Each set of parents, grandparents, relatives and significant others come with their own set of beliefs, philosophies and issues. You have to manage your team in a way that keeps them satisfied enough that they will stay with you whether the team has success or failure. Since many of their beliefs and desires can conflict with those of other parents on your team, this can be a difficult challenge.

What makes it worse is that nothing can really prepare someone to be a parent with a child in a competitive athletic environment. They may not know how to act and react in certain situations because they have never been in that position before. That is why I titled this chapter "Managing Parents" - you have to coach and teach them how to be good baseball parents just as you are coaching their children on the field. If you neglect this aspect of your job, you will not sustain any measure of success over multiple seasons.

So many coaches, especially professional coaches, overlook this aspect of their position. They are focused on the baseball part of the job—on-field performance, practices, player development, game strategy, etc.

That is why so many former professional baseball players with fantastic knowledge of the game fail as travelball head coaches. Nothing about playing professional baseball prepared them to handle parents of young athletes. They often never concern themselves about what the parents are thinking or feeling. You can be the greatest baseball coach in the world, but you will fail as a travelball head coach if you do not handle parents properly.

Parent-Manager Relationship

If I could describe my general approach towards parents on my team in one phrase, I would say that I am *friendly* to them but *not friends*. It is important to be civil to each other and get along. A parent is not going to keep their kid on your team if they personally detest you. However, it is also not necessary to be best friends either. In fact, I think it can be a serious detriment for a head coach to be close friends with other parents on his team. The other parents will perceive you as favoring the children of your friends. Also, these friends may eventually use that relationship to try and subtly persuade you to give their kids more playing time, or to play a certain position. They are rarely blatant about it, but they will use their access to you in social situations to try and advance their child in subtle ways. Again, this is such a natural parental instinct that parents often do it without even realizing it. You will feel it and notice it though, and it will put you in very uncomfortable position.

I am friendly with all of the parents on my team. I don't want anybody on my team that does not like me personally. I stay at the same hotel as the rest of the team. I go out to dinner with the team when we do a group outing at a tournament. However, I am very careful about how I go about these things. I never *share* a room with another parent at the team hotel. I also will not go out to dinner with parents unless *all the other parents* have been invited. Many may choose not to go because they have other plans, but I make certain before I attend a social event with parents that all the parents have at least received an offer to attend. If your team becomes divided into "cliques," and you join one of these groups for social functions, your team is destined for a breakup.

Playing Time Issues

The vast majority of the issues and conflicts you will have with parents are over playing time and positions. A few parents will be primarily concerned about being on a winning team, but most are focused on the opportunities you afford their son. You have an obligation to be fair with each of your players, and if you have players who are not getting a chance to play and develop you are naturally going to have unhappy parents. You must have an open door policy with parents to discuss their concerns about these issues in the proper manner. I emphasize to them that I am always willing to discuss whether I am giving their son an ample opportunity to develop.

What I absolutely *will not ever* discuss with a parent is the playing time and opportunities I give to *other players* on the team. You have to coach these parents by persuading them that how much their son plays *compared to other players* is not what is important. If they truly only care about the development of their son, the only thing that matters is whether he is getting enough opportunities to improve and play at a high level. Whenever they bring up another player on the team, I tell them that I am not going to discuss that player, but I am happy to discuss their own son with them.

Let me give you an example of a situation that happens often. I had a parent complain to me about their son's playing time after a long spring season. Since I keep detailed stats (as you should for just this reason), I pulled out the stat sheet as we spoke. Her son had played over 300 innings that season in the field. He also had 170 plate appearances. That is an enormous amount of playing time for a thirteen year old during a single season. You could look at those numbers in a vacuum and not comprehend how a parent in this position could complain about playing time. However, this parent had an issue because the top three players on our team averaged 370 innings and 240 at bats that same season. Therefore, her problem really was jealously and a perceived slight towards her child. You have to explain to these parents as tactfully as you can that they only have a legitimate complaint if their son is not playing enough to get better. It is a difficult process to change their way of thinking. Over time, most parents will soften on these jealousy issues and will not concern themselves as much with the playing time of their son's teammates. You play an important role in their education, though.

I also emphasize to my parents that there is a time, place and proper manner to discuss playing time issues. Before you can buy a firearm, or get a divorce, all states require you to wait a certain time period first. This is often referred to as a "cooling off period." Many people in anger or distress want to take desperate, serious, immediate action to remedy the situation in a way that will leave wreckage in their wake. That is why the law doesn't let them get a divorce or a gun until they have had a few days to think about it. I borrowed this approach because parents who are upset over playing time after a game or tournament can become a lot like people looking for a gun or divorce!

So often I have observed parents hopping mad over their son's playing time after *the first game* of a weekend tournament! It may have been my plan to play him every inning of the next three games, but if a player sits out some or all of the first game parents get stressed and are often ready to pack up and leave. By the end of the weekend these same parents are happy because everything balanced out and after 4-6 games their son ended up playing a lot of baseball. That is another reason for my "cooling off period" rule.

This rule is very simple - no parent is allowed to talk to me about these issues until twenty-four hours after the last game of a tournament. That is their cooling off period. So many parents drive away from a tournament upset either over playing time, a benching, or some other issue that happened between the coaches and their son. They are emotional and upset and if they talk to the head coach while they are in that state they will often say things they will later regret. The coach will then return fire and may say something that he regrets. A very high percentage of people who quit youth baseball teams do so in the parking lot fifteen minutes after the last game of a tournament. I am willing to bet that over half of them would not have done so if they had twenty-four hours to cool off.

Another reason for the waiting period is my own sanity. Travelball events can be mentally and physically draining for a coach. I am completely spent after each of them. The only thing I want to do after the last game is have a quiet ride home and reflect on the positives and negatives of the entire weekend. It is my time to think about what I can do to make the team better based on what just transpired that weekend. I evaluate each player's performance and think about my handling of the players and strategy decisions. This quiet time on the drive home and the shower when I get there is the time when I am able to do some of my most productive thinking about the team. However, if I had a parent in my ear complaining about some issue as I walked to my car, I guarantee that is the only thing that will be on my mind the whole way home, and it will be tough for me to get to sleep that night.

My hours of quiet reflection, and joy if the team performed well, have just been stolen from me. So, the waiting period is also there for selfish reasons. All coaches need this window of time for quiet reflection, and no parent should be permitted to take that from us.

I have argued in a few chapters of this book why I think it is important to keep and maintain comprehensive team statistics that include innings played and plate appearances. The discussions with parents over playing time will be a lot easier for you if both you and the complaining parent have access to these numbers.

I think the fact that I publish these to the parents every single week in ranking order for each category prevents a lot of complaints. I guarantee that if you do not keep stats, or if you keep them but don't disseminate them to the parents, almost all of your parents will think that their child is doing significantly better in every category than is reality.

Parents don't do this intentionally, but if nobody is keeping track they just naturally believe their child is batting at least .100 points higher than they are. Since I rank all the players in every category and send them to the parents each week, there is never any dispute about how my players are doing relative to their teammates. When a player is 7th or 8th in every category - on base percentage, batting average, runs scored, RBIs, and slugging percentage – it is very difficult for his parents to complain when he is also 7th or 8th on the team in innings played and plate appearances.

If you don't keep these stats, that same parent will argue that their son is no worse than 3rd on the team in each of these categories – then you will be stuck making your argument on their biased perception rather than reality.

Financial Stresses on Parents

Travelball can be expensive for everyone involved, especially for families with several children. The gas, hotels and meals while traveling add up quickly and can put a lot of stress on the family budget. I never want to lose a player because of money. Parents of a lot of outstanding players stay away from travelball for financial reasons. I believe that one of the major reasons why my teams have been so successful is that I have been able to attract talented athletes from families with limited financial means who are not able to play on other teams because of the money involved. If you pay attention to the financial stresses on parents and are able to alleviate their concerns in this area you can recruit better athletes because you have removed one of the major obstacles for a lot of parents.

A significant percentage of travelball teams are run by professional coaches or sponsored by baseball "academies." These coaches enjoy working with kids and many do an excellent job with instruction. However, the primary purpose of these programs is profit – the coaches make a living teaching and coaching kids. Therefore, rarely is a player turned away who can write the monthly check (regardless of ability), and kids from lower income families cannot afford to pay these coaches on top of the expenses of travelling. I often refer to these programs as "rich kid teams" – there will be a lot of nice cars in the parking lot when they are playing and they will have all the best uniforms and gear. They may have a few very good players, but they also almost always have several kids who have no business being out there except their parents are writing checks to get them on the field.

If you are just a parent-coach, and you are not charging large fees to make a living off your team, you have a recruiting advantage over programs that put added pressure on families' finances. To give me an even greater advantage, I do fundraisers that my parents must participate in that pay for all the expenses of the team like tournament fees, equipment, baseballs, etc.. These fundraisers have allowed me to run my teams without asking for a single dollar from any parent in team dues. Finally, I pay attention to the parents who are struggling to pay for travel. They often have a lot of pride and won't ask for help. They will make up an excuse why their child is unable to attend a particular event because they don't want to tell you they simply cannot afford it. If you sense that money is becoming an issue for a player, offer to have you or your coaches take that player with them to a tournament. An even better approach is to have the parents of his best friend on the team call them and offer to take him. They may not feel comfortable accepting help from a coach, but they will have no problem sending their son to a tournament with the parents of his best friend.

Grumbling in the Stands

On all travelball teams, there will be parents in the stands grumbling. They will be stewing over the performance of their own kid, other players on the team, the umpire or the decisions you made as head coach. There is nothing you can ever do to stop that and you should not even try – parents need to vent from time to time just like you do when you are frustrated. When a parent pops off or outwardly expresses frustration on occasion it is relatively harmless. Other parents will generally ignore them and focus on the game. However, where this becomes a problem is when a parent or small group of parents *persistently* complain about the job you are doing as manager – game after game, week after week. Some of these people just like to gripe like fans in the stands of a Major League game. Others have ulterior motives and hidden agendas. It is important for you to *identify* your critics in the stands and then determine which of them pose a threat to the health of your team.

You will rarely ever hear these critics. They grumble quietly off in the corner of the stands or away from the other parents along the fence of one of the foul lines. Eventually, they may attract one or two other parents who gravitate to them and commiserate with them. If you notice a group of two or three parents gathered off to the side away from the other parents during games talking to each other quietly and giving of negative body language, that is an indication you may have a problem. Inevitably, a parent that is loyal to you and appreciates the job you are doing will come to you and make you aware of what is going on and what is being said about you by the malcontents. Once you have identified the nature of the problem and the people involved, how you handle the situation becomes critically important to the survival of your team.

Although there may be a few people griping in the stands, there is always one parent who is the ringleader. This parent can be a cancer which can spread and cause the team serious illness or death. However, also like a cancer it can be cured if identified early enough and treated aggressively. If this particular parent is a "baseball guy" – someone who has coached in the past or has the ambition to be a coach – then he is probably doing this out of a calculated desire to break up your team and take most of the good players with him. I have seen this move played out so often that I can almost predict it is going to happen to a team after sitting in their stands listening to parents for ten minutes. These teams are destroyed because their head coaches are either oblivious to it or ignore it because the grumbling parent's son is a very good player.

Would you rather lose one of your best players, or half your team? That often becomes the choice. If you realize that one of these parents is trying to undermine you so that he can leave at the end of the season and take other players with him, the best thing you can do is get him away from the other players and parents as quickly as possible. This parent is just using his spot on your team to gain frequent access to your players and parents so that he can whisper in their ears about a better opportunity he has for them at the end of the season. If you realize what is happening in the middle of the season, and get that parent off of your team right away, you have a couple of months to "cure" your other infected parents and bring them back into the fold. No matter how good a kid his son is, or how good a player, you have to get this parent away from your team as quickly as possible.

Team Meetings After Games

All baseball teams get together after games to discuss what just happened – the good, the bad and the ugly. I was a travelball parent for one year, and one of the things that bothered me the most was that the coaches would conduct these meetings with the players *away from the parents* so that we could not hear what was being said. We waited for fifteen or twenty minutes wondering what was going on, then had to rely on our nine year old sons to tell us what the coaches said. We would inevitably get a nine year old summation, "Coach said we sucked," or even worse, "Coach said I sucked."

Kids are not going to accurately relay to the parents the full content of what you said, and parents are not going to know the tone or context of your speech if they have to get it filtered through a child. That is why one of the first policies I implemented when I started my own team was that I would include all of the parents in these team discussions after games. They certainly weren't being invited to say anything, but I wanted to make sure they heard everything I said directly from me.

This meeting can be extremely important – especially after a tough loss. I rarely single out any player in these post-game meetings, for either praise or criticism. You can do that later when you pull the player aside and speak to him individually.

If you praise one or two players for an outstanding performance, there will always to one or two you missed who also did something well and their parents will feel snubbed in front of the team. They will also feel terrible when their son is singled out for criticism in front of all the other players and parents. It is important to recap the things you did well or poorly *as a team*. Use a lot of "we" in this speech instead of individual names.

I begin the meeting and always go through the mistakes, how to correct them, and areas where we can improve. I then invite my assistant coaches to chime in with things they think we did poorly or at least could have done better. When this is over, I always conclude the meeting on a positive note, talking about all the good things that happened and praising the team for improvements they have made. It is important for all of the parents and players to leave these meetings feeling good about the future direction of the team, even if the game did not go as well as they hoped.

Parent-Coaches Relationship

The relationship between assistant coaches and the parents is usually quite different than the managers. The head coach has to make the difficult decisions that can upset parents – playing time, starters at each position, the batting order, etc.

I spent one year as an assistant coach when I was helping with my younger son's team while I was still the manager of my first Meteors team. It was so different serving as an assistant coach. The parents were a lot friendlier to me because I was never put in a position where I had to do anything they disagreed with. Suddenly I was the person they would come to and gripe about the head coach. They would tell me during these conversations that they wished I was the head coach, etc. This was an eye opening year for me because I was able to experience life as an assistant and realize how parents' relationship with assistant coaches differs from the one I had experienced as the head coach with my older team.

Once I realized how parents confide in and communicate with the assistant coaches, I understood how to use that to become a better manager. Parents will say things to an assistant that they just will not ever tell the manager, and these are often things you will want to know. I encourage my assistant coaches to engage in these conversations with parents, they relay the information back to me.

I think *spying* would be too harsh a way of describing this method of obtaining information. I prefer to think of it as using my assistants to help me accurately gauge the pulse of the parents on my team. Are they unhappy about something I am doing? Do they think the schedule is too heavy or we are travelling too much? Do they dislike a new player we have brought in? Are they being recruited by another team? There are a number of things you will only find out if you have someone else get the information for you.

Assistant coaches can also be your primary liaison to the parents. They can smooth things over if they are upset because they have a friendlier relationship with them. They can also convey information you want them to hear but cannot say directly to them yourself because you don't want them to quote you to other parents. Assistants can be great ambassadors for you and can help the communicative process that is so critical between parents and the head coach.

Parents and Tournament Officials

Tournament directors can have a big impact on the experience your team has at a tournament, including your ability to win the tournament. They decide what teams you are going to be matched up against, what fields you are going to play on, what times you are going to play, and who is going to umpire your game. Trust me, I don't care how good your team is, if a tournament director really does not want your team to win his tournament he can do a lot to ensure that it won't. When you think about it in these terms, your relationship with tournament directors and officials should become a lot bigger priority than you may have made it in the past.

I have been a director and host for ten major tournaments sponsored by my teams as fundraisers. It is an extremely stressful and difficult job. Tournament directors take flak from all directions – coaches, umpires, parents, and the organizations that control the fields being used. They get hit with many of the same issues you have to deal with, multiplied by the number of teams in their tournament. That is why I go out of my way to make sure that everyone associated with my team is polite, respectful and thankful to the people hosting and running tournaments we play in.

My policy is that we *NEVER COMPLAIN*, even if we don't like something. The way to get treated better in the future is not to complain. If you want a better draw, better scheduling, or something else, praise the tournament director and thank him for working so hard. Next time you will probably notice that you will get treated a lot better. Other teams have complained for years about the treatment Meteors teams receive in tournaments. Tournament directors always tell me how much they enjoy our parents, coaches and players and how nice and respectful we are to them. If we do get preferential treatment, it is only because tournament directors like and respect our team.

One time we were playing at a national tournament and I noticed that there was quite a scene being caused at the gate entrance. One of my parents came up to me and told me that a dad of one of our guest players was complaining loudly about the $7.00 entry fee for the tournament and was refusing to pay it. I walked out to the gate to see what it was all about, and this parent was really giving a hard time to the woman trying to collect the fee at the gate. This woman happened to be the elderly mother of the national director of the organization hosting the tournament. I was mortified, and thankful that he was not wearing a Meteors T-Shirt during the ruckus. I told him to go inside and I would handle it. I did not want to show him up and upset him – his son was only playing with us for one weekend and I didn't want to make waves unnecessarily.

After he left, I apologized profusely to the woman and paid the parent's entry fee out of my own pocket. I then called the national director, who was at another site but had already been called by his mother, and expressed to him how sorry I was and promised that it would not happen again.

Parents often complain bitterly to tournament officials if they are required to pay money to enter an event to watch their child play. It is quite common for officials to get complaints about entry fees, but not from the parents on my team who understand that they should never get in a disagreement with a tournament official. When I spoke to the tournament director, he was very surprised that one of our parents was complaining because he "never expected it" from one of our parents.

I was glad to hear him say that, and assured him that this particular parent was a guest with us and didn't understand how our parents are supposed to act at an event. Be proactive and aware of how your parents deal with tournament officials. The reputation of your team with them can be tarnished by one unruly parent. It is difficult enough to win a travelball tournament, you don't want to make it nearly impossible by turning the tournament director against you.

Parents and Umpires

Umpires, like tournament officials, normally do not go into an event wanting a particular team to win or lose. They are just out there to do a job, call the game to the best of their ability, get paid and go home. I think the manager's relationship with umpires is so important that I devote an entire chapter to it later in this book. When it comes to your parents, it is important to stress to them that it is your job to deal with the umpires, not theirs.

If you have a parent or group of parents continuously chewing on an umpire's ear, he may gradually turn against your team even if you have done nothing wrong and have not given him a hard time. You must lay down these ground rules and police the parents in your stands. If you go over to a parent who is berating the umpire and tell him stop, the umpire will notice that and appreciate it. By the same token, if he is getting a hard time from your parents and you do nothing to stop it, he will likely hold you responsible. The bottom line is that if there is an issue with an umpire, you are the person best equipped to handle it, not a parent in the stands.

Parents and Their Own Kids

A parent who really knows the game and cares about his son's performance can be a valuable ally to your coaching staff. Most of the really good young players became that way because a parent has worked with them individually for countless hours. You will also have parents who have spent a lot of time drilling their kids but they really don't have clue what they are doing. Both kinds of parents, unfortunately, can fall victim to the seemingly irresistible temptation to meddle with a young player while he is trying to perform. It is another one of those natural parental instincts that fades away gradually for most as people become accustomed to being a baseball parent. Most of the time, a parent is just giving harmless encouragement or "tips" that they think their son cannot live without. This section is for the parents who take it beyond that point - the ones that become a distraction to their child and a problem for the team.

Ideally you will have all of your parents only shouting encouragement to their sons and the team while it is playing a game. Although that is the case with most parents, there will be a few who continuously shout instructions to their child while he is trying to hit or pitch. You have to handle this situation delicately because if you jump on a parent too hard you may end up pushing them off your team. These parents tend to live and die with each game their son plays. They are keyed up and desperately want them to perform well. What they don't realize is that these attempts to help their son actually end up hurting them more often than not because it is tough to focus on a highly skilled task when you are receiving information from your parent about where you hands, hips, or shoulders should be. If you come on too strong, many of these parents will become defensive and feel that you are crossing the line and interfering with their parent-child relationship. Remember, you are dealing with a unique set of circumstances so try and *nudge* the parent in the right direction.

Never get on these parents or show them up during a game. Wait until after the game is over, then quietly take them aside away from the other parents and their own child. Explain to them that you really value the work they have done with their son and that their passionate commitment to his game is one of the main reasons why he is good enough to play travelball. Tell them that you consider parents like them partners in the success of your team and their dedication to their son better helps the team and you appreciate that. You should let them know that you have no problem with the parent providing constructive criticism to their son *after* the game is over.

However, when the games are being played they must understand that the coaches on the field are the only ones who should communicate with the players on baseball fundamentals and plays. You are not saying they cannot cheer their son on and provide encouragement. The only thing you are asking them to do is refrain from trying to give *instruction* during the games. If you explain this to them the right way and in the proper manner they will gradually begin to get with the program and leave their son alone.

An even bigger problem than the "coaches in the stands" are the parents who loudly criticize or berate their sons when they make a mistake or fail to produce during a game. Players can usually handle a coach who tightens them up on occasion because that is a natural part of the coach-player relationship. However, when his own parent berates him in front of his teammates, coaches and opposing players, it can be mortifying for the player. A player who receives a tongue lashing from the stands rarely recovers from it during the same game, and that is when a parent can actually hurt your team's performance on the field.

Some of these parents lash out because of frustration and/or anger. Others truly believe that their criticism actually *helps* their son because it motivates them by instilling a fear of failure. While fear of failure can often be a powerful motivator (Jerry Rice and Michael Jordan both cited it as the thing that motivated them the most in their Hall of Fame induction speeches), that must come from within not from an external source like a parent. Normally the worse offenders are rookie baseball parents at the younger age groups. Some of these parents will gradually get it out of their system and will behave once their kids reach 13-14U. However, some never learn and only stop when their son quits baseball after he becomes old enough to make decisions for himself.

Again, you have to be careful how you handle these parents to make them stop. They can be very high strung and intense people who take their son's baseball very seriously. You want to persuade them to change their behavior and become good baseball parents, but if you offend them and push them away they will continue to reoffend with another team.

The best way to approach it is to explain to them that you share their frustration when their son makes a mental error or mistake, and you understand why they get upset. However, you have to impress upon them that the time to criticize, if it must be done at all by a parent, is *after* the game. You must convey to them that when the game is going on, you must be given the exclusive authority to discipline each individual player and the team as a whole. Explain that when they step into that role, even for a few seconds, it infringes on your ability to handle the situation in a manner you see fit. You have to impress upon them that you (1) notice what they are doing, (2) it bothers you, (3) you understand where they are coming from, and (4) you need them to stop. Don't expect immediate results, but if you continue to speak to these parents the right way they will gradually get better and the player who is at the receiving end of the verbal abuse will really appreciate you for making it stop.

Opposing Parents - My Incident with a Dad Named Cal Ripken, Jr.

Just as fans heckle the opposing team at professional sporting events, it will happen to you at some travelball games. Parents, grandparents and relatives will make comments to you about any number of issues during games. Of course, the most intelligent thing to do is completely ignore this commentary and not respond to it. If it gets completely out of hand the umpire or tournament officials can step in and handle it, but if you are jawing back at forth at somebody in the opposing stands it drags you down to their level and distracts you from being able to coach your team. Most of the time, that is exactly what the heckler is hoping to accomplish.

I must confess that in my early years of coaching I took the bait many times. I really kind of loved giving it back as good as I got it and did not shy away from these confrontations. Finally, in my third year coaching, a wise older umpire pulled me aside and said, "Come on, Ron.

You should know better than that by now. You can't listen to anything that comes from the stands, and if you do you certainly shouldn't engage them."

I nodded my head and knew he was right. From that point forward I steadfastly refused to even acknowledge that I heard these comments coming from the stands. There was one notable exception, and that is when it came from a dad in the stands named Cal Ripken, Jr.

In 2005 we travelled to Minnesota for the 12U AAU National Championship tournament. It was a weeklong event at what was once a great tournament, and all of us looked forward to the opportunity to play some of the best teams from around the country. Our first pool game that week was against a team called the Baltimore Buzz from Maryland. We noticed on their roster a player named "Ripken" and we knew since he was from Baltimore he had to be related in some way to one of the Ripken brothers that played Major League Baseball. We won the game 7-1, and after the game we were able to talk to the coaches of the Buzz. They were really nice guys with great knowledge of the game.

I asked them if their "Ripken" player was related to the MLB players and they told me he was Cal's son. I asked them if Cal was at the tournament because obviously it would be a great thrill for our players to get to meet him. They told me that he was busy with business matters and said he may be able to fly in to watch his son play if they qualified for the Final 8 after the first three days of pool play. I asked them if he was one of the coaches on the team from time to time and they said he was not and when he came to the games he would just sit in the stands.

Sure enough, both of our teams made the Elite 8 and we faced each other in a rematch of our pool game on the first day. When we arrived at the field to warm up we noticed Cal walking around outside the fence near the Buzz dugout. That got us all talking and my assistant Rick Mullen suggested we ask Cal to take a picture with our team on the field after the game. I thought that would be really cool, especially since we were playing against his son's team. We decided not to bother him before the game started and figured we would ask him after it was over.

All the quarterfinal games at the park started at the same time. However, our game was tied 3-3 at the end of six innings and we went extras. The game seem to last forever and was tied 4-4 heading into the 10th inning. By this time, all the other games had long finished and we had a huge crowd from all the other fields around ours watching the game. I am sure most of the crowd was well aware that a Hall of Famer was sitting in the middle of the Buzz stands.

The Buzz changed pitchers in the top of the 10th inning and Cal's son came in to pitch. He had a little bit of a quirky delivery where he would rock back behind the rubber from the windup and lift his plant foot off the rubber. I wasn't paying much attention to it, but my first base coach Jerry Frye was all over it. He started talking to the base umpire standing next to him about how this move was essentially a balk on every pitch. Of course, I was completely oblivious to the whole thing over at third base.

After about five pitches our hitter popped a pitch to the first baseman. However, the base umpire threw up his hands and called a balk as the pitch was halfway to the plate. He walked to the home plate umpire and explained his call. The home plate umpire then called both managers to the plate to let us know what the call was. He said that he wanted to call the Chief Umpire to get a rule interpretation. I said fine and stood at the plate while he got on his cell phone. Suddenly I heard a voice from behind the backstop, "Hey man, why don't you just let the kids play!" I looked over and it was Cal Ripken, Jr., up against the fence calling out to me.

Normally, I would have completely ignored this kind of a comment. But I had one of those moments where a light bulb goes on in your head. I realized that I had a chance to go over and get into an argument with a Hall of Famer in front of 300 witnesses at the AAU National Championship, and there was no way I was going to pass up that chance! I walked over to the fence and asked him politely what he said. He repeated, "Why don't you let the kids play? Let the kids win it on the field."

I them asked him if he was a coach on the Buzz, and he replied that he was not. I said, "Then you need to sit back in the stands with the rest of the parents." Now the crowd began to gather around him to hear what was being said between us as things were getting interesting.

I told him that I did not make the call and didn't even know why the umpires made it until they explained it to me. He repeated his protest that it was all nonsense and that the call should not have been made. I said, "What exactly do you want me to do, decline the penalty like in football?" He replied that if I had any class I should do something like that and tell the umpire to forget about it and move on. I felt at this point that I was clearly winning the argument - the fact that it was his son was causing him to take a position that was kind of silly when you think about it.

Then he said something I did not expect, "It's not like lifting his plant foot gives him any kind of an advantage." That got me thinking about the purpose of the rule and I replied that it could possibly give a pitcher a slight advantage because it could give his body extra momentum going to the plate. At this time one of the moms on our team, a feisty woman named Tammy Van Brandt, had wondered over and was standing a few feet from Cal listening to what we were saying.

Cal then responded, "That is one of the most ridiculous things I have ever heard!"

Tammy, who didn't exactly know who Cal Ripken was, then couldn't resist chiming in, "How do you know it doesn't give him an advantage!"

That got a lot of people in the crowd chuckling and Cal looked a little stunned as he turned to Tammy and said, "I guess you think you know more about baseball than me?"

"Well maybe I do!" Tammy bellowed as the entire crowd burst into laughter as a mom on my team challenged one of the greatest baseball players on all-time. At that time I decided an argument that had been going rather well for our side was taking an abrupt turn and I needed to go back and join the meeting at the plate with the umpires. The balk call was sustained, but we failed to score that inning and later lost 5-4. After the inning I walked back to the dugout and sat next to Jerry and Rick on our coaching buckets. As soon as I sat down, Rick deadpanned, "I guess we're not getting that picture." Jerry and I fell off our buckets laughing!

CHAPTER 21:
<u>HANDLING UMPIRES</u>

Baseball is a game where the people who officiate it have an enormous amount of discretion. Every time a pitch is thrown and the ball is put in play an umpire or multiple umpires are called upon to make a decision that has an impact on the outcome of the game. So many of these calls can be decided one way or another by an inch of distance or less than a second in time. Because of this, an umpire can influence the outcome of baseball games more than the officials of any other major sport. All baseball coaches should have a full understanding and appreciation for this obvious fact and act accordingly.

It can be extremely frustrating when an umpire makes what you believe is a bad call that really costs your team in key situation. It can cause you to lose your cool and get very upset, and that is a natural reaction. However, you have to learn to internalize any frustrations you have with the umpires because usually complaining or lashing out at an umpire will only cause them to turn against you on future close calls and make things worse. I found that I was able to handle calls that went against me much better after I realized and accepted three important things: (1) youth umpires are as far away from the major leagues as we are, (2) they only want to do a job and don't care who wins, and (3) they almost always have a lot better vantage point to make the call than I do.

Travelball umpires are a mixed bag. Some also do high school and college games and are highly trained and professional. Others went to a weekend class for a few hours and bought some gear. The bottom line is that youth umpires are the lowest paid guys in their profession, so many of them are going to be mediocre or downright terrible. You should go into every travelball game hoping that you will get excellent umpiring, but expecting that it will be average at best. If you go into the games with lower expectations for the officiating, you will be a lot less frustrated when things don't go your way.

It is also easier to handle when you appreciate that the umpire is not against you and is probably just as bad for your opponent. However, you are a highly biased observer of your own games and usually don't notice all the calls that go your way. Your perception of all the close calls in your favor will be that they are "correct" and the close ones that go against you were "bad." However, keep in mind that the opposing coaches probably viewed those calls exactly the opposite way and are just as upset as you are. When you think about it, an unbiased below-average umpire is going to make bad calls that were 50% wrong in your favor and 50% wrong against you. The problem is that you never appreciate or recognize the ones that helped you, and the ones that hurt you are magnified.

Even the very best umpires make big mistakes that affect the outcome of games because they are human like the rest of us. In 2010, a Major League pitcher lost a perfect game on a blown call by one of the most highly regarded umpires in baseball. Let me give you an example of something that opened my eyes a little and helped me accept things a lot better in this area. A fairly good umpire made a really bad call on a play at the plate during my second season as a travelball coach. I came running out of the dugout, got close to the umpire and told him very emphatically that he had just made a horrible call. He calmly looked at me, waited for me to finish venting, then said, "You're right, I'll make it up to you on the next one." I was speechless, and was completely disarmed. What can you say when an umpire admits his mistake, then says he is going to even things out? The truth is that umpires usually realize a few seconds later when they blew a call and will try and make it up to you later if you let them. I guess it was refreshing to actually hear one of them admit it!

You also have to allow for the seemingly incredible possibility that you are wrong and the umpire is right on occasion. It is so silly to see coaches and parents sitting off to the side down the line hooting and hollering over whether a pitch was inside or outside. The umpire is a couple of feet away, and directly behind the edges of the plate. These coaches and parents are 40-100' feet away from the plate and looking at it from 45-90 degree angles. It is utterly foolish to argue inside and outside on balls and strikes from these comparative vantage points. Yet it happens on almost every close pitch in every youth baseball game in America.

How you react to close calls establishes your reputation and the reputation of your team with umpire crews in your area and in your state. As I said earlier, umpires almost never care which team wins or loses. However, the rare exceptions occur when an umpire cannot stand a particular coach or team because he has been persistently abused by them. Although umpires try to be professional and ignore criticism, when it is over the top and nonstop they will begin to retaliate in their own subtle way and all the close calls will go to the opposing team. Some umpires will do this consciously and others subconsciously. They are human beings and people tend to be nice to the people who are kind to them first. If an umpire is bad, let the opposing team ride him and tell him how horrible he is. When this starts to happen, I keep my mouth shut. Pretty soon, those 50% of bad calls that go against me are down to 10% by the fourth inning!

Coaches make mistakes all the time during baseball games. They choose the wrong starting pitcher or make a pitching change at the wrong time. They bat a player too high or too low in the order. They give the steal sign to a runner on a pitchout. They send a runner home who gets thrown out. Everybody associated with baseball games - coaches, players, and umpires - makes mistakes during games. However, when was the last time you saw an umpire run down the third base line to berate a coach for sending his runner home and getting him thrown out at the plate? Just imagine an umpire getting in your face, yelling at you in front of your players and your parents every time you made a bad move as a coach. Imagine what that would feel like, and you will begin to understand how they feel when you do it to them.

I try to go out of my way to thank the umpires for doing a good job. When a close call goes against my team and my parents voice their displeasure, I nod my head and tell the umpire he was right and made a good call. When an umpire hustles to get into proper position to make a call I thank him for working hard for the kids. When one of my assistant coaches argues a call and I think he is wrong, I will stop him and tell him in front of the umpire that I think the call was correct. Youth coaches who do these things are very, very rare. Umpires will really appreciate it and will never forget these gestures. They have a very difficult job, and when a head coach helps to make it easier he has just made a friend in that umpire.

Coaches all develop reputations with umpires in their area and in their states. It is very common for umpires to spend a lot of time hanging out with each other - at the ballparks between games and away from the parks. They love sitting around after a long day of games to tell stories about what just went down that day in their games during a tournament. If you constantly berate the umpires during your games, word will get around and a set of umpires working your game for the very first time will have a negative opinion of you and your team before they even walk onto the field. All coaches, and by extension teams, acquire reputations with the umpires as either "good guys" or another description I will not name. Believe me, life is a lot easier if you are considered to be one of the good guys by the boys in blue.

CHAPTER 22:
TOURNAMENT AND GAME STRATEGY

I am certain that I have coached in at least as many travelball tournaments as any other coach in the country.

This chapter highlights the things I have learned that are unique to travelball tournaments and can make a big difference on the ability of your team to navigate its way to the championship game.

Many of these things may sound silly, simple or obvious, but I included them here because I feel they are extremely important and frequently overlooked.

Crazy Little Things Make a Big Difference

The Coin Toss

Most plate meetings before the game begin with the umpire tossing a coin to determine which team is home or visitor. The winner of the coin toss will be given the choice of either home or visitor. It is the natural reaction of almost all coaches to choose home because home teams in every professional sport win more games than teams on the road. However, most of the reasons for this - sleeping in your own bed, familiarity with the park, home fans cheering you on - do not apply to travelball tournaments. Therefore, the only advantage the home team has is knowing how many runs it needs to score if it is behind heading into the last inning. Although this can be a slight advantage in some games, the negatives of choosing home in travelball tournament games so far outweigh this that I *never* choose home if I win the coin toss until the championship game.

There are no fewer than five major advantages to choosing visitor. The first are associated with the nerves young players feel at the start of tournament games. The younger the age group the more jittery the nerves, and it is a lot more difficult to pitch and play defense when you are nervous than it is to hit. I believe the toughest inning for a young pitcher is the top of the first inning of a game. After that, the game is underway and a lot of the nerves are gone. If the visiting team has just been able to score a couple of runs, that makes their pitcher and the players on defense even more relaxed when they take the field in the bottom of the inning because they are already playing with a lead. Also, many teams do not warm up their pitcher until the last minute and I don't want to give them any additional time before he has to take the mound to start the game.

Another reason why I choose visitor is to save pitching. In tournaments you usually have to play 5-6 games to win the championship. Saving your top pitchers as long as possible is the #1 priority for a manager working his way through a tournament. You may have decided to pitch one of your top two pitchers in a particular game early in bracket play. However, if you jump out to a big lead and score a bunch of runs to open the game in the top of the first, you can change your strategy and put a different pitcher on the mound. Every inning you are able to get your pitcher off the mound early opens up the possibility that he will be able to pitch later in the tournament. If my team is going to score a bunch of runs off a particular opponent, I want to know that as soon as possible by hitting in the top half of each inning.

Getting early leads in the top half of innings also allows you to get your bench players into the game an inning earlier. It is always my goal to get my substitutes into tournament games as early as possible. This affords them the opportunity to develop and become more productive in the future, and allows me to rest my starters for the next game. The sooner you are able to get your pitchers and catchers for the next game off the field the better.

Perhaps the most important reasons for choosing visitor in pool play games are the "runs allowed" and "runs scored" tie-breakers. Many teams end up in ties after pool games because they have the same record after these games. A lot of times whether a team advances or earns a "bye" and the overall seeding for bracket play is decided by the total number of runs a team allows in pool play or the total runs scored. Choosing visitor automatically increases your chances of scoring more and allowing fewer runs. If you are the home team, you will not get a chance to bat in the final inning if you have the lead. Therefore, you lose the opportunity to score additional runs that could be needed in a tie breaker. Also, if you are the home team, once you reach the number of runs needed to satisfy the "mercy rule," the game is over and you cannot continue to score. If you are the visiting team, you receive the benefit of these two things. You do not have to pitch the last inning and give up any runs in that inning if you are behind, and your opponent cannot continue to put up costly runs on you once he gets to the mercy rule. If you need to score additional runs to earn a bye for bracket play, you can continue to score in the top half of the last inning even if you have already passed the mercy rule. For each of these reasons, there is no way you should ever choose home if you win the coin toss during pool play.

Staking Out the Right Dugout

I know this one sounds really silly, but travelball tournament days can be very long and hot and most of the dugouts are not well protected from the sun. Get to the field as early as you can and take a look at which dugout is going to have the most protection from the sun at the time your game is likely to start. Once you see which one that is, you want to "claim" it by placing as many of your team bags and equipment near the entrance to that dugout as you can as early as possible. Tournament etiquette is "first come, first served" on who gets a particular dugout.

Losing the Tournament at the Hotel

It always seems necessary to remind all of the players and parents at the end of the first day of each tournament that they can lose the tournament at the team hotel. So many kids view their time back at the hotel as the highlight of the weekend for them and can't wait to cut loose and party all night. While I don't discourage fun, and recognize this kind of bonding is good for a team, I emphasize to everyone that you can take this stuff too far and defeat the main purpose for going to a tournament.

You should set a curfew for all of your players and then make sure someone is patrolling the halls at the time to enforce it. If your players stay in the hotel pool until 10:00 at night or play football in the parking lot for two or three hours, they are not likely going to be at the top of their game the next day. My teams have always had a lot of free spirits who like to party - coaches, parents and players. There is nothing wrong with that as long as you don't go so far with it that it affects your performance on the field the next day.

Nutrition and Hydration

Players and parents must be reminded to properly hydrate their bodies *the night before* playing and throughout the day. Tournament baseball can include a lot of long, hot days. Water and electrolyte drinks are very useful to keep hydrated and prevent cramps. Make sure your players stay away from sodas and carbonated energy drinks. These give you a short term rush but actually result in lower energy levels as the day wears on and the heat takes its toll.

Warming Up at Tournaments

The space to warm up can be very limited at tournaments. It is very common for there to be only one or two batting cages, or no batting cages, available for several teams. Since these are first-come, first-served, you want to make sure you have at least one coach or player get to the cages very early to stake a claim to it. If a facility has no batting cages available, you want to try and bring a portable net or whiffle balls. If you are unable to have your players hit live pitching in a batting cage, the very least you can do it get them swinging the bat some other way.

Time Between Games

At tournaments there will often be a significant time gap between games on the same day. It is important to keep track of your players and monitor what they are doing during these breaks. Let's say you finished your first pool game at noon and you don't play again until 4:00 PM. That leaves four hours for your players to potentially wear themselves out playing tag, tossing a tennis ball, or throwing the football around. Kids do not understand the concept of staying rested for the next game, and they will play until they drop if you let them. Try to get your team to a local restaurant in the air conditioning so that they are out of the sun and heat, eating and drinking. I try and keep my entire team together if possible during these breaks so I can keep an eye on them and make sure they aren't wearing themselves out.

Game Management

There are several good books on the market written by experienced professional and college coaches about how to manage different scenarios during a baseball game. This section addresses the peculiarities that accompany travelball tournament games and the most common mistakes made by youth level managers during these games.

Managing the Clock

This is something that no college or professional baseball coach ever has to worry about. Managing the clock is something you normally only hear about in other sports - football, basketball, hockey or soccer. However, the clock can become a significant factor in travelball because almost all tournaments games are run on a time limit. Travelball tournaments have a lot of games booked on every field back to back. To ensure that the scheduled games stay on time, a time limit is normally imposed on all games except usually the championship. What this means is that no new inning is allowed to begin after the designated time limit is reached. As long as there is at least a minute left on a clock after an inning is completed, the teams will begin another inning and play that inning to completion. However, these time limits can often be reached in the fourth or fifth innings of high scoring games, so it is important for a manager to have one eye on the clock at all times.

Many coaches who are leading tournament games will begin to "milk the clock" just like football or basketball coaches do late in games. When it becomes obvious that a team is doing that, the coaches and parents on the opposing team will begin to hoot, holler and complain about it. The rules of baseball present a lot of opportunities to stall. You are permitted one offensive timeout per inning. You are permitted trips to the mound to talk to your pitcher. Players get hurt, which can delay the game. Hitters call time out in the batter's box. Defensive players and base runners call time to tie their shoes. There are any number of creative ways to delay a baseball game and run the clock out within the rules.

I suppose a topic for heated debate among all travelball coaches is whether it is ethical to slow the game down when you are ahead to attempt to end the game early when there is a time limit. My own general opinion is that it is not unethical to manage a game within the rules to win the game for your team, within limits. It is pretty silly to see a team that is a big underdog take every opportunity to delay a game from the second inning on after they have jumped out to an early lead. I have no problem if a team runs a little time off the clock when there are just a few minutes left late in a close game. That is just smart strategy, and although it can be very frustrating when you on the receiving end of

318

it, there is nothing inherently unethical or illegal about it as long as the time you are taking is legitimate and within the rules. However, if you are make a mockery of the game - having players untie and tie their shoes, faking that they are hurt, etc., then you deserve whatever abuse and scorn you get.

When you are losing and an opposing team is obviously stalling to run out the clock, it is tough to take. Often coaches in this position will start to yell at the opposing coaches and complain to the umpire. There is not much an umpire can or will do about a coach taking trips to the mound or calling timeout. The rules of baseball clearly specify the exact number of times a team is allowed to do these things, and as long as they stay within these rules an umpire cannot help you. You should, however, alert the umpire to the fact that the other team is deliberately trying to stall the game to run the clock out. A good umpire will at least be able to keep the game moving and make sure that there are not any unnecessary delays or attempts to bend the rules by taking too much time between pitchers or calling time frequently in the batters' box.

Playing the Infield In

One of the most common mistakes youth baseball coaches make is playing the infield in too often during games. This is a defense that is employed to try and prevent a runner at third base from scoring with less than two out. Each of the infielders is moved in from normal depth to just inside or outside of the baseline. Although this gives the infielders a better chance to throw out a runner trying to score from third on a groundball, it also decreases the infielder's range and ability to field balls that are not hit directly at him. A few studies have been conducted to try and determine how much of an impact playing the infield in has on the batting average of a hitting facing that alignment. Coaches speculate that it can add as much as .100 to a hitter's average, but the data on Major League games suggests it is between .30-.80 points depending on what variables you are willing to count.

Although the data suggests that playing the infield in is not as detrimental to the defense as experienced coaches may suggest, it still provides an advantage to a hitter and should only be used in limited situations. It is common at the youth level, however, to see coaches move the infield in *every time* a runner reaches third base with less than two out. I have seen teams move the infield in even in the first inning countless times. Unless you truly believe that the game is going to end up 1-0 or 2-1, it is foolish to move your infield in early in a youth baseball game. This should be viewed only as a desperation move, and therefore should not be employed unless you are in the late innings of a close game.

Resting Catchers and Pitchers

You should have a pitching plan in mind for each game of the tournament. Since most or all of your pitchers will also be position players, be aware of how many innings they are playing in the field and how much they are running the bases on the days they are later scheduled to pitch. If your starting pitcher for the next game is playing shortstop, you should try and get him off the field and on the bench to rest as early as you possibly can. If one of my pitchers is also a catcher, I will make sure to have him pitch the first game of the day because it is almost impossible to be an effective pitcher after working behind the plate earlier in the day. Be very conscious of the amount of innings your future pitchers and catchers are logging at other positions throughout the rest of the tournament.

Using DHs, EPs and Courtesy Runners

Most travelball tournaments track high school rules and allow the use of a Designated Hitter (DH), an Extra Player (EP) or Extra Hitter (EH), and Courtesy Runners for the pitcher and catcher. Many organizations will also allow you to "bat the order" and have your entire roster in the batting order with free defensive substitutions. Whether you decide to use any of these things is entirely up to you because each one is optional.

If my team is playing a pool play game that is just for seeding purposes only, I will either bat the order or at least use an EP. Keep in mind that the more players you have in your batting order the tougher it is going to be to score runs. Instead of your nine best hitters in the lineup, you will also add one or more weaker hitters to the bottom of the order which can lead to some quick innings on offense. Also, you will be unable to turn your batting order over more often, and the more at bats a hitter gets in the game the more productive he is likely to be. So, whenever you decide to use an EP or bat the order you must do so with the understanding that you will be a less potent offensive team. Despite that, I will bat more players in pool games because these games are not as important to our ability to win the tournament and the extra players in the order gives me an opportunity to develop players who may be on the bench when the bracket games begin.

A DH is a very useful tool to a manager and I use it almost every single time it is permitted in a tournament. This rule allows you to create what I call a "two-headed monster" - utilizing the strongest half of two players to make one highly productive spot in the lineup. The player who is named the DH is only permitted to hit when the game begins. You must then "designate" the defensive player he is hitting for in the batting order. The player being "DH'd for" is permitted to play any defensive position but does not hit.

This can be useful to you on so many levels. It allows you to take a very strong hitter who is weak defensively and only have him hit. It also permits you to put a player on the field who is an outstanding defender but a weak hitter. Additionally, it allows you to keep players rested. I love using players who are going to pitch or catch later in the day as a DH in an early game. That way, I can get offensive production out of them if they are a good hitter, but they don't have to throw or take a position on the field when we are on defense.

The only downside to using a DH for the youth coach is the bruised egos of parents and players. Many players and parents and players detest the DH because it only allows them to play one part of the game and they take it as an insult as if you are saying you don't believe in their ability in a particular area. Whenever I employ the DH with a player who is new to my team, I go out of my way to explain to the player and his parents what I am doing and why I am doing it. This is another area where they may not agree with what you are doing, but if you take the time to explain your thought process they will at least be able to live with your decision a lot easier.

Manipulating Runs Allowed

As I stated previously, the first "tie-breaker" after pool play to determine seeding for bracket play is almost always total number of runs allowed. Many coaches will look at the scores of the early pool games to try and gauge where they stand in the seeding. There may be a particular team or a certain pitcher that they are hoping to avoid, and sometimes they will go into their last pool game knowing exactly what kind of a result will help them steer clear of a tough bracket matchup. On occasion, a team may get an easier draw if they lose their last pool game rather than win it. Or, they may avoid an outstanding pitcher if they drop down a slot in the seeding by giving up a couple of extra runs.

This is another aspect of travelball that is unique - sometimes your team is better off in the long run if it performs worse in the short term. That can entice coaches to try and do things to manipulate bracket seeding by sitting out some of their best players, pitching a pitcher who not one of their best, or experimenting with players at certain key defensive positions. I try not to ever do these things with the intent to manipulate my seeding because I always viewed it as "bad karma" and that the baseball Gods would make me pay for it later in the tournament. I cannot say that I have never done it, because I did a couple of times in major events where I was really trying to steer clear of a great pitcher that could send us home early.

Since I have done it myself on very rare occasions, this is another area where I will not preach to a coach about whether to do it or not. What I would say though is that if you are in a position to try this, do not make a mockery of the game. I have seen coaches actually tell their players to intentionally make errors, strike out on purpose, or have their pitchers walk batters with the bases loaded to give up runs. If you do some of these things, you can rest assured that it won't be just karma that catches up with you - your players and parents will be furious and may never come back because they are too embarrassed to play for a coach that would make such a mockery of the game. There is a right way and a wrong way to do this. If you put a pitcher on the mound who you are trying to develop, or you give a kid a chance to play shortstop who has been working hard there in practice, and these things result in a loss or a few extra runs allowed nobody can complain that much.

CHAPTER 23:
<u>RECRUITING NEW PLAYERS</u>

In this chapter I assume that you have already assembled a new team or have taken over an existing team and have a nucleus of players already in place. This chapter is about making that team better by improving the talent on the team through recruiting. Of course, the best way to improve your team is great practices and good coaching. However, as the great football coach Lou Holtz once said, even the best coaches in the world have to have good "raw material" to work with. When you add players to an established team, you should be looking for players who will bring something to the table that your team is missing - a lefty pitcher, a hard thrower, a shortstop, a leadoff batter, a big power hitter. Don't bring in a player in just to have more players, look for guys that bring something unique to your team that will make it better as soon as they put on your uniform.

I want to make it clear that the purpose of this chapter is not to encourage coaches to constantly turn over their rosters with a steady stream of new players. I do not advocate that approach to travelball because it can never be sustained. The guys who do that burn through every good player in their area in a few seasons and end up without a team because their mercenary players have no loyalty to them. Ideally, you want to keep a core group of 9-10 players together from season to season where you both remain loyal and committed to each other. This chapter is about how to get those other two or three players that will help take your team to a higher level. There are four different places you can look to find new players to add to your team: rec ball league teams, other travelball teams in your area, older travelball teams, and kids moving into your area from another state or region.

Rec Ball Leagues

The rec ball leagues in your area - Little League, Pony, Cal Ripken, etc., are the easiest places to recruit. There are lots of players there at each age group and many will be more than willing to jump onto a travelball team if the opportunity presents itself. The benefits of recruiting a rec league player is that you don't have to worry about an irate coach from a team you compete against hating you for "stealing" his player. Also, these players will tend to be more loyal to you and your team because they are from your area and they have not played travelball for anybody else. The drawback to recruiting players from these leagues is that many of them are very raw and have not played at a high level yet. Most of them are "projects," and if you already have an established team you are usually looking to add players who can make an impact to your team right away. However, if you are a younger team and their ceiling is really high, you should be willing to pick up guys like this.

When recruiting a rec ball player, I hang out around the stands of his team while they are playing and try to identify who his parents are by listening. However, that will not always be obvious and sometimes you are not able to find out who the parents are until you watch the player leave the dugout after the game and see who he walks up to. If I figure out who the players' parents are during the game, I will normally stand beside them and strike up a conversation about the game. Once I get them talking about general things, I mention to them that "#24" (who happens to be their son), is a really impressive player. They will beam proudly and point out that he is their son. I say, "Oh, really?", and proceed to say some of the things I like about him as a player. At this point they warm up to me because every parent loves to hear nice things about their child. I continue to stand next to them and compliment every little thing their son does on the field. Eventually, I begin to talk about my team, who I am and what I do. Then I mention to them that I have an opening on my team and that we could really use a player like their son on our team.

You should be careful to have the latter part of this conversation where the other parents on the rec ball team cannot hear it. Parents can be very jealous of other kids and if they hear your conversation they may try to talk the parents of your prospective player out of doing travelball. They may also be concerned about losing the best player on their rec ball team if he decides to play travelball exclusively, and will often tell them horror stories about it, or mislead them about you or your team. It is also common for the best rec ball players' parents to be coaches on the team. I have found over the years that coaches' kids are the easiest to recruit because they are more ambitious about their son's baseball future. If your team presents an opportunity for their son to get better they will not hesitate to make the move to travelball. It is also a lot easier to recruit these kids if you are willing to bring their dad in to help with your team as an assistant coach.

Some rec ball parents get excited about the opportunity to play travelball and jump on it right away. Others are more apprehensive for a variety of reasons. They may have heard bad things about it from other parents or are concerned about the time and money involved. They may also have other children involved in sports and other activities and they don't want a big commitment. If they seem reluctant, you should try and find out all of their concerns from them. They may not tell you unless you ask them, so try and draw them out. Most of the time you can allay their fears by simply explaining to them what your program is all about. The best thing you can do in this conversation is to be *flexible* if you really want the player. Tell them they can come as much or as little as they want at first. Assure them that you are not expecting them to quit the rec ball team they are on and that you will work around their schedule.

Many parents are willing to dip their toe in the travelball pool but are not willing to dive in completely right away. Don't scare these parents away by throwing a lot at them in these first conversations. If you have a good program, they may come out intending to play with you part time, only to change their mind later to a full time commitment. I can't tell you how many of these players came onto my team with the intention to play one or two tournaments with me, then want to play full time with us after the first day. Talented players love travelball when they get in the right situation because they are challenged like never before, get to play in great events, and get to play with great players equal to them in ability for the first time. They will be like kids in a candy store and won't want to leave. All you have to do in the initial recruiting process for a rec ball player is get them to come out and see what it is all about. The rest will take care of itself if you are doing things the right way.

Recruiting From Other Travelball Teams

This is a controversial subject because when you recruit a player off another team at your age group, feathers get ruffled to say the least. Coaches often view their players as their property, and when they leave to go on another team they see it as "stealing." Anybody who works with young players can understand why coaches feel like they have a vested interest in these players. They recruited them and coached them and taught them the game. They have invested hundreds of hours of time and sweat to make them better. It can be very painful when a player you have so much invested in turns his back on you to go to another team. When a coach from a rival team is actively recruiting a player from your team, it can make you justifiably angry and frustrated. All travelball coaches go through this and have players leave their team for situations they (or usually their parents) perceive as better for them.

The best advice I can give to new travelball coaches is that you have to understand that this can be a very ruthless, cutthroat business. There are no drafts or contracts, and any verbal commitment you receive from a player or parent is utterly without meaning. The bottom line is that every single player is a free agent every single minute he plays travelball. He can leave your team after the season, during the season, even during a game. Some sanctioning organizations have tried to limit "team hopping" to some degree with roster rules, but these policies are largely ineffective because there are so many different travelball organizations out there that a player can always find another place to play that won't restrict him. This is the main reason why many new travelball coaches retreat back into rec ball after a season or two. They cannot stand the Darwinian, wide open free market for players and want to return to a more stable, structured system that rec ball leagues provide.

Outstanding, aggressive, motivated coaches, however, see this free market system as a great opportunity to succeed. Many people prefer to work in a steady government job or for a large corporation. They may not be able to get rich quick, but they enjoy a steady paycheck and benefits. Others strike out on their own and become entrepreneurs. They have an idea and a vision and they are prepared to sink or swim in the free market - boom or bust. Travelball coaches are the entrepreneurs and rugged individualists of the youth baseball world. It is a rough and tumble business where you can enjoy great success one season then lose half your players to a rival team a month later and have to start over. Once you accept that this is the nature of the business, it becomes a lot easier to roll up your sleeves and get to work because you stop viewing your players as property and don't take their lack of "loyalty" too personally.

Some coaches believe that before you recruit a player off another team you should contact the head coach of that team. This certainly may be the polite thing to do, but unless that coach is a good friend of yours you are likely going to hit a brick wall. Why would another coach willingly allow one of his best players to play for another team? Even if you present it as a part-time or "guest" player situation, it is highly unlikely he is going to let that kid put on the uniform of another team. If he is given advance notice that you are interested in a particular player, he will take steps to try and prevent you from recruiting him. So, even though asking permission may seem gentlemanly, it is sort of like asking a guy if you can borrow his wife for the weekend. Coaches who are friends may share players from time to time, but anybody who lets their best player go off and play with a coach he can't completely trust needs to have their head examined.

Since asking permission is pointless, and since this is a free market, "survival of the fittest" environment, I don't talk to an opposing coach about a player I am recruiting unless he is a good friend. I always feel when I am recruiting a player that I am going to put him in a more competitive environment that is going to be beneficial to him in the long run.   If he and his parents do not perceive my team as a better opportunity, they are not going to leave the team they are on.

That is why I feel no sense of obligation to the coach of the team he is coming from. If that coach was doing a good job and the player and parents are satisfied with the team, I have no chance of recruiting him. Almost every player I recruited from other teams was essentially rescued from a bad situation and were looking for the first good opportunity that presented itself. Therefore, you should never feel guilty about recruiting these players from other teams because you provide them the opportunity to take their game to a higher level, and that is what travelball is all about.

People ask me all the time how I am able to recruit so many outstanding players. My short, simplified answer is that I try to identify the best players on bad teams. Outstanding players in great programs are not the best players to try and recruit. They are likely playing all the time, are already on a successful team and are usually happy as a result. From time to time one of these players' parents will contact you, but don't spend a lot of time looking at these guys. I focus my time and attention on weaker teams that play a soft, limited schedule. These teams are fertile ground for an elite team to recruit from because you can offer something to these players that they are not getting from the team they play on.

I probably spend more time watching bad travelball teams play each other than any other coach in America. I go out as much as possible to watch teams in my age group in the lower divisions play tournament games. Even though the overall quality of play may be poor, and the games may not be very entertaining, the best player on the field in a particular lower division game may impress you. Chances are, if he is an outstanding player and his team is not very good, he and his parents are unhappy with their situation. The coaching may also be very poor, or it may be a "daddyball" team with poor coaching that they can't wait to escape from as soon as possible. It may also be the case that they just want the opportunity to play bigger events against tougher competition.

When I decide to recruit one of these players, I generally follow the same pattern as the rec ball kids in that I try and identify who their parents are and strike up a conversation with them while watching their game. The difference from rec ball parents is that these parents understand what travelball is all about, and before they are going to leave the team they are on they are going to want to be certain that your team will provide their son a better opportunity. With these parents, there is a lot more salesmanship involved on your part, and you should get their email address and phone number so you can follow up because they will rarely commit quickly. This is where a comprehensive and impressive team website becomes valuable, because you can send them a link so they can read all about your program, including past accomplishments.

Probably the best method of recruiting players on other teams is to invite them to come out and play for you as a guest player on a weekend their current team is not doing anything. This is a "no strings attached" arrangement where there are no promises or obligations on either side. You will have a chance to see if the player fits with in your program, and they will have a chance to see if they feel comfortable with your team. If it doesn't feel right to either party, you can quickly and easily go your separate ways. If everything goes well, then they will likely ask you for a full time spot and leave the team that they have been on. Make sure that they make a phone call to their current coach to notify him about the move, because some parents will just leave without saying a word and that really isn't fair or right.

You should also pay attention to the teams in your area playing at an age group one year older than yours. Many coaches ignore these teams because they never play against them and are therefore not concerned about them. However, many travelball teams have a player or two who are "playing up" on their roster. That means that a player at your age group is on an older team to play against tougher competition. These players often become available because inevitably, as they climb the ladder in age, it becomes a lot more difficult to play up than it is at the younger age groups. The most common time for these players to go back and play on teams their own age is the 13U year. That is because this is the year teams transition to regulation fields and it is very difficult for a 12U player to be able to do that because it is tough enough for good thirteen year olds.

Identify which players in your area are playing up on older teams and open up the lines of communication with their parents. Let them know if they ever decide to come back to their own age group you have a place for them on your team. You rarely have to worry about their coaches getting upset at you for talking to the parents because these kids are not usually the best players on the older team, and they understand when a struggling player simply wants to play with kids his own age. A good idea to recruit these kids is to invite them to guest play for you when their team is not playing. Most of these kids will go from a minor role on the older team to a star player on your team. They will usually really enjoy having a lot of success and may decide to make the move even sooner than anticipated. As I tell their parents, you only get one childhood so why not let them enjoy it by having success. I understand the concept of challenging kids, but playing up in travelball can be really difficult - especially at the elite level.

Finally, you should also make your team known to kids moving into your area so they can find you. One of the best players who ever played in my program moved to our area from Kansas. He heard about our team before he moved here because we were nationally ranked and played in a lot of big national tournaments. His dad had also found our website on an internet search and read all about our team. When he moved to Florida, we were the first and only team he called. Any team would have grabbed him in a second, so we were very lucky he called us first. This is another area where a great team website can help you because it can be your best advertising in our internet era. Put a few team highlight videos up on YouTube, because that is another way your team will pop up on a search engine. You should also not be shy about posting on youth baseball message boards, because I have gotten a few good players that way. The only drawback of these message boards is that you just have to be prepared for fearless message board posters who may take an occasional anonymous shot at you and your team!

Travelball teams are a lot like college football and basketball teams - you recruit or die. The largely unrestricted ability of players to move from team to team makes turnover common. If you have a great program and do the right things as a coaching staff, you will have fewer of them turn over than others. However, even the most successful programs with the best coaches turn over a number of players on their roster each season for a variety of reasons. You have to constantly keep potential new players on your radar screen by watching other teams and visiting rec ball leagues in your area. You may enjoy coaching more than recruiting, but if you don't have the talent to work with you will get frustrated in a hurry. Recruiting is an important part of the job of being a travelball coach, and should be taken seriously by anyone hoping to have success.

CHAPTER 24:
HOSTING A TOURNAMENT

Some travelball teams and organizations decide to host tournaments at different age groups as a fundraiser. Hosting a tournament is something that can look deceivingly easy to someone who has never tried to do it. Tournaments are also not as lucrative as many people think because the costs involved can be quite high. However, if you are able to pull it off and do it right, hosting tournaments can be one of the most valuable fundraising tools available and will raise the profile of your organization.

I never even considered attempting to host a tournament until after I had been a travelball coach for three years. By that time, I had been to enough tournaments from different organizations that I thought I had a pretty good feel for the process. Although I understood a lot by playing in many events, there is just no way you can fully appreciate how difficult it is to pull off a successful tournament where you make a substantial profit and make most of your guests happy at the same time. I have now hosted tournaments each of the past ten seasons as a fundraiser for my Meteors' teams. Each time our tournament has gotten bigger and better through trial and error. A lot of mistakes were made along the way, and hopefully this chapter will help you avoid most of the problems and issues that we had to work through over the years.

Sanctioning and Insurance

The first thing you have to decide is whether you are going to have one of the major travelball organizations sanction your tournament. What this means is that you reach an agreement with them where they will insure and promote your event in exchange for a sanctioning fee. They will also agree to award tournament "points" and count the game results in their state or national rankings. This provides an added incentive for many teams to play in your tournament. Since you fall under their insurance umbrella, you will not have to purchase your own insurance for the event to cover you in case one of the participants gets hurt. These organizations will also allow teams to register and pay with a credit card online, then they reimburse your team once the payment is received. So, there are a lot of benefits to being affiliated with a major sanctioning organization.

Of course, sanctioning organizations are businesses and their benefits come at a price. They will charge sanctioning fees, but these are highly negotiable. Once you settle on the organization that is your first choice, contact the person in charge and try to negotiate these fees. Let them know that it is the first time you are hosting an event and you intend to continue the event each season for the foreseeable future. Tell them that you are doing it as a fundraiser, not as a for-profit business, and that you need to keep costs as low as possible. You should also mention that you are undecided which organization to use, and the cost of sanctioning will be a major factor in your decision. If that organization does not already have a strong presence in your region, they will have an incentive to work with you because you can help them attract teams in your area to their other events. I have seen many organizations charge no sanctioning fee for a first-time event, then charge a fee in successive seasons based on the number of teams participating.

Registering Teams

By far, the most difficult part of hosting a tournament is signing up teams to play. So many people who try to start events think that teams will flock to their banner as soon as they post something on a website or send out some emails. Travelball tournaments are like local restaurants, 90% of them do not survive their first year. The main reason for this is lack of customers. Because of the costs involved, you simply cannot sustain an event without a significant number of teams in each age group. There are a lot of ways to market your event to other coaches, but the bottom line is that you better be prepared to work at it every single day for at least a month or you will fail.

Coaches registering for events can be very fickle. They sit back and wait as long as possible before signing up for a tournament. Part of it is that they just don't want to part with their money until they absolutely have to. However, the main reason why teams stay on the fence is they want to see which other teams are going to enter. This part of it can be very frustrating when you are trying to promote your event. I have had as many as seven or eight teams at a particular age group simultaneously tell me that they will play as soon as we receive registrations from two or three other teams. That is when you have to tell them that if they would all just step up and stop waiting for the other guy you can have a pretty good event at their age group. Usually at this point these coaches will call each other and decide to get in at the same time.

So how do you sign up teams to play? There are a number of ways to do it. If you are with a sanctioning organization, they will put it on their website and send out email "blasts" to their members at each age group to promote your event. You can also go to the coaches meetings for different organizations and quietly promote your tournament. I also try to find popular, influential coaches at each age group to help me. I tell these coaches that if they help me sign up at least four teams I will let their team play for half price. If they sign up six teams, I let their team play for free. You have to be prepared to provide incentives to other coaches who are willing to help promote your event.

You also have to be very persistent and work the phones and email. Constantly update the list of teams that have committed to your event and continue to send that out via email to coaches. The primary incentive to play a particular event is the number of other teams signed up and the level of competition. There is a herd mentality in travelball, and once you reach at least six teams in an age group several others will jump in because it is starting to look like a good event. If you call coaches you can find out why they are reluctant to play. Most of the time they have scheduling issues, and if you are flexible you can assure them a pool game schedule that will make it a lot easier and convenient for them to play.

Choosing the Location

You may already have a home park that is going to let you host the event for little or no cost. If you have access to that, you have a huge advantage over other organizations trying to host events. I have paid as much as $4,500.00 to rent fields and facilities for my tournament. Most county Parks and Recreation Departments now charge significant "user fees" for their facilities that can wipe out your profit margin. The best way to combat that is to contact your local tourism board or Chamber of Commerce and get them on your side. Travelball tournaments bring a lot of families into a community - families that rent hotel rooms, eat at restaurants, buy gas, etc.. Make the people who benefit from that aware that your local government is making it impossible for you to host an event in their area. These organizations will either help finance the costs of facilities or put pressure on local elected officials to be more reasonable.

Don't choose a park simply because it is cheap or it is your home field. Teams are traveling a long way and pay a lot of money to play in your event. If you have substandard fields, or your park is in a bad neighborhood, there is a good chance your customers will not come back next season. A really nice facility can also be a great selling point when you market your event. Try to find the best fields you can at the right price, and make sure they have enough hotels and restaurants close by.

Awards

Napoleon once said that all he needed to conquer the world was a lot of colored ribbon. What he meant was that small trinkets and awards can really motivate people and make them happy, and if he had enough ribbons to pin on soldier's chests they would do anything for him. This concept is even more true with kids, whose eyes get wide every time they receive a medal. Although awards can be costly, you can keep them affordable if you shop around. The best advice I can give you is don't be too cheap with your awards. Parents, players and coaches get really upset when they have paid a lot of money, won several tough games in a row, then get handed an award that cost $1.50. Awards like this send a message that you are cheap and that you don't show appreciation for their achievement.

You don't have to spend a ton of money on awards, but a little extra cash goes a long way when it comes to quality. You should have team trophies to give to the coaches for First, Second and Third place, and at least thirteen medals to pass out to the players on each of these teams. If you have 5-6 different age groups, you should be able to pick up a nice set of trophies and medals to cover all of them for a total of $1,000.00.

Tournament Director

There should be one person in charge of the tournament that each team can contact if any issues arise. I have always served as my own tournament director, but many teams hire someone to take on this responsibility because it can be very stressful and difficult. A common fee for a good tournament director is $500.00 for the weekend. This is not expensive, because your tournament director must be at the complex and accessible to coaches, parents and umpires every single minute that games are being played that weekend.

There are so many things, expected and unexpected, that can happen during a youth baseball tournament. Kids get hurt, umpires don't show up, teams fight with one another, players and coaches get ejected, lights go off and sprinklers come on in the middle of games, teams show up at the wrong complex - the list is endless. In the last tournament we hosted, a woman took the metal lid off a trash can and was banging it on the metal bleachers whenever her team did something good. Some parents on the other team complained to me about it, and after sizing up the woman I really did not feel like confronting her. I grabbed a young coach I knew walking by and gave him $5 if he could get her to stop. He did, and it was the best $5 I ever spent!

The bottom line is that after serving as a tournament director for your tournament, you will never complain about little things at another event you play. After you have been a parent for a while, you appreciate your own parents more because you realize how difficult the job is. Hosting an event can serve as the same kind of eye-opening experience for you. That, and the cost savings, is why I recommend you serve as your own tournament director when you host an event. You will learn more about travelball coaches and parents serving as a tournament director as you ever will as a head coach.

Umpires

You have to find a good, organized, reliable umpire in your area to serve as your tournament's Umpire-in-Chief (UIC). A UIC will usually charge you a small fee to recruit and schedule umpires to work the games for your tournament. Let your UIC know that you want him to find the highest quality umpires in the area, because bad umpires are a leading cause of teams not returning to an event. Get your game schedule to your UIC as early as possible, and make sure it is clear and easy to understand. The worst thing that can happen to you as a tournament director is to have an umpire crew not show up at a particular field for a scheduled game. This can cause a "domino effect" where all the games on that field will fall behind. You must have your UIC's cell phone number to contact him whenever something like this happens. It is also important for you to let your UIC know the playing rules for the tournament as early as possible so he can brief all of the umpires before the event begins.

Turning a Profit

You cannot make a significant profit on team entry fees alone. Most of the time you are fortunate if these entry fees cover the costs associated with your event. The best way to turn a profit at your event is to charge an entry fee and run your own concession. Keep your entry fees very reasonable, because a lot of organizations have gotten really greedy, charging parents and siblings too much to watch youth baseball games. At our tournament we charge $7.00 for a weekend pass, and only charge people ages 18 and up. This is very reasonable compared to other events, but teams appreciate it. Teams are given four free passes for coaches when they enter. Parents on your team should be put in charge of collecting the entry fees at the gate.

The concession stand is usually the most profitable part of a travelball tournament. Do not contract this out to an independent entity if you want to make money - it should be the responsibility of the parents on your team. Visit local vendors to try and get them to donate food. Distributors of food and beverages all have a budget built in each year for charitable donations of their products. At our last event, all of the bread products were donated by a local company, and a local distributor donated 900 free assorted drinks for us to sell. Visit these businesses and tell them about your event. They will be more than happy to help you with free product to sell, which can make your concession very profitable.

ABOUT THE AUTHOR

Ron Filipkowski has coached the "Meteors" travelball teams from 2002-2011. He started his first team for his oldest son when they were nine years old and coached that team until they began high school after their 14U year. Ron then started over with a new Meteors team in 2007 when his third son was eleven years old.

Ron compiled a 644-217 record in tournament games. His teams have won 54 travelball tournaments and 6 Florida State Championships.

The Meteors were ranked in the Top 25 in the nation by Travel Ball Select for four consecutive years, and were ranked #1 in the country in 2010. Ron was awarded 13U National Coach of the Year by Travel Ball Select for 2010.

All of the players from his first Meteors team started for their high school teams. Twelve of these players have signed full baseball scholarships to major Division I programs like the University of Florida and the University of Miami. One player was drafted in the 3rd round of the 2010 MLB draft and several other players are professional prospects for the 2011 MLB draft, with one player projected to go in the 1st round.

A BONUS GIFT FOR YOU

For a free copy of *"Ron Filipkowski's Top 20 Travelball Tournaments to Play In"* for the current travelball season, go to Ron's personal blog at:

http://travelball4kids.blogspot.com/

Made in the USA
Lexington, KY
16 December 2019